BUSINESS COMMUNICATION
Methods and Strategies

BUSINESS COMMUNICATION
Methods and Strategies

DR. K.C. SHARMA
ANUPAMA SHARMA PATHAK

Foreword by

PROF. JAI NARAIN SHARMA
Professor and Hon. Director
Gandhi Bhavan, Panjab University
Chandigarh

DEEP & DEEP PUBLICATIONS PVT. LTD.
F-159, Rajouri Garden, New Delhi - 110 027

BUSINESS COMMUNICATION
Methods and Strategies

ISBN 978-81-8450-373-9

Typeset by RAHUL COMPOSERS
358, Pocket-B, Phase-2, Sector-16B, Dwarka, New Delhi - 110 075

Printed in India at MAYUR ENTERPRISES
WZ Plot No. 3, Gujjar Market, Tihar Village, New Delhi - 110 018

Published by DEEP & DEEP PUBLICATIONS PVT. LTD.
F-159, Rajouri Garden, New Delhi - 110 027 • Phone : 25435369, 25440916
E-mail : ddpubs@gmail.com • ddpbooks@yahoo.co.in
Showroom :
2/13, Ansari Road, Daryaganj, New Delhi - 110 002 • Telefax : 23245122

Dedicated to

MRS. VIDYA SHARMA
(ANGIRAS)

Contents

Foreword

Brian Tracy, an eminent authority on the subject, has rightly said, "your ability to communicate effectively is closely tied to your ability to perform effectively, to get the results for which you were hired. The quality of your communication with others will determine the quality of your life as a manager". Judged from this brilliant quotation, let us examine the utility of effective communication.

A manager or for that matter any person in whatever activity he or she is engaged, can not remain oblivious of this fact. Apart from social necessity, all information passes through communication of sorts. In offices, in factories, in educational institutions, in the corporate world or elsewhere, even in personal life, things are better managed if communication skill is at its best.

I find that all aspects of business communication which are material for developing, and increasing proficiency in business world have been suitably included in the book. The highlight of the book contains in the fact that the style is the authors' hallmark and the presentation is as simple as it should be for the learners and professionals in our country. The authors are knowledgeable and well experienced in teaching of communication and they have brought these to bear upon this written work, keeping also in view the general standard of English readers in our country, especially those pursuing management, technical and professional courses. I expect more such publications from them in the coming time.

The book should be very useful also to the management teachers, not only to the management students and others, keen to learn. The importance of communication is in sharp focus in the modern times due to the globalization process which would establish regime of free trade, ushering in an era of heightened competition in the global market arena. As of now, we are ahead of China only because of our English medium of education. We have to strengthen English speaking, writing and management education to remain competitive. On overall assessment, I find the book an invaluable asset in any library and like a Bible with the students and teachers.

PROF. JAI NARAIN SHARMA
Professor and Hon. Director
Gandhi Bhavan, Panjab University
Chandigarh

Preface

It is a fact that communication brings people together and establishes commonness among them. A message is the developed idea which is carried by the media to the people in an environment. The situational relationship created in the environment is the purpose which it serves to achieve.

This book is a sum total of more than 40 years of experience of the authors who bring relevant part of the communication as it relates to business; business includes services and concerns all those related to or connected with business in any kind of relationship.

This book contains nineteen chapters packed in summarized form what a student or professional looks for becoming skilled in communication. There are chapters on communication in general, objectives of communication, verbal and non-verbal communication, official correspondence with some examples, commonly used business terms, business enquiries and replies thereto, claims and adjustments, banking, strategies for interview, presentations and interviews, group discussion, committees, conferences, group dynamics, etc.

The authors feel that the book will be useful to all who deal with business including students at post-graduate level commerce and management education.

DR. K.C. SHARMA
ANUPAMA SHARMA PATHAK

Acknowledgements

During the course of our project of writing of this book, many friends and colleagues have been generous with their suggestions and ideas what to include, what to exclude from the scope of this book. We hereby thank them collectively as, being numerous, it would not be possible to name them individually. Well, there are a few of them who remained in contact throughout and continued to enquire about the progress. It would be proper to mention a few of them by name.

We thank Mrs. Anjana Sharma, who is Master of English, apart from M.Ed. and M.Phil. (Education) and has been teaching English for the past 25 years at under-graduate and post-graduate levels with distinction. Her contribution to this book is tremendous.

We thank Dr. Charu Sharma, Associate Professor, Government Post-Graduate College, Dharamsala (H.P) for her valuable, weighty and spontaneous guidance from time to time.

We thank Dr. Ashu Pasricha, Associate Professor, for her help and encouragement and going through the manuscript.

We thank Mr. Parveen Malik, Mr. Ajay Khurana, Ms. Tanuja Pathak, Associate Professors; Mrs. Shipra Parmar Sood, Dr. Uttama Pandey, Ms. Riju Sharma, Ms. Ritu Aggarwal and Mr. Som Nath Jagtap, Assistant Professors, for their views and support during the course of this work.

DR. K.C. SHARMA
ANUPAMA SHARMA PATHAK

CHAPTER

1

Introduction

WHAT IS COMMUNICATION?

Communication is as old as the human race. Several communication scholars have stated that the word "communication" is derived from the Latin verb "communicare", which means to make common or to share.

By 'communis' is meant to communicate and share, to impart a piece of information, a message, an idea or concept. In short, communication is sharing/exchange of information, data, finding, message, report, opinion, viewpoint, advice, knowledge, experience, etc.

COMMUNICATION AS A PROCESS

It can be explained as under:

(1) Communication is not just an act. It is a process. The process of communication includes transmission of information, ideas, emotions, feelings, skills, knowledge, suggestions, commands, directions, etc.

(2) For this to happen, tools like symbols, words, pictures, figures, graphs, drawings, illustrations are used.

(3) The act of communication is referred to as transmission.

(4) It is the process of transmission that is generally termed communication.

(5) It is again a process by which we understand and, in turn, try to be understood by others.

(6) It is dynamic, constantly changing and shifting in response to the overall situation.

DEFINITION OF COMMUNICATION

Communication is the interchange of thoughts or ideas, which is the same as transmission of information, consisting of discriminative stimuli, from a source to a recipient. Some important definitions are given below:

> "Communication is an exchange of facts, ideas, opinions or emotions by two or more persons".
>
> —W.H. Norman and Summer

> Communication is defined as "the process of passing information and understanding from one person to another. It is essentially a bridge of meaning between the people. By using the bridge, a person can safely cross the river of misunderstanding".
>
> —Keith Davis

> "Communication is the sum total of all the things that a person does, when he wants to create an understanding in the mind of another. It involves a systematic and continuous process of telling, listening and understanding".
>
> —Louis A. Allen

> "Communication may be broadly defined as the process of meaningful interaction among human beings. More

specifically, it is the process by which meanings are perceived and understanding is reached among human beings".

—D.E. Mc Farland

Features of Communication

From the above definitions, the following features of communication emerge:

(a) Communication is unavoidable. It exists even when we observe silence; our facial expressions, signs, gestures always remain. Our behavioural ways communicate too.

(b) Communication is not only a process but also it is a continuous process. There are activities which are inter-related and inter-dependent; all these activities and actions communicate.

(c) Communication is a two-way traffic. G.R. Terry remarks: "communication is not complete unless the receiver has understood the message". There has to be feedback, recipient's response; simply talking and/or writing may create misunderstanding if due regard is not given to the recipient's response as it is conducive to understanding the message for desired required response.

(d) Communication is always selective because our sensory receptors are limited and they detect only part of the phenomenon (these are the five senses—sight, hearing, taste, feel and touch).

(e) Communication is universal phenomenon. Notice that all human beings, birds, beasts, etc. communicate—human beings have developed language but they use also signs and symbols as animals and birds do.

(f) Communication is a social process as it enables all the members of society to satisfy their basic needs and desires through exchange of written, spoken or non-verbal message.

IMPORTANCE OF COMMUNICATION IN BUSINESS

Communication is as essential to business as blood is to a human body. As business has become voluminous and complex, its importance has increased further. Effective communication boosts business; in its absence, business will be standstill. The following points will make the position very clear:

(a) It is essential for the efficient working of business. Healthy and conducive environment is created in business; goals and policies are conveyed to the employees; resources are coordinated; environment of understanding is created and smooth working follows.

(b) The communication failures prove costly to the organization. There can be stoppage of production leading to loss of man-hours and development of ill-will between employees and managements. Low morale and lowering of productivity level will result. Production loss means lower profits and adverse effect on shareholder value, etc.

(c) According to George R. Terry, "communication serves as a lubricant for fostering the smooth operations of the management process. The management functions are POSDCORB. The following management functions are carried out smoothly through communication:

   (i) *Forecasting/Anticipating*: There are statistical and mathematical tools to forecast demand and to have thereby the anticipated sales of products, to find out future of the company's products and prospects in emerging social, economic and political environment of various countries, continents and regions. So, gathering and processing of information, data and other particulars requires communication, especially when groups and committees deliberate to arrive at common approach and effective corporate policies and strategies. Trends have to be anticipated and action plan evolved to sustain and further enlarge clientele base and improve market share.

(ii) *Innovation and Creativity*: These require formation of strategic business groups, quality circles and special committees, etc. for market research, research & development, product innovation and changing delivery system through proper or new method of distribution to give satisfaction rather delight to consumers.

(iii) *Planning*: This includes framing of policies, plans, programmes and revamping/improving procedures and undertaking systemic changes in response to changing environment. All these require communication. There is continuous monitoring and mid-course review, warranted by situations. Communication makes all these functions conducive, participatory and effective.

(iv) *Organising*: Organising means decision taking for various activities for business, creating or merging departments for these business activities and to delegate powers to the functionaries down the hierarchy for timely and prompt decisions for better results. There is sometimes need to decentralize certain functions for terminating final decisions at lower/branch/department levels to avoid delay and to develop decision-making skills at junior level management.

(v) *Directing as well as Leading and Motivating*: The entire process in these areas requires effective communication, at least communication whether effective or not. Researchers have observed that 98% of a manager's time is taken by communication. While Directing involves the issue of commands, the other functions of motivating and leading require continuous communication for the purpose of discussing, persuading, counselling, rewarding and educating employees and managers. Sometimes, incentive schemes are necessary to boost morale and enhance motivation. Issue of orders, inviting suggestions, creating open working atmosphere for frank exchange of views in informal and even in formal meetings require communication.

(vi) *Monitoring and controlling*: Performance reporting is the effective tool to exercise control over the various activities in the departments, divisions and sections. The budgeted level is compared with the actual performance and variations discussed. Negative variances are disturbing and, therefore, causes are found out for appropriate tactical planning by conducting field research/survey. Remedial actions are taken and, if warranted, review of budgeted level is done to peg targets at lower levels.

(d) *Strengthening Customer relations and building human relations*: Both external and internal publics are cared for. Happy industrial relations are conducive to higher productivity. Two-way communication promotes co-operation. The management can convey expectations and concerns to the employees and, with skillful handling, can involve them more efficiently; the process brings about loyalty in the workers towards their organization. In this connection, William Onchen III says, "Communication is the chain of understanding that integrates an organization from top to bottom, from bottom to top and from side to side".

(e) *Total Quality Management (TQM)*: As involvement of various departments and specialists is essential for TQM, communication plays significant role. For this, there has to be consensus and commitment among the specialists and departments. Michael J. Stahl says in this regard, "Untill consensus is reached between the executives and the employees about how to go in for achieving quality, there will be a great deal of wasted efforts or no effort at all". Further, Total Quality strategy involves continuous change and, therefore, organizational members must be kept informed about the change otherwise there will be avoidable chaos.

(f) *Zero defect Marketing and Quality services to customers*: Customer is the king. There is severe competition. Zero defect products and prompt and efficient services are the hall mark of present day marketing. Proper and healthy communication of company employees/representatives/executives with the customers is very essential. Present day customers are money rich but time poor; they can not be ignored at any cost, else the company may lose business.

(g) *Job satisfaction and Job enrichment among the Staff*: Defective or deficient (bad) communication results in misunderstanding and illusions among the employees and the executives. Consequently, their behaviour pattern changes, which manifests in low morale, low productivity, unhappy industrial relations, absence of loyalty and no sense of belongingness, etc. Effective communication removes misunderstanding and clears illusions, develops conducive working environment and generates cordiality in overall relations, and commitment to the organizational goals.

(h) *Maintaining professional and cordial relations with external publics*: Effective communication is the key to uninterrupted working. It helps in maintaining good relations with the external publics (parties) like customers, creditors, suppliers, bankers, trade unions, research institutions, consultancy organizations, government, local authorities, trade associations, etc. Globalization has been introducing sweeping changes in the format, systems and practices of business. Information technology has developed to great extent and must be adopted for any kind of business to sustain and grow. In this scenario, communication is indispensable and imperative.

(i) *Strategic Management*: Communication is essential for strategic management, which means taking decisions and formulating action plans to devise strategies for implementation. The aim of the strategic management is to adopt courses of action to out-perform the competitors. Industrial Darwinism eats up small organizations and collaborates with the big ones to grab all business. The MNCs are the colossal corporations which are making their presence in all the sectors, countries and trading blocks.

Therefore, flawless and free communication among all levels of management ensures understanding each other's business plans and actions and to know the objectives of the organization. The lower and middle level managers formulate tactical strategies, which they communicate to the top management.

The above points highlight the importance of communication in organization. All businesses have to maintain a system of communication and must encourage every manager to practice healthy and effective communication.

BARRIERS TO EFFECTIVE COMMUNICATION

Stephen Cavey says, "Diagnose before you prescribe is a correct principle manifest in many areas of life".

Communication is complete and perfect when the receiver understands the message in the same sense and spirit as the communicator intends to convey. Practically, it has been noticed that such perfect, complete and effective communication does not take place because of certain obstacles or other factors known as communication barriers.

Proper identification of these barriers is as important and imperative as diagnosis of ailment for its remedy. Most of the behavioural problems in some organizations stem from improper communication of business executives, the people responsible to discharge their functions better and ensure smooth running of the enterprises. They have to overcome these communication barriers through their right understanding and effective actions.

There are a lot of causes of misunderstanding and misinterpretations of message communicated. As the process of communication involves sender, channels and receiver, the problem of communication usually lies with either one or more of them. There may be certain flaws in encoding and decoding the message; the channels used may be defective or faulty. These barriers may be categorized into the following groups:

(a) Semantic Barriers.
(b) Physical Barriers.
(c) Organizational Barriers.
(d) Psychological Barriers.

(A) Semantic Barriers (Meaning of Words)

Semantic barriers are concerned with problems and obstructions in the process of encoding and decoding the message into words or other impressions. There is absence of correct and contextual understanding of the messages. The use of different languages, different interpretations of different words and symbols, poor vocabulary and poor grammatical knowledge are some of the semantic barriers.

(1) Different Language (known to receiver)

Employees in organization have generally no common language. This is obvious barrier when there is no common vehicle to convey ideas and feelings. This problem is more acute in culturally diversified organizations and multinationals. Even competent translators fail to convey the exact meaning of different words of different languages because of cultural or social background to them.

As company's operations expand and extend to different countries, this language barrier widens.

(2) Different Context for Words and Symbols

"The meaning of words are not in the words; they are in

us," Hayakawa (author of Language in Thought and Action) profoundly remarks: "Words and symbols used have several meanings depending upon the context in which they are used". For example,

(a) Give me water to drink (Here water means glass of water).
(b) The Water dispute of Punjab, Haryana (Here water means water of river).
(c) Kauveri water dispute between Karnataka and Tamil Nadu means water of river, Kauveri flowing through Karnataka and Tamilnadu.

Unless the context of words and symbols used is known, the receiver may misinterpret them because of his preconceived ideas. Misunderstandings become the rules, rather than exceptions, because of different presumptions and perceptions.

(3) Poor Vocabulary

Poor vocabulary is handicap with communicator to convey written or verbal message in the right and intended sense. The communicator should know the clear and precise meaning of the used words and their appropriate replacement, if needed. If the inappropriate and inadequate words are used, they will not make the communicated ideas clear.

(B) Physical Barriers

Some of the physical barriers are as follows:

(1) Noise

Any disturbance or interference that reduces the clarity and effectiveness of communication is called noise. It may be physical or psychological; written or visual. Noise distracts the person communicating and acts as barrier to communication. Loud noise of microphone, playing outside or noise due to machines, affects listening process of persons communicating (physical noise) with others (audience). Mental trouble and turmoil affect the receiver's listening and understanding the message. Similarly, inattentiveness and indifference of the listener make communication ineffective (psychological noise). Bad handwriting and incorrect typing irritate the reader what to speak of understanding the contents (written noise). The late arrival of employee, results in distractions of superior's attention (visual noise).

(2) Improper Time

Improper timing of communication also hinders the process of communication; e.g., an order at the closing hour to execute an urgent work, may cause resentment in the employee who has to catch train for going back to his house. Message requiring action in distant future may be forgotten. Phone call at midnight, interrupting sleep, further irritates the receiver if message is not urgent.

(3) Distance

The distance between sender and receiver acts as a barrier in the communication process as the sender has to speak loudly to convey the message. In import/export transactions, because of distances of miles, communication may be ineffective if proper use of fax, telephone is not made.

(4) Inadequate or Overloaded Information

Inadequate information falls short to convey the message and overloaded information distracts the reader's attention and dilutes the theme of message.

It is imperative that information should be adequate, neither less than desired, nor more than warranted. If this is not so, it fails to serve the purpose of communication.

(C) Organizational Barriers

(1) Organizational Rules and Regulations

Organizational rules and regulations prescribing the different formal communication channels for each subject-matter may restrict the flow of messages and act as hindrance in the communication process.

Sometimes, it happens that important messages are omitted or manipulated. Observance of rigid rules and regulations relating to communication causes delay in receipt of message and action thereon, and discouragement to employees in conveying their creative and innovative ideas. On the other hand, where such rules and regulations are flexible and communication is free, employees feel encouraged and motivated to come up with new ideas and opinions. We call it an open culture.

(2) Hierarchical Relationship

Hierarchical formal boss-subordinate relationship in organization structure also restricts free flow of communication, especially in the upward direction. The greater the difference in hierarchical position, the greater is the communication gap between employees and executives. The employees are expected to contact executives through their immediate bosses. *Original Message (top to bottom)*

In such types of cases, it has been noticed that upward communication is intentionally distorted and designed either with exaggerations or understatements, sometimes with false and fabricated stories, to suit the purpose of middle level bosses.

This leads to distrust and disappointment among employees and disruption of the congenial communication

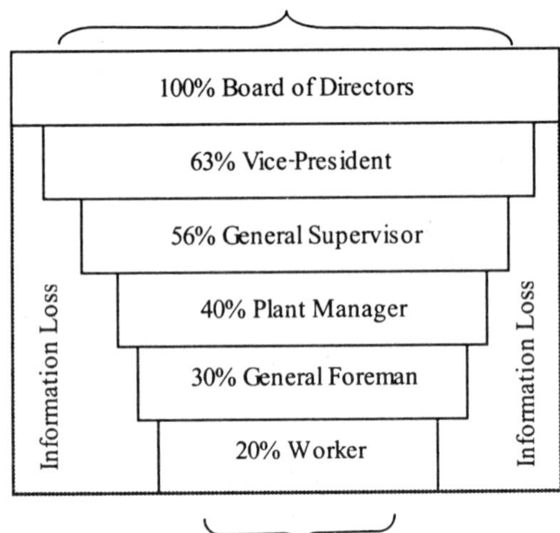

Source : Dalmar Fisher, Communication in Originisations, Jaico Publishing House, Mumbai, 1999, page 38.

environment. The modern theory gaining ground currently is that managers have to don mantle of leadership to collaborate, guide and lead colleagues from the front; results are better.

(3) Non-Conducting of Staff Meetings

Certain organizations conduct staff meetings to know the grievances and collect suggestions of employees and to overcome the above barrier.

In organizations where such meetings and conferences are missing, free flow of communication is interrupted and the communication gap between persons being ruled and the ruling ones widens.

(4) Wrong Choice of Channel

There are many mediums and channels of communication available. No communication channel is ideal and perfect in every situation. For persuasion by sales manager, more suitable is face to face communication than talking on phone.

Written communication is required in case of formal relations. But in communicating with literate people, this channel fails. Illiterate people are to be communicated orally and with support of pictures.

(D) Psychological Barriers

Psychological barriers arise from motives, emotions, social and cultural values, different perceptions, etc. These create a physiological distance, cause misunderstanding among people at work and hinder the communication process.

(1) Selective Perceptions

Our sensory receptors have their own limitations. As a result, we perceive not the whole spectrum, but only a few selective symbols based upon our needs, motives, experience, background, etc. as already explained. We do not see the reality, as it is, but interpret what we see and call it reality.

We communicate only a part (not the whole of the subject) because of our selective perceptions; and natural words conveying a positive message convey the opposite meaning as they reach the receiver, resulting in misunderstandings and misinterpretations and makes communication ineffective.

(2) Premature Evaluation

It is human tendency that we try to evaluate quickly. We do not listen or read the whole, but try to infer from certain part of the message; we become impatient. The moment we try to evaluate, we stop further message visible to our sensory receptors. So, effective communication does not take place because of premature evaluation. This barrier can be overcome by empathic listening or suspending judgment for the time being.

(3) Different Comprehension of Reality

Reality is not an absolute concept; it is relative to different persons. Each person has unique sensory receptors and mental filters. As a result, our abstractions, inferences and evaluation are different. Abstraction is the process of focusing attention on specific details and ignoring others. Due to abstracting, we fail to comprehend the situation as a whole and even fail to understand other person's point of view as we think ourselves right. Our inferences are different, beyond verifiable and confirmed facts. For example, one person told the other that he would leave by specific train; the other person infers his arrival at the station at the right time of train. It may prove to be correct or wrong. In the same manner, we infer beyond facts.

(4) Attitude of Superiors

The general attitude of the superiors about communication affects the flow of communication. If the superiors are afraid of delegating authority and lack confidence in themselves as well as in their subordinates, they will obviously try to conceal, colour or filter the information. They intentionally do so to twist the situation to their favour or to mask their weaknesses.

(5) Attitude of Subordinates

The negative attitude of subordinates also affects the communication flow. Their inferiority complexes, unwillingness to share information and fear of action are the obvious barriers to communication. Organizational communication becomes ineffective.

(6) Poor Listening

Poor listening is one of the psychological barriers in the effective communication. Most of the people just hear; they do not listen. If they listen at all, they listen only selectively, taking the desired part and ignoring the 'undesired part' of the message; they listen what they want to listen. This poor listening retards the communication flow and prevents understanding of the real meanings.

(7) Egotism

Egotism is diametrically opposite to the transmission of understanding, the most vital aspect of communication.

The self-centred persons think that their own ideas are more important and others are wrong. Such people are very bad listeners. They keep their minds closed and alienate from the people; the communication process is hindered.

(8) Emotions

Positive emotions such as love, affection and compassion make the flow of communication smooth whereas negative emotions such as hatred, anger, anxiety obstruct the communication process.

Excited, nervous, afraid and perplexed individuals cannot think rationally and consequently transmit their negativity to others. They cannot receive the message as it is.

Therefore, effective communication requires a soothed heart and a silent mind.

BASIC MODEL OF COMMUNICATION

The process of communication involves a procedure consisting of only a few steps. Berlo has suggested one model to comprehend the process properly, which includes:

(a) Communication source or an encoder,
(b) A message,

(c) A channel, and
(d) A decoder or a communication receiver or a destination.

We can illustrate this procedure as under:

(i) The information source decides to communicate and encodes a message, transmits it through a channel to the receiver, which is then decoded and acted upon. There are noises or distortions in between.
(ii) Thus, we see that there are six elements of communication: a code, a channel, encoding, decoding, encoder and decoder.

The six elements are described as under:

Sender/Encoder

A message is communicated or a piece of information is conveyed by means of a mechanism. This is necessary with a view to being able to convey the message or information fully and completely.

There is a sender of the message who is also called an encoder; he understands the code just as a computer understands the language of a code.

Channels

(i) A channel or device is used to communicate. It could be a radio or a television set, newspaper or magazine and the like.
(ii) The encoding process means putting the message together or arranging the ideas in a recognizable and understandable form for conveying it to the receivers.
(iii) Unlike in telegraphy, the encoder her is a human agent. The encoder decides the content of the message.
(iv) Similarly, decoder is the destination where the message lands.

The receiver has to wait for the words to be spoken or written. He/she selects them according to his/her knowledge, experience, assumption, and attitudes.

When two people communicate who are equally matched in intelligence, social background and comprehension power, the whole bundle of advantages and disadvantages pass from one to the other.

The encoder, the initiator of the communication activity, chooses his subject and the channel of communication and makes the first impact on the mind of the decoder.

Decoding of message is one of the most important and very crucial elements of the communication process. The entire process of communication comprehension hinges on the decoder.

Of course, the message will be received, recorded and interpreted differently by different people according to their knowledge, experience and understanding levels.

Two other communication specialists, Claude E. Shannon and Warren Weaver have given another view of the communication process as:

Sender
to
Signal
Through
Mechanical and Semantic Decoder of the Receiver
With
Mechanical and Semantic Noise
Working all through the process

What we mean by 'noise'—whether mechanical or semantic—is when the communication process is on, some loss of the message or information is bound to take place. There are varied reasons for it: it may be due to human ignorance, chaotic conditions in the system, and distortion at some point in the system. Whatever quantitative or qualitative may be the loss due to any kind of disturbance, the receiver can decide about the value, worth or the use of the message only on the basis of what he/she has decoded.

These elements factors in communication operation—communicator, receiver, purpose, expression, perception, interpretation, response, channel and occasion—compose the communication process.

According to Berlo, the basic purpose of communication is to enable human beings to meet their basic human needs and to be able to grapple with daily requirements imperative for human existence, such as to "give and take orders, make request, comply with requests of others. We learn about acts, how things are made, destroyed, changed". Berlo says further: "Again, communication enables us to study social organizations, economic relationships, cultural values, etc."

In view the above discussions, we can say that it is crucial that the content and objective of the communication of a message are of relevance to human beings in their daily life.

The following situation, therefore, represents what communication achieves and what its parameters are:

WHO SAYS
WHAT
IN WHICH CHANNEL,
TO WHOM
AND
WITH WHAT EFFECT

Refer: Harlod Laswell's Model of Communication.

Harlod Laswell, Communication expert, asserts that communication is affected by all the steps stated above. Every step influences the consequences and the effects of the communication process.

Form and Content are of special importance: 'Form' involves how we communicate the message whereas 'Content' involves what we communicate.

ESSENTIALS OF EFFECTIVE COMMUNICATION

"Here are the first steps to successful communication, follow them and you will be on your way", say Levine and Crom.

(1) Make communication a top priority.
(2) Be open to other people.
(3) Create a receptive environment for communication.

An effective communication is most essential for the organization. Whatsoever the form—letter, memoranda or reports—it may take, whatsoever the media it may use, it has to be made effective by following certain scientific principles. These principles are not exclusive, but only illustrative as more can be added to them. According to Francis J. Bergin, communication should be:

(1) Candid	(2) Clear	(3) Complete
(4) Concise	(5) Concrete	(6) Correct
(7) Courteous		

More points can be added to these 7Cs of communication.

For our discussion, we shall divide the principles of communication into two broad parts:

(a) 7Cs of communication
(b) Other Principles of communication

7 Cs of Communication

(1) Candid

The message communicated should be candid *(straight forward, frank),* not indirect, multimodal or untrue. Gay Hendricks and Kate Ludeman profoundly remark, "If you make sure you are telling the truth, you won't ever have to worry about people listening to you. When people do not listen, it is usually because the speaker's got something else; he or she is communicating besides the truth".

To make communication effective, the message should be frank and straight forward. There should not be beating about the bush or conveying something that hinders the truth. It will lead to prejudices and doubts about the sincerity of the communicator.

(2) Clear

The message to be communicated whether oral or written should be clear. *Make thought and all other things clear to the recipient for anticipated action/response; the first and foremost requirement of communication.*

Clear message always stems from clear minds and clear hearts. As the message to be communicated is first produced in the mind of the sender, the sender's mind should have clear thought about the objectives of communication, to be effective on the receiver and the channels to be used.

The clearly thought out message should be presented with clear expressions to avoid ambiguities and confusion. Transmitter should be very careful about the meanings and organization of the words and symbols used in communication.

To make the expressions clear and free from multi-interpretations and inferences, the sender of the message should consider the following points:

(a) Clarity in expression is brought through use of precise and concrete words. For example, notice the following sentences:

Imprecise: After studying the market reports and other relevant data of different markets, we can infer that the share market is lucrative for investment.

Precise: After studying the market, we recommend that investing in shares is profitable.

(b) As far as possible, use simple and short words than pompous and heavy words:

Pompous	Simple
Terminate	End
Fascination	Attraction
Utilise	Use
Procure	Get
Deem	Think
Interrogate	Question

(c) Use words which are familiar to the audience and are appropriate for the situation:

Familiar	Pretentious
Home	Domicile
After	Subsequent
Deeply	Profoundly
For Example	e.g.

(d) Construction of effective sentences and paragraphs is at the core of clarity. For this:

(i) Prefer use of short sentences than long ones.
(ii) Insert no more than one main idea into a sentence.
(iii) Arrange words and clauses in such a way that the main idea occurs easily in a sentence and less important in subordinate (or dependent) clause.

(e) Heading, tabulation, graphs, line charts, pie charts, coloured capital letters or italic letters should be used in a relative way to improve the visual impact of the message.
(f) Use technical terms and business jargons while communicating to the professionals. But for communicating with ordinary reader or listener, it should be avoided. For example: Technical—the company earned 20% rate or return on equity.

Ordinary: The Company earned 20% rate of return on owner's money.

(3) Complete

Completeness is necessary for effective communication. Incomplete messages bread misunderstanding and misinterpretation that lead to further queries resulting into wastage of time and resources and irritates the receiver. Therefore, *every aspect and relevant detail should be incorporated in logical sequence.* Moreover, completeness contributes to the clarity of the message.

Herta A. Murphy, Herbert W. Hildebrandt and Jane P. Thomas aptly remark on the benefits of completeness of message, "Completeness offers numerous benefits. First, complete messages are more likely to bring the desired results without the expense of additional messages. Second, they can do a better job of building goodwill. Messages that contain information the receiver needs show concern for others. Third, complete messages can help avert costly law suits that may result if important information is missing. Last, communications that seem inconsequential can be surprisingly important if the information they contain is complete and effective.

To make the message complete, the following guidelines should be kept in mind:

(a) Provide all necessary information that the reader needs for thorough and accurate understanding. Check if the message provides answer to the five W. questions—who, what, when, where, why—and other essential, how.
(b) For example, while circulating the notice of conference, specify when the conference will be held, where it will be held, why it is being conducted, what the matters to be discussed are, which are going to address and how many members are expected to reach there.
(c) Answer all stated and implied questions which may arise in the mind of reader. For example, while drafting letter offering sale of goods, first anticipate customer's possible questions regarding price, quality, quantity, usage, etc. and then draft the letter to answers all these questions.
(d) Give extra information in the relevant context.

(4) Concise

To retain the attention as well as to save the time of the reader, it is essential that the message should be concise. *Conciseness means conveying the message in the fewest possible words without sacrificing its completeness and clarity.* It contributes to make the important ideas stand out. On the other hand, aimless and unnecessary details distract the reader's attention and consequently reduce the effectiveness of communication: these should be avoided.

Concise messages appear more interesting to the reader and show respect for recipients by not letting his personal as well as professional life bored with unnecessary information.

Communicated message should clarify the meaning in fewer possible words; include only relevant facts, avoid needless repetition of the same ideas and the words should appear in organized form. For this:

(a) Use single word substitutes instead of phrases without changing the meanings of the message:

Long Phrases	*Single words*
At the present time	now
Due to the fact that	because
Despite the fact that	although
Will you kindly	please
Keeping in view	considering

(b) Omit trite and wordy expressions:

Words Expression	*Concise*
I beg to state that I am going	I am going
Allow me to say how useful your suggestions were.	Your suggestions were very useful

(c) Use single and simple words instead of using two words, conveying the same idea:

Two words	*Simple*
9 a.m. in the morning	9 a.m.
Viable alternative	alternative
In my personal opinion	in my opinion
Period of one month	one month

(d) Eliminate unnecessary prepositional phrases:

Words	*Concise*
Wish to suggest	Suggest
Order for goods	Order goods

(e) Include only relevant material related to the main purpose of the message

(f) Avoid lengthy introductions and unnecessary explanations. Also, omit the information already known to the receiver.

(5) Concrete

The communicated statement should not be vague; *it should rather be concrete and specific*. Concrete expressions create specific visual images in the mind of the receiver which vague or generalized statement cannot. For example, consider the following statement:

(i) The price of washing machine is very high.
(ii) The price of automatic washing machine is Rs. 23,000.

The first statement is vague and general. To say that the price is very high conveys different meaning to different people depending upon their economic background and perceptions. The second statement specifying "automatic machine" and "Rs. 23,000", is concrete and specific as it presents definite facts.

While writing business letter, memo, advertisement copy, report, etc. always give concrete facts, no generalized statements. Concrete language reduces the chances of misinterpretation by the receiver and increases the likelihood that message will be understood in the way the sender intends.

"Moreover, concrete messages are more richly textured than general or vague messages, then they tend to be more concrete, dynamic and interesting", Murphy, Hildesbrant and Thomas rightly remark. Therefore—

(a) Use specific facts and figures.
(b) Avoid using words that lead to uncertainty and confusion: For example, early, low, many, large, quick, soon, slightly, least, very big, a few, small, about, slow, most, easy.
(c) Use active voice than passive voice.

Passive	*Active*
The goods were received by us.	We received the goods.
The conflict among workers was resolved by top management.	Top management resolved the conflict among the workers.

The message to be communicated should be correct in spelling, grammar, format, contents, statistical information, etc. Incorrect and inaccurate statements mislead the reader, lower his confidence in the communicator and tarnish the image of the organization. These may sometimes lead the management to erroneous and disastrous decisions. Therefore, it is imperative that the sender should verify the correctness of the information before presenting it to the receiver. To make the message correct—

(a) Ensure that facts and figures are accurate and verify statistical data, totals, etc.
(b) Check whether grammar, punctuation and spelling are proper or not.
(c) Use the right level of language. That language may be formal or informal.

"Formal writing is often associated with scholarly writing, doctoral dissertations, scholarly articles, legal materials where formality in style is demanded. Informal writing is more characteristic of business writing. Here, the sender uses words that are short, well-known, and conventional". [Murphy, Hildebrandt and Thomas].

(6) Correct

The message to be communicated should be correct in various aspects—spelling, grammar, format, contents, statistical information, etc. Being correct means creating credibility. If message is incorrect, it creates misunderstanding, shakes faith, misleads the receiver or reader, lowers the confidence in communicator and tarnishes the image of the organization.

Management may take erroneous or disastrous decisions. Business may be affected in the process.

(7) Courteous

Congenial and healthy communications environment is essential to ensure the effectives of communication. Courtesy in the message as well as manners plays dominating role in this regard.

While communicating, it is necessary to be considerate, not impatient and irritated by being aware of ourself. If it is necessary to criticize, we must be tactful in approach, so that our communication generates more light than heat. While communicating:

(a) First be in right frame of mind. Ensure that you are not perturbed or irritated, but are calm and quiet.
(b) Use polite and respectful tone. Courtesy is not merely policing with mechanical insertions of "please" and "thank you" rather it is sincere concern and respect for the other person.
(c) Always 'thank" the other person for his generosity and favour.
(d) Do not forget to sue the word 'please' for requesting something.
(e) Ensure that the other person's self-respect is not hurt. None wants to pocket insult and face indignation. Managers must realize that respect to individual pays rich dividends.

OTHER PRINCIPLES OF COMMUNICATION

In addition to the above 7Cs of communication, the following points deserve attention for making communication effective:

Misunderstandings are rules rather than exceptions because of unhealthy and uncongenial organizational environment. The neutral words attempting to convey positive message convey negative message because people possess different perceptions.

We notice defensive behaviour of employees because of lack of co-operation and trust among them in the organization. Communication can not be effective under such circumstances.

1. Concern of Top Management

The first and foremost requirement is to create synergetic environment. Synergy means whole is greater than sum total of its parts. Under synergetic environment, cooperation breeds co-operation and trust breeds trust at accelerating rate. For this, top management should take initiative and ensure trust and cooperation among employees at lower levels. They will respond with trust and cooperation sooner or later. When organization is operating at high degree of cooperation and trust among employees, communication will be automatically effective.

2. Two-Way Communication

Effective communication is never one-way traffic rather it is two-way canalization. The organization should ensure two-way communication, with sound feedback system, to overcome the communication gaps because of distortions, filtering, colouring, etc.

3. Strengthen Communication Flow

The organizational policy should simplify, streamline and strengthen the flow of communication both upward and downward through proper organizational structure, proper decentralization and delegation of authority. In addition to this, adequate and timely dissemination of information should be there, both through formal as well as informal networks.

Frequent meetings, conferences and social gatherings should be organized from time to time to ensure easy access of information to employees.

4. Proper Media

Proper media of communication should be followed. Any media is not ideal for very situation. Illiterate workers should be instructed through oral and visual communication. In case of formal relations, written communication should be followed. And for negotiation, persuasion, brainstorming etc., the best way is to have face-to-face oral communication.

5. Encourage Open Communication

Lack of transparency and denial of information breed rumours in the organization and consequently harms the organizational environment. To avoid this, management should make open doors policy and 'Manage By Walking Around' (MBWA).

In open door policy, employees are encouraged to approach immediate and higher superiors with any matter that concerns the organizational gap among executives and employees. Executives should follow this policy not only in letter but also in spirit so that not only their doors are open physically but also psychologically, and the employees can communicate without hesitation.

Executives should not restrict their operations by sitting in their offices but walk out through the door to make contacts with a large number of employees.

6. Use of Appropriate Language

Appropriate words, pictures, symbols should be used to make the message simple and easily comprehensible to the concerned employees. As far as possible, technical and equivocal words should be avoided and message should be supported by proper diagram.

7. Effective Listening

In oral communication, effective listening is vital. It is not only the sender's responsibility to make his message clear, complete and concrete, but also of the receiver to understand the message in proper sense through effective listening.

Listening should be made effective by keeping the mind free from prejudices and presumptions, paying attention to the spoken words and feeling the emotions of the speaker.

CHAPTER

2

Communication Log (DRILL)

Log is something like a diary, a record of events. So, the communication log of a manager should be the record of the various acts of communication that engage him during the day. The manager manages with the help of communication.

It works in all situations: whether he is motivating his employees to work with greater efficiency, negotiating with the union leaders to settle certain disputes, attending the meeting of a chamber of commerce, inaugurating a seminar, going through a report, or going to lunch with another manager with whom he wants to strike a business deal in the informal atmosphere of a restaurant, he is engaged in communication.

His work is tremendous, and activities, multifarious, but the time at his disposal is limited. He must plan his day's work, or he is likely to land into some embarrassing situations.

It is indisputable fact that the manager plans with the help of his communication log.

The day's activities: In the course of a day, the manager's time may be taken up by the following activities:

(i) Going through the incoming letters and dictating replies.
(ii) Making and receiving calls on the telephone.
(iii) Issuing orders and instructions to the subordinates.
(iv) Going through reports.
(v) Holding discussion with the departmental heads.
(vi) Holding interviews with the subordinates to discuss with them organizational matters, their performance and their problems.
(vii) Holding interviews with outsiders, clients, customers, dealers, agents, professionals, etc.
(viii) Inspecting the various sections of the office and/or factory and holding on the spot discussion with the employees.
(ix) Taking business lunch, tea or dinner with prospective suppliers, dealers, clients, pressmen, etc.
(x) Presiding over the meetings of the employees.
(xi) Attending meetings of the chambers of commerce and industry, trade, finance, taxation, etc.
(xii) Stimulating subordinates to do their work with greater zeal and sincerity.
(xiii) Negotiating with the trade union leaders, attending to the workers' complaints, intervening to settle the disputes arising among the workers themselves.

These activities can be put into five broad groups:

(a) Receiving both from internal and external sources environmental and competitive information that might prove helpful in the formulation of general policies and fixation of organizational goals,
(b) Internal communication aimed at the transmission of policies, business strategies, and procedures to the lower level employees, motivating them to achieve organizational goals, and appraising their performance and achievements.
(c) Giving information about the organization to the outsiders.
(d) Communicating with dealers, agents, client,

suppliers, other professional people like those handling the publicity media, bankers, chambers of commerce and industry, pressmen for the furtherance of the organizational goals, and

(e) Communicating with the employees as well as trade union representatives with a view to ensuring smooth working within the organization.

While preparing the communication log, the manager should take sufficient care to spare time for all these activities.

A SPECIMEN OF COMMUNICATION LOG (COM. DRILL)

The communication log of the normal day of any manager would naturally depend upon the nature and size of the organization to which he is attached.

It would also depend upon his professional qualifications and competence and the respect he commands in the field of trade and industry. So, no hard and fast rules can be laid down on how to prepare his communication log. What we are giving below is only a specimen to serve as a guide to the student or practicing manager:

THE ADVANTAGE OF MAINTAINING A COMMUNICATION LOG (DAILY AND PERIODIC DRILLS)

The major advantage of preparing the communication log of a day, or even a weak, (leaving scope for day-to-day adjustments) well in advance is that the manager can plan his activities much better. Let us suppose that he is required to interview some candidates on a particular day. If the communication log of that day is ready with him well in time, he can give instructions to the Personnel Manager to do preliminary screening of the applications so that before beginning the interview, he has a fairly good idea of the suitability of a few candidates and does not have to waste time on subjecting all the candidates to long interviews.

A Specimen of Communication Log

08.00 AM	Reading newspapers and trade journal over the morning cup of tea (tea gives better flavour and generates ideas).
08.00 to 08.30 AM	Fixing appointments on the telephone.
08.30 to 09.15 AM	Getting ready for the office/factory, leaving for the office/factory.
09.30 to 10.00 AM	Going through relevant letters, files, reports, getting ready for the day's work.
10.00 to 10.30 AM	Discussion with departmental heads and giving orders, instructions.
10.30 to 01.30 AM	Receiving visitors, sales representatives, dealers, professionals, etc.
11.30 to 12.00 PM	Going through important incoming letters (attending to the 'in-tray').
12.00 to 01.00 PM	Dictating letters, notes, etc. (out-tray).
01.00 to 02.00 PM	Business lunch with some guest (creating goodwill).
02.00 to 03.00 PM	Interviews with the employees (feedback and guidance).
03.00 to 04.00 PM	Visit to the various sections of the office/ factory and on the spot discussion with the employees (surprise checks and managing by walking).
04.00 to 05.00 PM	Presiding over seminars (creating open culture for informal and frank discussions).
08.00 to 10.30 PM	Business dinner with some guest building bridges of public relations).

Another example: Suppose on Friday, the manager instructs one of his supervisors to report to him on the progress of a new project on Monday. While preparing the communication log for Monday, he will make provision to receive the supervisor on Monday and he will neither have to say an embarrassing no to the supervisor nor hurry through his report.

Communication log can be extremely helpful to the over burdened manager who feels himself to be on the verge of nervous exhaustion. He can critically scrutinize his activities and spread them over the various days of the week in such a way that he is not over strained on any day.

Perhaps, he may also succeed in eliminating a few time consuming but fruitless activities. He may discover that most of his time is being consumed by incoming telephone calls.

He may then instruct his secretary to pass on to him only the urgent calls and either answer the routing calls herself or pass them on to the concerned departments. If it is correspondence that he finds burdensome, he can entrust it to someone else and make himself free to devote his time to more important matters.

A case in point in this regard is that of Imperial Bank of India. It would be found interesting and practical. There used to be a Daily List of usance accepted Bills to record the bills date-wise under the dates these fell due for payment. The officer-in-charge had to refer to this book (daily list) to take necessary action. If payment was not forthcoming, the bill(s) was/were returned to the drawers through the branches which sent them for collection of payment.

Similarly, the Agent who headed the branch (now designated manager or branch manager, etc.), used to maintain five long lists on hard-board, one board for each of the week-days, except Saturday which was half day. These cards mentioned books of accounts or entries constituting original record. One card relating to Monday was given on that day of the week to the Head Messenger to bring all the books in single lot to the Agent's room for scrutiny to see that the books were properly maintained and there were no unauthenticated cuttings or alterations. This was repeated every day.

Again, the Messengers were made to follow in a line outside the counters in the hall to see that they were clean-shaved, uniforms and badges clean and shining, shoes polished, etc. The bank used to supply uniforms, polish and paid for laundering.

Now that there is scientific management, things have been streamlined and the daily, weekly, fortnightly, monthly drills of the Agent (or manager) is reduced to Log in the computer and followed meticulously.

CHAPTER

3

Objectives of Communication

The main purpose of all communication in an organization is the general welfare of the organization. Therefore, effective communication is needed at all the stages to ensure this welfare. In view of the elaborate and complex structure of to-day's commercial and other organizations, communication is and can be used for any or all of the following purposes:

These are Information, Advice, Order, Suggestion, Persuasion, Education, Warning, Raising Morale and Motivation. Let us know about each of them in some details.

INFORMATION

Receiving or passing information is one of the most important objectives of communication. We can do this either by spoken word or through written language. There is no denying the fact that managers need complete, accurate and precise information, timely and in the form desired so that there is no need to refer back for more of it.

Information helps in planning and implementing the plans, and so on. Information can be External and internal.

External Information

1. Information on the following aspects is very vital for the welfare of the organization:
   Information about the products: whether these are being manufactured as per modern trend and whether the feedback of the customers is favourable or not.
2. Information about the availability of credit from financial institutions or suppliers and others, terms and conditions.
3. Information about the availability of raw material.
4. Information about the rules and regulations of the government.
5. Information about the advertising media.
6. Information about the latest developments in the fields of science and technology.
7. Information about the import and export opportunities and partnerships/collaboration abroad.
8. Information about market and business environment in own country and in the potential markets abroad.

Internal Information

1. Information on job assignments and procedures governing them.
2. Information on status and decision-making powers.
3. General information on policies and activities of the organization.
4. Information about the organization hierarchy.

Information for Planning

1. Environment Information.
2. Internal information about production and sales capacity of the organization; detailed information about the members of the staff, their academic and professional qualifications, their efficiency and reliability, their limitations, etc.
3. Competitive position in the market, market share

and strategies adopted to stay and win in the market.

For efficient and effective planning, this information is classified, analysed and brought up to date. It should be readily available in the files.

SOURCES OF INFORMATION

1. Old files in the organisation's various departments or in a centralized section.
2. Observations during supervision, inspection, audit and comments and suggestions as well as customers' feedback.
3. Mass Media reports, opinion and comments or articles and features appearing therein.
4. Library Research.
5. Chambers of Commerce and Industry, Confederation of Indian Industry (CII), NASSCOM, etc.
6. Meetings, Seminars, Conferences and Conventions, etc.
7. Personal Interviews with politicians, bureaucrats, business leaders, experts in professional fields and members of the general public.
8. Questionnaires administered periodically to elicit information which could be analysed and used, where found useful.
9. Trade fairs and Exhibitions.
10. Current Electronic Media Communication, in particular the Internet.

ADVICE

It is always supposed to be factual and objective. Since it involves personal opinion, it is likely to be subjective. It is neutral; the receiver may or may not accept it. Its purpose is either to influence his opinion or his behaviour. It may be helpful; it can lead to disaster, too.

Importance of Advice

All the economic and commercial activities in the modern world have become complex. None is expert to handle all of them efficiently and profitably. Managers need advice from experts in various fields like finance, marketing, engineering, construction, electronics, technology, public relations, etc. Business can succeed only if all support from the relative areas is available.

Advice flows horizontally or downwards. To make advice become effective, the following steps may be taken:

1. Advice should be both man-oriented and work-oriented.
2. Advice may not be given to a person to make him feel conscious of his inferior knowledge or skill. The advice giver should not assume patronizing tone, the receiver will reject it outright.
3. The advisor should genuinely feel the motive of betterment of the person who is given advice. Adopt a tone and phrase language in such a manner that the person concerned feels absolutely at ease.
4. Give the subordinates due freedom to react to the advice and you may possibly get a number of good suggestions.

COUNSELLING

It is very similar to Advice; counselling is objective and impersonal. The counselor has to be very skilled and tactful. He does his work without personal interest and involvement. While advice has a personal touch about it, counsel is eagerly sought. Good organizations keep a panel of experts like doctors, psychologists, psychiatrists and social workers to invite them to give counselling—for the welfare of workers, managers and senior executives—under physical or mental strains.

ORDER

Order is an authoritative communication. It is

synonymous with command. It is a directive and has to be followed. There are occasions when strict obedience is required. Otherwise, things may not move and organizations may fail to achieve the desired results. All the downward flow of information is dominated by orders.

Types of Orders

These are classified in the following ways:

1. *Written and Oral Orders*

Written ones are given in the following cases:

(a) If order is of highly responsible nature, its record is to be kept. It is made absolutely specific.
(b) When the task is repetitive in nature and it is inconvenient to issue oral orders again and again for the same task.
(c) The person being ordered is situated away physically and it is not possible to give him oral orders.

Oral orders are given in the following cases:

(a) The task or job is to be done immediately.
(b) It is an ordinary work and there is no need to keep its record.
(c) There is a kind of permanent superior-subordinate relationship between the order-giver and the order-receiver. The order-giver does not feel the need of giving written orders as the procedure is cumbersome.

2. *General and Specific Orders*

Orders relating to one activity are specific orders. If there are numerous activities with operational similarities, the general orders are issued.

3. *Procedural and Operational Orders*

When procedures are specified, procedural orders are issued. They are general by nature. Operational orders are more closely related to the job in hand and in mind. These orders specify how a particular job is to be done.

4. *Mandatory and Discretionary Orders*

Mandatory orders have to be obeyed; there is no alternative. Disobedience tantamount to insubordination and instantly invites disciplinary action.

Discretionary orders are in the nature of recommendations. They suggest what is desirable and what is to be done. The receiver of such orders will see the feasibility of the order and decide what can be done. He may ignore it altogether or partially implement it. He may explain his position and why he chose another course to do the job. For example, Head Office may issue discretionary order to do a particular job. The branch manager, being the person on the spot, may not find the order befitting the situation. He may not implement it.

Characteristics of Effective Order

(a) It must be clear, complete and understandable.
(b) It should be possible to execute it.
(c) It should be given in a friendly way; otherwise, it may be resented or carried out reluctantly.

Steps involved in the process of order-giving: Paul Pigors has mentioned seven steps in this regard. These are as under:

1. *Planning*

Planning is very necessary to make order complete and clear. The order-giver ensures on the following points:

(i) What action is actually required?
(ii) Is the order feasible?
(iii) Who is to perform it?
(iv) In how much time is it to be performed?
(v) Are any problems likely to crop up? Is there any provision to solve those problems?
(vi) What kind/type of order is to be given?

Human nature is not amenable to coercion or repression. The buyers and workers have to be manipulated tactfully to accept change; they have to be convinced that the change is for their advantage without making them conscious of the change. Persuasion is an art. Managers have to learn it and practice to master.

Art of Persuasion you can persuade others if—

(a) You are convinced yourself first;
(b) You do not impose but discuss and meet him half way and then proceed in case of one being headstrong.
(c) You are not rigid, and prepared to meet half way.
(d) You can look at the situation from the other person's angle also.

There are four steps you can take to persuade; these are as under: (1) Analyse the situation. (2) Prepare the receiver. (3) Deliver the message. (4) Prompt action.

EDUCATION

It is a very conscious process of communication. It involves both teaching and learning. The main purpose of education is to widen knowledge and to improve skills.

This is brought about in discussions, seminars, training and development, refresher courses, study tours to large corporate, organizing special lectures, sharing research results, etc.

It is carried on at three levels: Education for management; Education for the employees; Education for the outside public, etc.

WARNING

It becomes necessary to administer (issue) warning to the employees who do not abide by the norms of the organization or violate the rules and regulations.

Tardiness (laziness), negligence, defiance, tempering with the records, mishandling equipment, lack of regularity and punctuality, gossiping, pilfering office stationery and other material, spreading rumours and misleading new employees are some of the actions that call for a reprimand or warning.

Warning is a forceful means of communication, though negative in its import and effect. It requires immediate action. It should be used sparingly and discreetly to retain its effectiveness. The following points should be kept in mind while issuing warning:

(a) Some warnings are general like 'No smoking', 'No talking', Beware of dog', etc. They convey a kind of notice. They are almost in the nature of information.

(b) Warnings are given to particular persons (by name). They involve disciplinary actions, or advance notice of likely disciplinary action for negligence, lapse or wrongful action.

As reprimands are demoralizing and so, resented, care should be taken to ascertain the truth of the charges and imputations. Reprimands never spring from personal prejudices. The action should be fair and dispassionate as far as possible. It should never be accompanied with display of rage.

(c) Reprimand should never be administered in the presence of others. It will make him feel humiliated. The worker should be summoned to the privacy of the supervisor's room and talk to him dispassionately. He should be given opportunity to explain his position. If he fails to convince, tell him without losing temper what is expected of him, in his interest and in the interest of the organization.

(d) Investigate the employee's undesirable behaviour. He may be burdened with domestic or personal problems. He may be nursing some personal grudge against the supervisor or the organisation. If the supervisor succeeds in talking him out of the problems, it becomes constructive.

(e) The purpose of giving warning should be betterment of the organisation. It should be desirable to choose the right words and make the reprimand or warning less bitter by ascribing the mess to unknown reasons.

RAISING MORALE

Morale stands for mental health. Its constituents are courage, fortitude, resolution and confidence. High morale is the launching pad for operational efficiency, team-work and ends up in high performance—satisfying to the workers and management alike, and organisation attains ascendency.

Morale creates a sense of togetherness, promotes co-operation (*esprit de corps*), generates stronger bonds of loyalty with the organization and creates work-culture to forge ahead in the competition, assuming leadership in the market.

Factors considered conducive to strengthening and sustaining of high morale:

(a) Right man on right job and at the right time, suiting his experience, intelligence, aptitude as well as his physical and technical caliber. He would feel thereby that his work is important and it is appreciated by the authorities. He is accorded autonomy in his work: he is free to do his work as he likes. Besides, he is encouraged to give suggestions.

(b) The working atmosphere at the work-place is congenial in that the superiors are helpful, efficient with positive attitude Their interaction is constructive and they enjoy workers' respect.

(c) The workers are sure of their career path and they entertain no doubt about availability of promotion avenues.

(d) Grievances are looked into sympathetically and genuine ones are promptly removed.

MOTIVATION

Motivation is a need to engage in an activity. It is either generated by head or vented by the heart. Motivation activates and energises a person. It channelizes his behaviour towards attainment of desired goals. So, motivation and behaviour are intimately related to each other.

We observe that in Order and Persuasion, the communicator (superior generally) has the upper hand but in motivation, he is in the background.

A motivated worker does not need any supervision over him, rather he resents it. He does the work as his own. Motivated workers show much better results and they are liked by every body. The organization introduces many innovations to sustain the motivation level of the workers.

Monetary and non-monetary incentives are offered. Bonus, share in the net profits, sweet equity offers, leave travel facility for the entire family, medical benefits, dinner at late hour working, transport to residence when asked to work overtime, etc. and much more is thought of and implemented. These work wonders. After all, you dig deep into any activity, you find a man there.

However, monetary benefits (incentives) do not work well all the time. They get absorbed in the routine.

Consider the following points while discussing motiation as a form of communication: benefits and new ones, more of the non-monetary, are innovated.

Rewards generally work and motivate. Same incentive does not motivate all equally. An array of incentives has to be introduced with continuous improvements or variations to give them new look.

Consider the following points while discussing motivation as a form of communication: Motivation can be achieved through:

(a) Monetary incentives;
(b) encouraging the workers to participate in decision-making process;
(c) making achievement goals very specific and measurable with some challenge; and
(d) giving security and congenial working environment.

CONSENSUS

In political sphere, this concept of consensus is familiar enough. It is felt that election to high offices like President or Vice-President should not be made a subject of controversy as dignity of these offices is very important. A few names are thrown up and each name discussed. The name of one person, most acceptable, is approved. Election does not take place and the candidate gets elected unopposed.

Consensus does not imply unanimity. Unanimity in the perfect sense is just impossible. In official matters also, consensus is tried to be brought about; that ensures better working and the workers pull together and do not pull apart. Working efficiency results, and productivity and profitability improve.

The Chief Executive plays crucial role in the process. He places the situation before the house and invites views. He listens to the views and makes notes. He winds up the discussions, first by acknowledging the contribution of all members and then proceeds to explain implications of each proposal threadbare. He clarifies doubts and finally comes to the point which he feels is the most profitable solution.

In short—Consensus is the process of arriving at agreement through consultation. Consensus is not unanimity. Dissent is not expressed in the larger interests.

Its advantages are: decisions on the basis of consensus are easy to accept. It promotes harmony, checks conflicts and splits. Splits generate unending controversy. That leads to groupism and affects working.

It has disadvantages too. These are: Dissent is often stifled in the name of consensus. It may degenerate into a process of mutual accommodation. It may project false image of the management.

CHAPTER

4

Media and Types of Communication

In the current, call it modern time, it is possible to communicate through a variety of media. All the media available can be broadly classified into five groups as under:

1. Written Communication
2. Oral Communication
3. Visual Communication
4. Audio-Visual Communication
5. Computer-based Communication

1. WRITTEN COMMUNICATION

It includes letters, circulars, memos, telegrams, fax, telex, reports, minutes, manuals, questionnaires, etc.

2. ORAL COMMUNICATION

It includes face-to-face conversation, conversation over

telephone, radio broadcasts, interviews, group discussions, meetings, presentations, speeches, conferences, seminars, conventions, announcements over public address system, etc.

3. VISUAL COMMUNICATION

It includes gestures, facial expressions, tables and charts, graphs, diagrams, posters, slides, film strips, etc.

4. AUDIO-VISUAL COMMUNICATION

It encompasses television and cinema films with narration (dialogues, interaction, etc.)

5. COMPUTER-BASED COMMUNICATION

It includes E-mail, voice mail, cellular phones, fax, telex, etc. These have been taken up in detail elsewhere in the book.

TYPES OF COMMUNICATION

Each type of business entity has to have two types of communication, External and Internal. Externally, it needs to communicate with other business organizations and industrial houses, etc. like banks, government offices, the press, customers and the general public. Internal communication consists in transmitting information within the organisation. Internal communication is both downward communication and upward communication.

Downward Communication

This communication flows from superior to the subordinate; they are connected and related together by authority relationships. Generally, orders and instructions flow downwards.

The main objectives of this communication are as under:

1. To give specific directives and orders about the job being entrusted to subordinate(s).

2. To explain policies and procedures of the organization (policy guidelines for implementation).
3. To apprise the subordinates of their performance.
4. To give information to the subordinates about the rationale of their jobs to make them understand the significance and urgency of their jobs in relation to the goals of their organization.

Limitations of downward communication are the following:

1. Under communication and over-communication.
2. Delay as the message travels through proper channel.
3. Loss of information as delay often and particularly the comments made at various stages do the trick, more so in regard to oral communication or secret communication which is translated down the line in own words.
4. Distortion takes place due to interpretation and filtering process. There can be softening down the tone or exaggerations of the message.
5. *Built-in resistance*: It smacks of too much authoritarianism which subordinates do not accept in good taste as they do not participate in the decision-making process.

How to make it effective?
Read the following tips:
Managers need to be adequately informed.

Managers should be clear in their mind how much to communicate.

Some authority should be delegated to the lower levels in the organization to shorten the line of communication. Information should be passed on to the concerned person.

Orders, instructions and directives should be freely discussed among the subordinates in the open meetings to clear any doubts or to give clarifications. This will satisfy the subordinates.

DOWNWARD COMMUNICATION

- It flows from top to bottom of the organisational hierarchy.
- Its objectives are : (a) to give directions about what to do, when to do, who to do, how much to do, whom to report, etc. Next, to explain organisational policies, programmes, projects, procedures and systems: to know how effectively the personnel are doing their jobs; to motivate employees and raise their morale, and hear their grievances and complaints for redressal; and to educate subordinates for performing jobs better.
- It benefits employees, introduces work culture, removes bottlenecks, enhances competitiveness, improves productivity and increases market share as also to project better image of organisation.
- There are problems too in downward communication such as—distortion of message, delays in flow of orders and instructions, overloaded or underloaded messages (lack of clarity and lack of completeness), bureaucratic degeneration, etc.
- Pre-requisites of Downward Communication are—well informed managers, positive communication climate, prevention of over-concentration, proper channelisation and adequate and clear message.

UPWARD COMMUNICATION

Downward communication flows downwards and the upward communication is the reverse of that direction (channel). There is importance attached of late to this communication channel. The reasons are—

Feedback to the upper levels.
As outlet for pent-up emotions.
Constructive suggestions can and do emerge.
It is easier method of introducing new schemes.
Greater harmony and cohesion.

Methods of upward communication are the following:

1. Open door policy.
2. Complaints and suggestions boxes.
3. Social gatherings.
4. Direct Correspondence.
5. Reports.
6. Counselling

Limitations of upward communication are as under:

1. Reluctance on this account in the employees for fear of unfavourable action if the views do not get accepted.
2. Employees fear if they communicated their problems to the higher management, it would affect their efficiency. It may be interpreted that the supervisor is incompetent to handle the problems; it may adversely affect relationships and confidential reports.
3. Upward communication is more prone to distortion than downward communication. So, information which the superiors find unpalatable may be suitably edited to lose its originality and intended meaning.
4. Workers, sometimes, may become too bold in this process and may not mind bypassing their superiors. The officers so bypassed may feel inferior, slighted while their higher authorities become suspicious of the subordinates' intentions.

Strained relations between the subordinates and the superiors may mar the efficiency and create differences. Atmosphere may become incongenial and that is going to harm the organisation as a whole.

HORIZONTAL COMMUNICATION

When there is communication between departments and people on the same level in the organizational hierarchy, it may be termed horizontal communication; it is also called lateral communication.

This communication is the most commonly used communication. Workers of one department or of the same department exchange information among them; clerks of one department exchange information or discuss matters of common interest; supervisors hold coffee-break sessions and exchange information and even managers discuss inter-departmental working and matters of common interest among themselves. All of them are engaged in horizontal communication.

Importance of Horizontal Communication: This type of communication is extremely important for promoting understanding and co-operation among various departments. Common problems can be immediately solved.

As there is inter-department dependence for functional operations, this communication strengthens co-ordination and smoothens the working of the organization.

When organization is small, diverse functions are concentrated either in the same person or in a few persons. Horizontal communication in that organization solves all problems easily and immediately. Problem arises when an organization is large and its structure is complex. In that case, interaction does not take place freely.

Horizontal communication in such an organization becomes complex and difficult. Efforts have to be made to develop horizontal communication by establishing structured forums and encourage free discussions.

Some managers discourage horizontal communication. They feel that the workers become very free and pose problems for the management. They believe and feel that purpose is served better by issuing orders from the top and insist upon meticulous compliance. If authority is vested in one person at the top, problems can not be solved unless fresh orders are sent to the lower levels. This would obviously cause delay and, sometimes, disrupt functioning. Further, this kind of authoritarianism is likely to provoke bitterness and indignation among the workers.

GRAPEVINE

In all organizations, informal channel of communication exists; it is called grapevine.. It follows no set lines, nor any definite rules but spreads like the grapevine, in any direction, anywhere, and spreads fast.

A group of people working together or at the same place, interact amongst themselves and talk about promotions, transfers, retrenchments, or even domestic affairs. Women workers talk more freely and express even doubts and do spread rumours, too. The workers do talk about estranged relations of one worker with his wife, or romantic involvements of other. These matters are supposed to be secret but a few of the workers derive great pleasure out of these discussions. They find these interesting and spread fast. These are the leaders who control the grapevine. The top secret soon becomes common knowledge and matters reach the top boss.

Keith Davis rightly points out that the grapevine is more the product of the situation than it is of the person. Certain situations like insecurity of service, uncertainty about promotions, special increments to certain employees, certain innovations in the organization likely to affect the job prospects of the employees are sure to attract the attention of the leaders of grapevine so that soon all kinds of rumours have spread in the organization.

The grapevine is basically a channel of horizontal communication because it is the people working at the same level who interact freely and frequently, and with perfect ease. Therefore, the workers may have one grapevine, the supervisors another, and so forth. The grapevine operates in all directions; there is no fixed route or channel.

The management can take advantage of it by giving vague information about new technology to be introduced or second shift to be introduced to find out feedback to such moves.

If favourable feedback is available, the innovation or technology is introduced. Otherwise, process to persuade the workers by discussion in groups is initiated to prepare them for accepting change without any resistance.

Importance of Grapevine

1. It works as a safety valve.
2. It promotes organizational solidarity and cohesion.
3. It is supplement to other channels.
4. It gives quick transmission.
5. It gives quick feedback and its base is considerably wide.

Demerits of Grapevine

1. It gives distorted views and there is quite bit of distortion in transmission.
2. It gives incomplete information.
3. It has damaging swiftness.

Effective Use of Grapevine

1. Managers should spot out the leaders.
2. Grapevine should be used to feel the pulse of the employees.
3. If there is any false rumour, the management should immediately use the official channels to contradict and to dispel fears of the employees.
4. If the workers are associated with decision-making, the rumour-mongers are automatically frustrated.

CHAPTER

5

Important Business Terms

The list of commercial terms, given below, is not intended to be an exhaustible one. It contains only those terms, which are frequently used in various kinds of reports and commercial correspondence. Terms too technical to be within the scope of this book and too familiar to be listed have also been excluded:

Abate: To diminish or to come down.

Adjournment: Suspension of a meeting for a particular period or indefinitely.

Advances: Upward movement in price.

Agenda: List of items of business to be considered at a meeting.

Amendment: Alteration proposed in the terms or language of a motion before it is put to vote.

Arbitrage: Buying securities in one stock exchange market and selling them in other stock market in order to make profit out of the difference in the two markets.

Articles of Association: The set of rules and regulations, which govern the working of joint stock company.

Assignment: A transfer of title or of an interest in any property. Assignment may be automatic [in case of death or bankruptcy] or by arrangement between the parties themselves.

Audit Internal: An examination of the accounts of an organization conducted by the members of its own staff.

Auditor: A person appointed to examine accounts and to report on them. Every registered company is required to get its accounts examined and to report on them. Every registered company is required to appoint an auditor.

Backwardation: Premium paid by the seller [bear operator] to the buyer [bull operator] on the stock exchange when he wishes to defer delivery of shares he has sold.

Balance of payments: The difference between payments due to and from a country of all international transactions over a certain period.

Balance of trade: The difference between a country's recorded imports and exports of good. The balance of trade is said to be favourable when exports exceed imports.

Bank Rate: The minimum rate of interest at which the central bank will rediscount bills and advance loans to scheduled commercial banks.

Bazaar Bill Rate: The rate of interest at which bills of small traders are discounted by money-lenders.

Bear: A speculator on the stock exchange who sells for future delivery securities he does not possess, hoping thereby to lower prices so as to acquire the securities at a reduced price in time for delivery and thus earn profit.

Bearish: A gloomy sentiment in the stock market.

Bill of Entry: A document in which the importer of goods or his agent declares all particulars relating to the goods entering the country.

Bill of Sale: A legal document evidencing transfer of the ownership of goods from one person to another, the possession of the goods remaining with the former.

Bill of Sight: A customs document that allows an importer to inspect the good and prepare a statement because the information about the good dispatched by the exporter has not yet reached him.

Blank Transfer: Transfer of securities by written deed in which the name of the transferee is not specified.

Blue Chips: Equity shares of companies, which are supposed to be as safe for investment as gilt-edged securities.

Board of Directors: Shareholders' representatives responsible for the administration and operations of a company.

Bonus Shares: Shares which are issued free of payment to the existing member-shareholders of a company.

Broker: An agent who buys or sells on behalf of someone else on commission.

Bucket Shop: The office of a broker who is not a member of the stock exchange and who deals in highly speculative securities.

Bull: A speculator who takes securities with no intention of retaining them, hoping to sell them at a higher price, when the day of settlement arrives.

Bullish: A cheerful or optimistic tone in the stock market.

Bullion: gold or silver in mass or in bars, as distinct from coined or ornamental metal.

C&F (Cost and Freight): A price quotation covering all charges incurred till the goods have reached the port of destination.

Capital Market: Financial market in which long-term loans and capital transactions are carried out.

Carry-over (Budla): The postponement of the settlement of a transaction till the next settlement day on a stock or produce exchange; due allowances being made for the accommodation.

Cash Credit: A facility whereby a bank allows a borrower to draw money from the bank from time to time up to a certain limit, interest being charged only on the actual amount drawn; currently it is charged on daily basis.

Cash on Delivery: A price quotation according to which price is payable by the buyer as soon as the goods are delivered to him.

Cash with Order: A price quotation which requires the buyer to send the price of the goods with his order.

Certificate of Incorporation: A document issued by the Registrar of companies, from the date on which a company comes into legal existence.

Certification of Commencement of Business: A document issued by the Registrar of the joint stock companies after a registered public company has allotted shares of not less than the minimum subscription and completed certain other formalities laid down by the Indian Companies Act.

Chamber of Commerce: A voluntary association of businessmen formed for the protection and promotion of their trading interests.

CIF (Cost, Insurance and Freight): A price quotation, which includes the marine insurance premium along with cost and freight.

Clearing Agent: An agency firm, which undertakes the clearance of imported goods, and their transportation to the warehouse on behalf of the importer.

Closure: A motion in a meeting to bring to close a discussion that has been going on for a very long time.

Commission Agent: An agent who negotiates the sale of goods on behalf of others on payment of a commission.

Comprehensive Policy: An agent who negotiates the sale of goods on behalf of others on payment of a commission.

An insurance policy which covers a number of risks, like risks of fire, riots, burglary, etc.

Cotango: Payment made to seller (bear operator) by a buyer (bull operator) on a stock or produce exchange for grant of time till the next settlement day for payment to be made on the original deal.

Convertible Debentures: Debentures which are convertible into shares after a specified period.

Cornering: Speculative operation by which an individual or a group of individuals comes to hold the entire supply of a particular security or commodity.

Cover: A system under which the broker acts on behalf of the client on the basis of a deposit which is adjusted towards any losses that might be incurred on this account.

Debenture: A bond issued by a company acknowledging a debt.

Deflation: The state of market in which prices suddenly fall due to reduction in expenditure or increase in production and the purchasing power of money increases without a corresponding increase in money supply.

Demurrage: The daily charge made for detention of ship beyond the agreed number of lay days. The term is also used for the daily charge made for detention of railway rolling stock.

Devaluation: Lowering of the value of a currency in terms of gold or other currencies.

Dip: Sudden fall in prices.

Dividend: Share of profits given to the shareholders.

Dividend Warrant: A certificate entitling the holder to payment of dividend. It is negotiable and may also be crossed like a cheque.

Dunning Letters: Collection letters written to those customers who fail to make payment of the amount due within the stipulated time.

Earnest Money: The amount paid by a buyer as a security for due performance of his part of the contract.

E&OE (Errors and Omissions Excepted): Usually printed at the bottom left-hand corner of an invoice, according to which the seller has the right of making corrections of errors or omissions, if any, noticed later.

Endorsement: Signature made on the face or back of a negotiable instrument for the purpose of negotiation.

Equity Shares: The ordinary shares of a joint stock company. Dividend is payable on them only after the dividend on preference shares has been paid.

Estimate: The written offer to do certain work for a specific price, calculated ahead of execution.

Excise Duty: A tax levied by the Government on goods produced and consumed within the country.

Ex-dividend: A quotation ex-dividend, means that the price quoted does not include the dividend, about to be declared

Face Value (Nominal Value): The amount printed on the face of securities as opposed to their market value, which may be higher or lower.

Factor: A mercantile agent who sells goods (including debts) lying in his possession in his own name with the approval of the principal.

Featureless: A situation of no activity in shares.

Firm Offer: An offer made by a seller whereby he promises to execute an order for specified goods at specified prices within a specified time.

Fixed Capital: Capital invested in fixed assets, or the fixed assets themselves.

Floating Capital: Capital in the form of circulating assets.

FOB (Free on Board): A price quotation which includes the cost of loading the goods on board the ship but does not include freight.

FOR (Free on Rail): A price quotation which includes the cost of carrying the goods to a railways station or yard and loading them into the wagons but not the freight.

Forward Delivery: A term signifying that goods are sold for delivery within a specified future time, either by instalments or in one lot.

Forwarding Note: A note prepared in prescribed form by the consignor of goods, to be sent by the railways, giving the particulars of goods consigned and the name and address of the consignee.

Freight Forward: Words inscribed on a bill of lading if the freight is to be paid by the importer of goods at the port of destination.

Futures: The purchase of goods for delivery at some specified future date, providing the buyer with a form of insurance against a possible rise in the price of his raw material.

Group Insurance: Insurance on the lives of the members of a family or the employees of a business firm.

Hammering: The process of declaring that the prices are steady but there are no transactions.

Hard but Idle: A state of market in which the prices are steady but there are no transactions.

Hedging: The practice of covering the risks attaching to transactions in the cash market by contra-transactions in the futures market.

Hot Money: Short-term capital which is subject to speculative movement among different countries.

Hypothecation: The act of pledging or mortgaging property in order to raise a loan, the physical possession of the property remains with the borrower.

Hundi: Instrument of the nature of a bill of exchange. It is recognized in India as a negotiable instrument.

Indemnity: A promise whereby a person undertakes to save another from loss caused to the latter by the promisor himself or by another party.

Indent: An order placed by an importer directly or through an intermediary for goods for which he holds on import licence.

Inflation: An increase in available currency that has the effect of raising general prices.

Instrument: A negotiable instrument, deed, will, certificate, or any other formal legal document.

Insurable Interest: A term used in insurance to denote some pecuniary interest in the risk against which it is desired to provide. In the absence of an insurable interest, there can be no insurance.

Interim Dividend: Dividend payable prior to the making of the balance sheet, in anticipation of profits.

Invoice: An account sent by a seller of goods to the buyer, stating details of the quantity, description and price of the goods and showing the total amount due. It may also include the buyer's order number, the mode of dispatch and the terms of payment, etc.

Inward Mail: Letters received.

I.O.U. (I owe you): Acknowledgement of a debt containing no specified date for repayment, usually given as evidence of temporary loan for a small sum.

Jobber: A member of the stock exchange who buys and sells stocks and shares on his own account. He usually specializes in a particular class of securities and often in a limited number of securities in that class.

Joint Stock Company: An association of persons who unite to subscribe the necessary capital to carry on some trade or business. The subscribers are known as shareholders.

Krebs Market: A market in which purchases and sales of securities are carried on by jobbers and brokers before or after the official hours outside the stock exchange.

Knocked Down Price: The price at which the sale of an article is concluded at an auction.

Landed Price: A price quotation by the exporter which includes all expenses up to the landing of goods at the port of the importing country.

Legal Tender: That form of money which may be legally offered in settlement of a debt or in payment of goods supplied or services rendered.

Letter of Credit: A letter issued by a bank on behalf of the importer of goods in favour of the seller undertaking that bills or exchange drawn by him upon the importer up to a specified amount will be honoured by it.

Letter of Hypothecation: A Litter empowering the bank that has advanced money to sell the goods in case of default and to apply the money realized towards satisfaction of the outstanding debts due if the importer does not accept documents or bills received from the exporter. A bank may advance money for the working of factory and hold goods including raw material lying in the possession of the factory owner under lien to the bank.

Lien: The right to retain another's property until some debt or claim is settled.

Liquid Assets: Assets that can easily be turned into cash.

Memorandum of Association: The principal document filed with the Registrar of Companies upon the incorporation of a company under the Companies Act. It defines the company's relations with the outside world. It must be subscribed by seven or more persons through signatures and states: (i) the proposed name of the company; (ii) the domicile of the registered office; (iii) the objects of the company; (iv) a statement that the liability of the members is limited (if such be the case); and (v) the amount of authorized capital and the manner of its sub-division into shares, etc.

Minimum Subscription: The minimum amount, details of which must be stated in the prospectus of a company, estimated by the directors to be necessary to enable the company to function. It must be sufficient to cover the purchase price of any property to be acquired, preliminary expenses and working capital.

Minutes: A concise and accurate record of the proceedings at a meeting, stating the date and place (and venue) of meeting, the names of those present, the matters discussed and the decisions reached. Minutes are prepared by the secretary and signed both by the secretary and the chairman.

Monetary Standard: A monetary system based on standard value of the currency.

Money Rate: Interest rate charged on short-term loan in the market.

Negotiation: Transfer of ownership of an instrument to a person by delivery or endorsement or both so as to make that person holder of the instrument.

Nominal Capital: Maximum amount a company is empowered by its memorandum to raise from the public.

Non-Cumulative Preference Shares: Preference shares in respect of which the arrears of dividend due do not accumulate from year to year.

O.L. & S.O.L (Odd lot and Small Odd Lot): Abbreviations used with price quotation of shares to indicate that price relates to transactions in odd lots and small odd lots and that this price is not to be taken as a regular quotation for the shares concerned.

Open-Marked Operation: Purchase and sale transactions of securities in the open market by the central bank of a country.

Ordinary Resolution: A resolution which is passed by simple majority of votes cast by the members.

Outwards Mail: Letters sent by a company to various people.

Overdraft: An amount withdrawn from a bank current account in excess of the balance available.

Overheads: The indirect expenses of production such as rent, lighting and heating, administration and advertising, which cannot be precisely allocated to any cost unit. Overheads represent the difference between the prime cost and the total cost of a product.

Paid-up Value: The amount payable under a life policy if the insured stops paying the premiums due by him before the policy matures.

Paper Money: Bank notes and government notes which are used as money.

Partial Endorsement: Endorsement on a negotiable instrument with the intention of transferring only a part of the amount payable on the instrument.

Pledge: A contract whereby an article is deposited with a creditor as security for the repayment of a loan.

Point of Order: A question raised by a member regarding the procedure at a meeting.

Power of Attorney: A deed executed by one person authorizing another person to act on his behalf, e.g. to collect debts and to sign documents.

Preference Shares: Shares with a prior claim on the profits of a company. They are entitled to a fixed rate of dividend which must be met before any payment is made on the ordinary shares.

Preliminary Expenses: Expenses incidental to the formation and incorporation of a company, incurred for such items as legal charges, stamp duties and printing costs of memorandum and articles, etc.

Privilege in Speech: Protection given to speakers against legal action for having made defamatory statements at meeting provided the statements are made in good faith and without malice.

Private Company: A joint stock company which by its Articles limits its membership to fifty, does not invite the public for subscription to its shares and debentures and restricts the transfer of its shares.

Proforma Invoice: An invoice sent for form's sake. It is not entered in the books of account and does not debit the receiver with the amount. It is used :

(i) to serve as a quotation;

(ii) to cover goods sent on approval or on consignment, and

(iii) to serve as a request for payment in advance if the goods are required.

Promissory Note: A signed promise to pay a specified sum of money at a certain date. It is subject to the rules that apply to the bills of exchange, but, unlike a bill, does not require acceptance.

Prospectus: Any document inviting the public to subscribe to the capital of a company. Before it can be issued, a copy, signed by the directors, must be filed with the Registrar of Companies. It must state the contents of the Memorandum of Association and includes other statutory information to enable the public to form a fair judgment of the prospects of the company (risk factors to be included).

Pro-Tem Secretary: A person who temporarily acts as the secretary of a company in order to assist in carrying out all the preliminary work before its incorporation.

Proxy: A person who is nominated by another person to act and vote on his behalf, and it is also the document of authorization.

Public Credit: Loans and advances extended to the government, municipalities and other local bodies.

Public Deposits: Deposits made by the general public with companies, which invite such deposits to meet their financial needs.

Public Sector: The part of the economy directly under government ownership and control.

Quorum: The minimum number of members of a body necessary to constitute/form a meeting competent to transact business.

Quotation: An offer to sell goods at a price and under conditions specified.

Rate of Exchange: The price at which the currencies of various countries are bought and sold in terms of one another.

Rally: Recovery in the prices of shares after a fall.

Redeemable Preference Shares: Preferable shares repayable either on a specified date or on a date to be decided.

Reserve Price (Upper Price): The lowest price an owner of goods is prepared to accept for them at an auction sale.

Resolution: Decision of the members present at a properly constituted meeting.

Re-valuation (of currency): Raising the existing value of a currency in terms of gold or another currency.

Revocable Letter of Credit: Letter of credit under which the amount of credit can be withdrawn or changed at any time.

Rigging the Market: Forcing up the market value of particular shares artificially.

Scrip: Provisional or preliminary certificate of a person's holding in a joint stock company or government loan.

Scrip Dividend: Dividend paid by a company in the form of shares and debentures of other companies. Finance companies usually pay scrip dividend.

Security Listing: Inclusion of the securities of a particular company in the official list of a stock exchange for the purpose of trading.

Sentiment: The tone of the share market.

Share: A unit of the share capital subscribed by he members of a company.

Share Warrant: A document issued by a registered company in place of the share certificate. It entitles the shareholder to transfer the shares stated therein.

Shipping Bill: A document the exporter is required to fill; it has to be presented to the customs authorities for permission to export the goods stated therein.

Short Selling: The sale of a large volume of securities by bears without actually possessing them.

Sight Bill: A bill of exchange payable at sight, i.e. as soon as it is presented to the drawee.

Slump: A period of falling prices and generally low business.

Special Resolution: A resolution that requires three-fourths majority of members' votes to be passed.

Speculation: Buying and selling of goods or securities in anticipation of a rise or fall in their prices.

Speculator: One who is engaged in speculative activities.

Split Certificate: Split certificates are multiple share certificates issued on the request of a shareholder in place of an existing certificate to facilitate transfer of shares by him.

Spurt: A sudden rise in the prices.

Squeezed Bear: A bear that is compelled to purchase at high prices because of the pressure brought on him to close an open position.

Stag: A speculator who applies for a new issue of stocks and shares, not with the intention of taking them up, but anticipating a rise in their value, which would enable him to sell at a profit before he has to complete his purchase.

Statutory Meeting: The first general meeting of the shareholders of a public company which must be held within a period of not less than one month and not more than six months from the date of commencement of business.

Statutory Report: A report from the Board of Directors which must be sent to all shareholders at least 21 days before the statutory meeting.

Stock: Money contributed to the capital of an incorporated body, or advanced to the Government and forming part of the national debt. The essential difference between stock and shares is that the former may be transferred in fractional amounts, whereas shares cannot be sub-divided.

Stock Exchange: A voluntary association (now in India, a corporate body) concerned with regulating operations by players regarding buying and selling of stocks and shares.

Subsidy: A payment made from the national revenues to some industry or enterprise to ensure its faster growth or to keep down prices.

Surrender (of Shares): Voluntary surrender of shares by the shareholder of a company when he is unable to pay the unpaid capital.

Tariff: A list of the customs duties imposed on imported goods along with details of the goods exempt from duty, goods prohibited, and goods on which the duty has to be charged.

Tender: An offer, usually in response to a public advertisement, to supply goods or do work at prices quoted and under conditions stated in the tender.

Trapped Bull: A bull placed in a tight position owing to the pressure brought on him by other parties who deliberately keep out of the market to compel the bull to sell at lower prices.

Turnover: The total value of goods (money realized called sales) sold during a given period, usually one year.

Warranty: A contractual obligation which entitles the injured party to damages but not to rescind the contract.

Wash Sales: Factious transaction in which a speculator sells a security and then buys it at a higher price through another broker to create an artificial opinion about its price in the market.

Without Engagement: This term is used by the sellers while giving quotations and it means that they are quoting the market price of the day but they do not bind themselves to accept an order at this price.

Working Capital: The working capital of a new enterprise is the amount of invested capital remaining after the fixed assets have been bought; the working capital of a going concern is the excess of current assets over current liabilities.

CHAPTER

6

Need and Function of a Business Letter

INTRODUCTION

Every business, whether big or small has to maintain contact with its suppliers, customers, prospects, government departments and the like. In his regular work, a businessman has to exchange information of a varied type with different parties. Making and/or soliciting enquiries; placing of order for goods, acknowledging and executing orders, grating or applying for credit, sending statements of account to debtors, requesting for settlement of accounts, complaining about delay or mistake in supply of goods, etc. making adjustments for customers' grievances, canvassing for the firm's new lines of goods or ideas, and a lot of such matters require communication. Included in this list is also the correspondence with government departments, such as the Tax Section of the Local government, Sales Tax and Income Tax Officers, customs' authorities, etc.

FUNCTIONS OF A BUSINESS LETTER

As L. Gartside puts it, there are four main reasons for writing business letters:

(i) To provide a convenient and inexpensive means of communication without personal contact,
(ii) To seek or give information,
(iii) To furnish evidence of transactions entered into, and
(iv) To provide a record for future reference.

Another is that of building goodwill by creating in the mind of the reader an impression of the writer's organization as one that is efficient, reliable and anxious to be of service.

Recording and Reference: With a view to maintaining records of communication with the outside world the communication must be in writing. Written communication can be passed on to the concerned persons or departments as it is. Written letters enjoy a distinct advantage over other means of communication: they can be preserved for future reference. Back references are quite frequent in business communication. Where memory fails, records come to rescue.

Making a Lasting Impression

Oral Communication, whether in person or over the phone, is rarely remembered in full. However, a letter makes a lasting impression on the reader's mind because it stays with him, goes with him and does its work effectively every time it is read.

Widening the Approach

Frequently, a businessman finds it difficult to send his representatives to all the places of his business connections. It is the letter that reaches any place at whatever distance. In its effect, a business letter helps widen the areas of operation. Only letters can send the goods of a businessman to places thousands of miles away, even across the country. Executives, professionals, politicians, etc. are difficult to be approached in person. But a letter can find easy access to one and all. A letter knows what is the right time to reach different persons, and it enjoys the advantage of being able to wait till the reader has leisure and inclination to turn to it.

An Authoritative Proof

A commitment in writing binds the parties concerned to the text of writing. A letter, signed by a responsible person, is an authoritative proof of what is said in it. It can even be treated as a valid document that can be produced as evidence in a court of law in case of disputes.

Action can be taken, responsibilities can be fixed and mistakes can be pointed out only if communications are held in writing. It is for this reason that oral communications over phone or telegraphic communications need confirmation in writing.

Building Goodwill

An important purpose of a business letter is to sell the good reputation and friendliness of a company. It aims at building goodwill in the customer-company relationship, holding present customers and capturing new ones, reviving inactive accounts and inviting customers to buy more and varied products. The underlying purpose of all letters is to create customers by making them loyal (rather friends). Thus business letters are an indispensable means of communication for industry and commerce. Business letters represent the firm just as much as the personality of the firm's salesmen and the quality of its goods or services.

Therefore, business letters must try to make the best possible impression on those who receive them. Their functions must go beyond the essentials of presenting information clearly and courteously (which is the function of a salesman). They must make friends, build goodwill and add to the company's prestige (projecting proper image of company).

ESSENTIALS OF AN EFFECTIVE BUSINESS LETTER

Promptness

In business, it is a general practice to answer a letter the same day it is received. Since we are in business to keep friends and to make more friends, we must be prompt and courteous. Promptness creates a good and lasting impression.

Knowledge of the subject: Know your subject so well that you can discuss it naturally and confidently. If we have a full grasp of the subject, we know exactly what is to be communicated and can easily write a letter or draft a reply to cover all the necessary points.

Appropriateness

A letter writer should vary the tone and language of the letter according to the need for the occasion. Appropriateness of tone and style in writing and replying to letters leads to friendliness and good feeling. As a person varies his tone and language while writing to his wife, his father, his bosom friend, his employer, his colleagues, a business correspondent; he should also vary the style of his letter, keeping in view the relation and psychology of the reader as well as the needs of the occasion. Appropriateness, in many cases, necessitates the use of technical terms or terms that are frequently used in business. A correspondent should understand such terms fully and use them properly to make his letter attractive and intelligible. However, unnecessary use of phrases and words must be strictly avoided; simplicity in writing is as important as an appropriate style. High sounding words and phrases detract the attention of the reader from the idea denoted by them.

Accuracy, Completeness and Clearness

Accuracy, completeness and clearness of thought and expression help the writer in making his purpose perfectly clear to the reader. Facts, figures, statements, quotations, etc. must be very accurately mentioned. The message communicated by the letter should be complete so that it leads to the accomplishment of the purpose for which it is being sent. Accuracy and completeness go together and help in avoiding mistakes that may otherwise prove costly. Write so that you can be understood and never misunderstood.

Clarity consists, in other words, in making letters free from ambiguity. "Ambiguity may result from the omission of a word, faulty punctuation and faulty arrangement of words", as we can see from the following examples:

(1) A book-seller received the following letters:

"Please send me urgently two copies of Business English and Principles and Practice of Book-Keeping."
(The book-seller had to enquire whether the customer required two copies of each or two books in all).

(2) The following advertisement from a domestic gas distributor appeared in a paper:

"Using Charcoal?
Don't kill your wife with that.
We will supply you GAS".
(well, does the advertiser mean that he will supply gas instead of charcoal to kill your wife?)

See the fun of faulty punctuation in the following:

(a) On a busy road which was under repair, the following sign appeared:

"GO, SLOW WORK IN PROGRESS".
(In fact, the half-stop should have been at the end of Slow.)

(b) A Magistrate wrote in his decision as under:

LEAVE HIM NOT HANG HIM
He had forgotten to put the comma at the end of first HIM.

(He had acquitted the accused). But the clerk put the full-stop as under:

LEAVE HIM NOT. HANG HIM.
(The poor accused!)

(a) When a school inspector entered a classroom along

with the Principal, the class-teacher explained to the students how a little change in punctuation can give an altogether different meaning for the same sentence:

He wrote on the black-board:

"The inspector", said the Principal, "is a fool".
The inspector and the Principal were embarrassed.
The teacher then changed the punctuation as under:
The Inspector said, "The Principal is a fool".
(The Principal breathed in relief).
Where figures are concerned, the writer must be very clear. Ambiguity therein results in misunderstanding, bitterness of feeling, loss, and sometimes plays havoc.

Dr. Robert Ray Aurner brings out the importance of correctness in the following words:

"what good manners are to the gentleman, correctness is to the businessman. If the businessman does not observe the rules of writing-etiquette, he is not accepted in the best business circles".

Talking about ambiguity, Lord Chesterfield says:

"Every paragraph should be so clear and unambiguous that the dullest fellow in the world will not be able to mistake it, nor be obliged to read it twice in order to understand it".

•

Courtesy

In business, we must create friendliness with all those to whom we write. Friendliness is inseparable from courteousness; courtesy is considerate and sympathetic behaviour, a friendly attitude towards others. Impatience, irritation, sarcasm, criticism, an unfriendly tone, a fighting style, etc. should be kept out of our letter. That is what courtesy demands. "A person is known by the company he keeps and the language he speaks". We make known the personality of our firm by our language, style and tone. "Be courteous, friendly, polite, grateful and of thanking nature".

To say, 'Thank you' for a service performed or work done or order booked or complaint adjusted is the essence of courtesy; we should never forget to give thanks where they are deserved". Courtesy makes friends, and "a soft answer turns away wrath. If you don't make a friend, you will at least avoid making any enemy, if your letter is courteous".

Tact

Tactfulness ought to go hand in hand with courtesy. Maintaining goodwill of customers is one of the most important tasks of a correspondent. Therefore, he should write tactfully in order to avoid antagonizing the reader. Matters of delay in execution of order, refusing complaint and credit, requesting for early payment or adjustments, etc. always require tactful handling.

Persuasion

In writing a letter, complaint or adjustments or demanding claims, refusing requests or orders of regretting inability to grant credit of offer of substitutes of sales, etc., the writer must use persuasiveness. The writers mostly use persuasiveness. It is very helpful in selling goods, services or ideas. Even disagreeable things can be got done with the help of conviction which is achieved only through the art of persuasion. It requires making positive suggestions to the reader and offering an argument or a reason to convince him how and why it is to his advantage.

A persuasive style is mainly the one that arouses a reader's interest in what the correspondent says. Everyone is primarily interested in himself. Hence persuasion requires an appeal to reader's interests: economy, financial gain, saving, pride of possession, self-esteem, security, etc. requires an appeal to the reader's interests.

Brevity and Conciseness

A reader's time is invaluable. "Don't make him feel that he is wasting his time in going through your unnecessarily lengthy letter. Be as brief as possible." Brevity in expression effectively wins the attention of the reader.

However, brevity should not be effected at the cost of appropriateness, clarity, correctness, completeness or courtesy. In fact, there is no hard and fast rule for the length of a letter. A letter should be as long or as short as is necessary to tell the story effectively. A two-page letter may seem short, while a ten-line letter may seem too long. You can ask yourself these two questions: "Does it take too many words for what it must say?"

For shortness, avoid needless words and information; don't qualify your statements with irrelevant if's. But avoid telegraphic and shorthand language also. Use simple and short words as also sentences. That will make your letter accurate, correct and easily intelligible. For example, write 'often' in place of 'in a considerable number of cases'; 'nearly' in place of 'in close proximity to', 'enclosed' for 'enclosed please find herewith' or 'enclosed herewith'. Use 'prefer' for 'express a preference for', 'consider' for 'give consideration to', 'decide' for 'arrive at a decision'.

Salesmanship

As a business correspondent, we should know that every letter is a sales letter and it should have the requisites of salesmanship. We sell goods or services or ideas through our letters when we draft our letters with a view to routing every opportunity into a sales opportunity.

The importance of salesmanship for a business letter can be summed up in the following words of Mr. Herbert Casson:

> "From a business point of view, we must look upon ever letter as a sales letter . . . . Every outgoing letter is a traveller of your firm. It is a salesman. It carries a message. It is silent but not dumb. . . . It helps to make the reputation of the firm".

The 'You' Attitude

We know that we are primarily interested in ourselves. Naturally, every other person is interested more in himself than in a third party. It follows, therefore, when we write letters to others, they are effective and the readers respond to our letters well only when we write from their point of view. "It is an accepted truth that one of the most pleasant sounds to the average individual is his own name or self".

To make our letter more effective, we must avoid I's and We's and have as many You's as possible. In any case, we should not forget the reader's point of view in the whole of our letter.

The Positive and Pleasant Approach: A businessman will have many occasions when he has to refuse, say 'No', regret, disagree, complain, or say 'sorry'. To say this in plain words and in a straight forward style is not difficult, but its effect on the reader's mind and the repercussions on the firm are bad and far-reaching. We swallow a sugar coated pill without any grumble.

Similarly, in a business letter, the reader accepts calmly and coolly all the No's, Regrets, and Sorry's if they are expressed in a positive manner. An approach with a negative beginning or a negative connotation irritates the reader and makes him feel that the writer lacks business manners and gentlemanliness.

A positive approach, on the other hand, convinces the reader of the helplessness of the writer, or his genuine difficulties, etc. In other words, a positive and pleasant approach says 'No' but retains the customer's goodwill.

A business letter should leave a pleasant impression. "Get a smile into your letter, a bit of your personality, an atmosphere of goodwill. A sour letter, piqued or disinterested attitude, complaining undertone are comparable to an arrogant or uncivilized manner in your conversation".

The following phrases have a built-in smile:

We shall be glad to . . . .
It is a pleasure . . . .
Thank you . . . .
With our compliments . . . .
Your kind letter . . . .
Many thanks for your . . . .

We are pleased to . . . ...
You will be glad to . . . .

THE LANGUAGE OF A BUSINESS LETTER

The language of a business letter should be familiar. Many people think that a special language called 'Business English' which is supposed to be somewhat different from everyday spoken English is to be used in business letters.

This concept frequently complicates the job of writing to a person with whom one is doing business. "it is false to think that the English used in trade and commerce is of a different kind or quality from that used in other walks of life".

The average business letter is written not in some special 'Business English', but in the familiar language, which we use all day. 'Basically, every letter, memorandum or report written in the course of business is a piece of prose composition, and the general rules relating to English composition apply to them also.

Every profession and each branch of commercial or business world has its own special terms and vocabulary which arise from the precise needs of the particular business or profession. "Formal style is now outdated. There was a time when 'peculiar' expressions were used in business letters, which made them stiff and formal. But today the tendency is to write in a simple, natural and almost conversational style".

Business correspondence ranges from letters that are almost as brief as telegrams to more lengthy and intimate letters, depending on how well the writer knows the person with whom he is communicating, and the requirements of the subject matter.

The best way to write a business letter is to make it conform as closely as possible to spoken English.

It was during the Victorian period that 'Commercial English' was in vogue, particularly in the British business circles, but it was just a meaningless jargon consisting of flattering, stiff and trite words. Its style was prone to verbosity and it lacked sincerity.

The American influence, however, changed the tendency of businessmen and the use of natural, forceful and conversional language gradually replaced the so-called 'Commercial English'.

Some formal expressions that should be avoided: we give below a list of a few 'Commercial English' terms and the proper terms to be used in their place.

Formal and Stiff	*Simple and Preferable*
(1) This is to acknowledge. . . We acknowledge	Thank you for your .... Thanks for your letter . . .
(2) We will contact you at an early date	We shall write to you soon.
(3) Attached hereto, attached herewith, enclosed herewith, enclosed please find.	Attached, ... or Enclosed.
(4) Would you be good enough	Would you please
(5) Contents noted	(This phrase should not be used).
(6) Your letter of even date	Your letter of 23rd July.
(7) We hand you our latest quotation, enclosed herein	Enclosed in our latest quotations
(8) Your letter of the 26th to hand	Thank you for your letter of 26th
(9) Beg to say, beg to inform	Avoid beg
(10) Instant, inst. (of the same month)	-do
(11) Prox. or Proximo (of the next month)	-do-
(12) Under (by) separate cover	Either avoid this phrase or say, separately.
(13) We regret to	(Be positive)
(14) We shall advise you	We shall let you know
(15) As per, in accordance with	According to
(16) And oblige	Avoid it, or say, Thank you,

THE LAY-OUT OF BUSINESS LETTER

(i) Physical Appearance

As in the case of any other article, the appearance of a letter is as important as its contents. The letter takes the place of a salesman and represents the firm sending it. Like a salesman, the letter should create a good impression on the mind of the reader.

A salesman representing his firm will create a poor impression about the firm if he is poorly dressed or shabbily combed; if he has unshaven chin, if his shoes are unpolished, or if he does not know the etiquette of approaching and presenting himself. Similarly, letter which has an unpleasant appearance, fails to catch the reader's eye even if it contains an attractive proposition.

> "A Letter is looked at before it is read, and the first impression which it makes on the [reader's] eye is often an important factor which influences the reader's opinion of the sender of the letter.

(ii) Mechanical Structure

The mechanical structure of a letter constitutes the different parts of letter that should have their customary place in it. The arrangement of the different parts of business letter is fixed by custom and makes a world of difference in the impression it conveys. A letter being sent in an inappropriate form is as bad as a salesman follows no acceptable code of dress. The person receiving it may well discredit the standing of the company that has sent it out.

A couplet from Dryden really deserves quoting here:
Set all things in their own peculiar place;
And know that order is the greatest grace;

The usual parts of a business letter are as under:

1. Heading
2. Inside address
3. Salutation
4. Body of the letter

5. Complimentary close
6. Enclosures and postscripts, if any.

Heading

The heading contains the following information:

(a) *Name of the firm and address*: While writing the address, if the house number or the street number is being mentioned, no comma need be put after it:

'T' Phone: . . . ...

SULTAN CHAND AND SONS
Publishers and Booksellers
SCO 1-2-3, Sector 17-D
Chandigarh

(b) *The Date*: The date consists of day, month and year. It is written below the address or the heading, leaving some space for a better look.

The following are the only two commonly [and, let us add, correctly] accepted methods of writing the date:

23rd July, 1981 OR
July 23, 1981.

Do not use abbreviations for month and do not cut short the year, as, 81 or 82

When the address of the firm is combined with the date they are written in one of the ways:

23, Daryaganj, New Delhi
23rd July, 1981.
OR
23, Daryaganj, New Delhi
July 23, 1981.

(c) *The Reference:* This is a part of the letter-head. It is printed either below the date line [if the date is written close to the left-margin] or on the same line in the right-margin. In both cases, the reference is written close to the left margin. It serves to identify either the department and its section from which the letter is being sent or the particular file in which the correspondence is to be found. The purpose of the reference is to enable replies to be linked with the previous correspondence and also to send replies to this letter to the proper office or department. Stating the 'reference' helps handing it quickly to the proper official or department. Stating the 'reference' helps also in quick and easy future references. Therefore, addressees are requested to quote this reference in their replies. The usual form of giving the references is:

	(1)	Reference No . . . .
Left–Side Margin	(2)	Ref. No. . . . .
	(3)	In reply, please quote . . .
	(4)	Please quote reference in future correspondence . . . .

Inside Address

The inside address contains the name and address of the firm or the individual to whom the letter is written. Also, it should start from the left-side margin and may be written either in the indented (step) form or in the block form.

While the outside address (on the envelope) is to be written in full, the inside address may be written in brief:

Outside Address:	*Inside Address:*
Shree Ram Mills Ltd. Ferguson Road, Lower Parel, Mumbai-13 (BC)	Shree Ram Mills Ltd., Ferguson Road, Mumbai-13 or Shree Ram Mills Ltd., Mumbai-13

However, it is advisable to have the inside address on the letter-head and the address on the cover both in full.

Mode of Address

(a) *Addressing Individuals*: (i) Mr. or Esq. or Shri, (ii) Mrs., or Smt. Or Shrimati; Miss, Mmes, and (iv) Messrs. are the ordinary courtesy titles used for addressing correspondents.

(a) Mr. (Mister) or Esq. (Esquire) or Shri is used for men, both married and unmarried.
(b) Miss is used for an unmarried woman.
(c) Mrs. (Mistress) or Smt. or Shrimati is used for a married lady.
(d) Messrs. (Messieurs) is used as the plural for Mr.
(e) Mmes. (Mesdames) is used as the plural for Mrs.

Examples:

M.H. Haridas, M.A., Near Veeranarayan Temple, Ramaduram	Shri, G.C. Honnolli, Commerce College, Jamnagar
Dr. R. Vasant, M.B.B.S. Mangalwar Peth, Harkuttai	R. Vasant, Esq., M.B.B.S., Mangalwar Peth, Harinagar
Miss. Vrinda Joshi, 124, Shanti Path Kalka	Dr. (Miss) Suman Deshpande Principal (Mrs.) D.S. Desai

A married woman should be addressed by her husband's name, e.g., Padma Joshi, the wife of Prahlad Joshi, should be preferably addressed as:

Mrs. Prahlad Joshi, Tagore Nagar, Ujjain	or	Shrimati Padma Joshi Tagore Nagar, Ujjain

(b) *Title or Rank*, such as Sir, Reverend, Doctor, Professor, Colonel, Rao Bhadur, Padmashri, etc. are used as under:

Dr. J.K. Irani,	or	J.K. Irani, Esq., M.Com., Ph.D.,

Prof. G.M. Shetti,	Sir Frank Worell, M.Com., L.L.B.
Rev. W. Ryn,	Colonel B. Ghooi,
Rao Bhadur S.S. Manvi,	Padmashri (Dr.) R.B. Patil, M.B.B.S., F.R.C.S.

We use either the title or Mr. or Esq. etc., but not the two of them together. Both 'Sir Frank Worell' and 'Frank Worell Esq.' are in order but it is incorrect to write 'Sir Frank Worell Esq'.

(c) Use of 'Messrs': This plural form of Mr. is used in addressing firms with titles that contain personal name or names:

Messrs. Hombali Bros., Messrs. Desai & Co.

However, when addressing (i) an individual, or (ii) an anonymous official in the firm, or (iii) when the title is impersonal, or (iv) when it starts with 'The', or (v) when the courtesy title is included, Messrs. should not be used:

(i)	Dr. (Miss) Vedavati, Central College New Delhi	(ii)	The Personnel Manager, Tata Mills Ltd. New Delhi
(iii)	Mysore Stores, Belgaum Galli, Hubli	(iv)	The Patel Tea Depot, Subhas Road, Dharwar
(v)	Sir Isaac Steels Ltd.	(vi)	Mr. S.K. Dhar J.K. Mitra & S.K. Bose
(vii)	Multi Steels Ltd.	(viii)	The Birla Mills Ltd.

(d) *Addressing a Limited Company:* In the following examples, a particular officer is being addressed. Therefore, Messrs is not prefixed to the name of the Company:

The Advertising manager, J.L. Morrison & Sons Ltd.,	The Secretary, Brooke Bond (India) Ltd.

(e) *Use of 'For the attention of ....' Or 'Attention of ....':* This phrase is used when the writer of a letter, addressed to an organization, wishes to direct it to a particular person or official. It is written below the inside address but above the salutation, usually in the middle of the line and is underlined:

Phoenix Mills Ltd.,
Modi Nagar,
Mumbai-1

Attention : Mr. Abhimanyu, General Manager

Salutation

The salutation is the complimentary greeting with which the writer opens his letter. It is the written equivalent of the conversational 'Hello'. It should be written below the inside address (or 'Attention of ....', if any), leaving some space. It should start flush with the left side margin and end with a comma.

For ordinary business purposes, 'Dear Sir' (or 'Dear Madam' for both single and married women) is for addressing one person and 'Dear Sirs' (or 'Mesdames') for addressing two or more persons, i.e., a firm or an association.

Salutations commonly used are:

Sir : This is rather formal and used only in official correspondence. It is not proper for use in business.

Dear Sir, Dear Sirs or Dear Madam or Dear Mesdames are used, as appropriate.

Body of the Letter

It is that part of letter which contains the message or the information to be communicated and is, of course, the most important part. The body consists of the following:

(a) Subject or Reference,
(b) Opening Paragraph,
(c) Main Paragraph
(d) Closing Paragraph

(a) Subject or Reference

A brief, one line mention of the major theme of the letter right in the beginning adds to its clarity. In case of lengthy communications, it is almost indispensable. It is usually written below the salutation, beginning from the place from where the first line of each paragraph starts, or it is placed in the middle of the line.

(b) Opening Paragraph

There is an old German proverb that 'a good beginning is half the battle (won)'. And that applies doubly when it comes to writing successful business letters. It is here that the reader's attention should be attracted and he should be made to 'go ahead' with interest and concentration. If the letter fails here, it has failed totally to achieve its purpose.

(c) Main Paragraph

This paragraph contains the subject matter of the letter. It should be brief and to the point, but care should be taken to see that no relevant details are omitted from it. It should be written in unambiguous, sincere, simple and correct words.

(d) Closing Paragraph

Like a perfect day, every letter must come to a close. The letter ending must motivate the action that the writer wants from his reader. "It must be natural and logical, must be final and complete". It must be gentle but firm, friendly but forceful". It should stress the 'You' point of view and, wherever possible, should use different forms of 'Thank you". Closing with an important statement, a question, an offer or a request is also suitable.

Complementary Close

The complimentary close is merely a polite way of ending a letter. As the use of Dear Sir, etc., is conventional so is the use of Yours faithfully, Yours truly, and similar expressions; just as the salutation is the written equivalent of "Good Morning", so the complimentary close is the written equivalent of "Good Bye". Salutation and complimentary close should correspond to each other.

Important points to be noted here are:

(a) Only the first letter of the closure is capitalized.
(b) At the end of the closure there is a comma.
(c) Participle endings like

Thanking you,

Yours faithfully,
ABC
Manager (Marketing)

Signature

Signature is the assent of the writer to the subject matter of the letter and is a practical necessity. It is usually hand written and contains the writer's name, status, department, the firm, etc. Signature is put just below the complimentary close. It should be, as far as possible, legible. If not, the name of the signatory should be written legibly, in parenthesis below the signature.

Yours truly,	Yours sincerely,
Uttkarsh	Abbu
Executive (Sales)	Chief Manager (Personnel)

Enclosures and Postscripts

Sometimes a letter carries along with it some other papers, such as price list, catalogue, prospectus, order, invoice, railway or lorry receipt, bill, cash memo, or cheque, draft, etc. In such cases, a mention should be made of these enclosures in the letter after the signature, and at the left side margin, as below:

Encls: Four, or
Encls: (1) . . . .
(2) . . . .
(3) . . . .
(4) . . . .

STYLE OR FORM AND PUNCTUATION

This style or form is the lay-out of the different parts of a letter in a particular form. The various forms and their explanation are illustrated in the next specimen letters.

Punctuation refers to the marks of 'period' at the end of each line of the letter head and the inside address. It may be closed punctuation with full stops and commas at the end or open punctuation without comas and full stops, except where the last word of a line (in the heading and inside address) is in an abbreviated form as Cp. Ltd. Bros. etc.

CHAPTER

7

Enquiries and Replies

ENQUIRIES

A letter of enquiry should be:

(a) Straightforward, compact and courteous,
(b) Positive and confident in tone.
(c) Brief and to the point, yet clear, complete and correct.

Hints for Drafting an 'Enquiry'

(1) State the purpose of your letter, whether you need goods, service or information.
(2) Request for price list, catalogue, etc.
(3) Ask for samples or demonstration, if needed.
(4) Tell the seller how you got his name whether someone personally recommended him or you learnt about him through an advertisement.
(5) State the details of your business and what you are interest in.
(6) Ask for terms related to discount, credit, mode of

delivery, package, etc. These will enable you to prepare the order.

(7) Give an idea of the quantity you need in order to enable the supplier to quote the best possible price.

(8) If you are asking for a concession, give reasons like large and continuous orders, your ability to promote more sales in your area, etc.

Don'ts

(a) Avoid lengthy and unnecessary statements.

(b) Avoid repetition.

(c) Avoid apologies—do not say
"We beg you to send . . . ."
"Thank you", etc.

Replies must replace salesmen. So, they must contain something capable of arousing the reader's interest and creating in him a desire to buy. They must carry to the customer some of the convincing force of a good salesman's talk.

Hints for Drafting a 'Reply'

(1) Thank the party for his letter and show appreciation for his interest in your company, its products or service.

(2) Refer to the date and/or number of his letter.

(3) Answer, in a cheerful tone, all the questions in the letter of enquiry.

(4) If possible, add relevant information in the form of a short description of goods, prices, advantages, favourable terms, etc.

(5) State the terms clearly and concisely and tell the time required to execute the order, if placed, place and mode of delivery, terms of payment, discount (trade and cash), packing, etc.

(6) State the time for which the offer is open, if time is an important factor.

(7) State whether the price-list, catalogue, samples, etc. are enclosed or they are being sent separately.

(8) Use some sales talk to stimulate the interest of the buyer.

(9) Show your willingness to serve or help the customer in the form of additional information, etc., if needed.

Example 1:

Ask a firm dealing in furniture to send their price-list and catalogue.

Modern Furnishers,
535/2, Diwakar Road,
Jamnagar.

Tel. No. . . . .
Fax No. . . . .
Mobile No. . . . .

Ref. No. . . . . . . 30th March 2008

To

Messrs J.K.S. & Co.
Hanuman Street, Vidyanagar,
Ahmedabad - 105 067.

Dear Sirs,

Subject : Home and Office Furniture

We inform you that we are dealers of all kinds of furniture. Our firm was established in the year 1990 at Jamnagar. It has now branches at 10 important centres in the country including Mumbai, Kolkata and Hyderabad. Our annual turnover is about Rs. 2.75 crore.

We want to add your furniture items in our stock. Therefore, please send us your latest illustrated catalogue and price-list of 'Home and Office Furniture'.

Yours truly,
For Modern Furnishers

V.K. Sharma
Proprietor

Example 2:
Reply to the above Enquiry.

J.K.S & Company,
Hanuman Street, Vidyanagar,
Ahmedabad - 105 067

31st March 2008

Reference No. . . . .

Tel. No. . . . . Fax No. . . . . Mobile No. . . . .

The Proprietor,
Modern Furnishers,
535/2, Dwarka Road,
Jamnagar (Gujarat)

Dear Sir,

Subject : Home and Office Furniture

Thank you for your enquiry of March 30, vide your reference No. . . . . We are glad to enclose the illustrated catalogue and price-list of 'Home and Office Furniture', both wooden and steel. Our furniture is very popular among the elite.

We have 120 dealers throughout India. You may get our dealership. The terms and conditions for the same are being forwarded with this letter on separate sheet. Any further query will be welcome.

Our furniture is made of high gauged steel sheets and pipes and is designed to suit the 'Luxury Class' customers. Our traditional type is wooden but elegant and antique looking.

We believe the catalogue and price-list fairly describe our products. However, if you need further details or assistance in meeting your customers' special requirements, we shall be pleased to be of help.

Yours faithfully,
For J.K.S. & Co.,
J.K. Shayam (Partner)

Encls:
(1) Catalogue
(2) Price List.
(3) Dealership literature.

ORDERS AND THEIR EXECUTION

Orders

The quotations are the 'offers' made by the seller and the orders by the buyers are the 'acceptance' of the offer.

Order Form: Practically, all firms use 'Order forms' or 'Order blanks' to place orders. These are standardized order forms printed with columns for necessary information.

Hints for Drafting an 'Order'

(1) Thank the seller for his quotations especially when special terms have been offered, or add a note of appreciation, in the case of repeat order.
(2) Give specifications of the goods:
    (a) Exact trade name, catalogue and trade name, size, colour, style, design, quality, etc.,
    (b) Price and discount,
    (c) Quantity desired for each item,
    (d) Alternative goods, if acceptable,
(3) Give shipment or forwarding directions, goods to be sent by parcel post, goods or passenger train, motor truck (lorry) or ship.
(4) Give special instructions, if any, for packing, marking, insurance, etc.
(5) State the manner of payment:
    (a) Debit to account,
    (b) Cash sent with order (C.W.O.).
    (c) Cash to be paid on delivery (C.O.D.).
    (d) Invoice to be sent by post or through a bank,
    (e) Bill to be drawn by the seller.

(6) Close with what you wish to emphasize:
   (a) Quality,
   (b) Prompt execution,
   (c) Discount,
   (d) Time factor, etc.

Example: Place an order for certain goods which you reserve the right to reject if delivered after more than 15 days of the date of order. State that they are to be sent by parcel post.

Modern Emporium
Namjoshi Road, Gadag.

Ref. No. . . . . . . 31st March 2008

Messrs, J.K. Das & Sons,
10 Corporation Building,
Durgad Bail,
Hubli (Karnataka)

Subject: Our Order No. SRY/27/09, dated 30-03-2008

Dear Sirs,

We hereby enclose our order No. SRY/27/09 and we request you to execute it promptly. The articles have been selected from your latest catalogue.

The articles are required urgently by one of our regular and valuable customers. They may be sent by parcel post so that they reach us early. The time factor being quite important, we insist that the articles should reach here within fifteen days from the date of this order and we reserve the right to reject the goods if received late.

Yours faithfully,
For Modern Emporium
Anju Rani
Manager

Encl: The Order

EXECUTION OF ORDERS

The receipt of every order must be promptly acknowledged either by a ready printed post card or by a special letter. Every order is an opportunity for the seller to build an abiding, profitable relationship with the customer.

The acknowledgement of an order is a legal acceptance of all the points mentioned in the order. Hence the order must be read carefully before accepting and acknowledging it.

(I) Prompt Execution—in full

(1) Thank the party for his order.

(2) Specify the goods you have dispatched or the time by which you will dispatch them.

(3) State the total amount of the invoice and attach the Invoice to the letter.

(4) Refer to the need of prompt payment but do not stress this point. If the Bill has been debited to the party's account, make a mention of it or if the invoice and other papers have been sent through a bank, request the party to arrange for getting the papers released from the bank.

(5) Mention the mode of dispatch, post parcel, passenger or goods train, motor lorry, etc.

(6) Reference may also be made to the quality and popularity of the goods and also the expression of hope that the goods will satisfy the consumers' requirements.

(7) Maintain a personal tone throughout and show your eagerness to serve the customer in all possible ways.

(8) Impress on your customers the fact that this order has been given personal attention.

(II) Prompt but Part Execution

(1) Thank the party for the order.

(2) Mention that you are supplying the goods immediately.

(3) State the reason for not being able to execute the order in full.
(4) Give the probable date by which you can supply the rest of the order.
(5) Suggest a reminder to keep the order alive.

Defective Order

Sometimes, the sellers receive orders with incomplete information. Such orders, if executed, may not fully meet the customer's requirements. Hence, it is always a good policy to write back to the customer asking for exact specifications regarding colour, design, price, size, pattern, etc. before executing the order, and to enable the customer to furnish exact specifications, sellers should enclose or send separately the necessary catalogue and price list. Tact, suggestion and the tone of being helpful are the most important qualities of such letters

Hints for Drafting Replies to Defective or Incomplete Orders

(1) Thank the party for the order.
(2) Be tactful to point out that the order did not specify the requirements clearly.
(3) Be informative and suggestive.
(4) See that the tone of your letter does not offend the customer.
(5) Help the customer in specifying his requirements clearly; giving necessary details. It is preferable to enclose catalogue, price list and other literature, if any, to guide the customer.
(6) Indirectly, make it clear that the information is sought in the interest of the customer.

DELAY IN EXECUTION

Hints for drafting letters intimating delay in the execution of orders:

(1) Thank the party for his order.

(2) Explain clearly in a personal tone the reason for delay.

(3) Make the customer understand that the circumstances are beyond your control.

(4) State, if possible, the date when you can execute the order.

(5) Assure the party that his order will receive prompt attention on the date being mentioned.

(6) End your letter with a reference to the inconvenience your customer might be put to and hope that he will not mind it.

Example: (Stock Exhausted)

You have received an order for 500 meters of curtain fabric. As the cloth is not in stock, you request the customer to allow you more time for the execution of the order or to accept a substitute. Draft the letter.

SHREE RAMRATAN STORES
Wholesale and Retail Cloth Merchants

Broadway, Kolkata
Ref. No. .... 31st March 2010

Messrs. B. Bommyaya & Sons
K. Kamraj Road, Chennai.

Dear Sirs,

We are pleased to receive your order No. C/24/8-19 of 31st March 2010 for 500 metres of 'SWASTIK' curtain fabric of the model patterns sent by you.

The quality and the pattern selected by you is an imported article and since we have exhausted this fabric at present, you can get it only after 31st May 2010.

And we are afraid if our foreign manufacturers do not have the patterns selected by you, there may be a further delay. We, therefore, request you to extend the time for the delivery of the goods by 3 more weeks. We assure you that you will certainly receive the consignment in the third week of April if you can hold your order till then.

However, if your requirement is very urgent, we offer you a substitute, DIAMOND curtain fabric, which is quite satisfactory for all general purposes. We enclose sample patterns of the same and the price this fabric-list.

We suggest, however, since you are a regular user of SWASTIK Brand, it would be better for you to suspend the execution of your order unless such a course is unavoidable.

We hope you will confirm your order subject to extension of time.

Yours faithfully,
Vee. Kay. Angiras
Manager

Encls: Six sample patterns,
One price-list

Refusal of an Order

Even though the seller may be having the goods ordered, he may have to refuse to deliver them because of the following reasons:

(A) Prices mentioned in the order are less than quotations, quantity ordered is too small, orders on hand are large in number, production difficulties, etc.
(B) Dues have not been cleared by the customer.
(C) Sale is through authorized agents only.

(A) The order is declined because of the unsuitability of prices desired or heavy orders on hand.

Hints for Drafting

(1) Thank the party for his order.
(2) Draw the customer's attention to the price-list or quotations supplied by you or bring to his notice the minimum quantity of an order that can be executed, or inform the customer of the exact reason which makes you decline the order, or explain that it was

not a firm offer and placing the order within the stated time was important.

(3) Convince the customer that the price quoted by you is the lowest and you cannot afford to sell the goods at the reduced price asked by the customer in his order.

(4) Show your willingness to execute the order at the prices quoted by you or at the new prices.

(5) If goods can be delivered after the lapse of a particular period, ask the customer whether he can wait till then.

(6) If the refusal is on account of heavy orders on hand or production difficulties or inadequate stocks apprise the customer of your difficulties and make him realize that although you earnestly desire to serve him, you are compelled by your circumstances to refuse the order. However, offer your services for filling future orders from the customer.

(B) The order is declined because earlier dues have not been cleared

Hints for Drafting

While drafting such letters, the writer should be simple, straightforward and accommodating. The tone of the letter must not scare away the customer. The customer should not be made to feel that he is being avoided by the seller. Rather he should be convinced that the seller is trying to be as accommodating as possible. It must be remembered that poor drafting not only results in bad debts but also in loss of business reputation in general.

(1) Thank the customer for his order.

(2) Do not refuse the order straightway; simply regret that you cannot fill up the order immediately.

(3) Show the customer your confidence in him, but convince him of your difficulties with large number of open accounts and tell him of the disadvantages of long-term indebtedness.

(4) Refer to the amount due and make a request for its prompt payment.
(5) Express your desire to serve him.
(6) Make it clear that the order can be filled up but you are awaiting his remittances.

(C) The order is declined because sale is undertaken only through authorized agents

Hints for Drafting

(1) Thank the customer for his order.
(2) Tell him of your policy of sale through agents only.
(3) Indicate your appreciation for the customer's interest in your goods.
(4) Give the full address of your nearest agent.
(5) Make it clear that it is the general policy of your firm to serve the customers through agents only.

In your letter, do not show your disinterest in the order because the order is for your goods, though sold indirectly. You should endeavour to please the customer and make him purchase your goods only through your agent.

CREDIT AND STATUS ENQUIRIES

A substantial amount of trading involves credit. Credit is a means through which goods can be bought and sold without cash payment. It is the buyers who conduct business with comparatively less capital and the sellers attract larger sales. The sellers get the additional advantage of regular sales and guaranteed market for their good.

Although credit increases sales, it involves risks, particularly of bad debts and delayed payments. A sound credit policy, careful selection of credit customers and prompt collection are essential to successful functions of credit customers and prompt collection is essential to successful functioning of the system. Before allowing credit, the Credit Department must get the following essential information about the customer:

(a) His character which indicates industry, honesty, reputation for fairness and justice, reliability, trustworthiness moral conduct; prompt payment for which the customer is known.
(b) His capacity which includes business experience and knowledge, commercial acumen and judgment, ability and resourcefulness.
(c) His capital including the tangible assets, their market value, the reserves, and the ratio between assets and liabilities.
(d) The condition of the customer's business in particular and the external conditions of the business on the whole, which certainly affect individual business. The above factors (the four C's) are considered to be the foundation or criterion of a sound credit policy. Relevant information about the four C's can be obtained from the following sources:

(i) Internal Sources

(a) The sizes and values of the past orders placed by the customer, if he is a regular cash customer.
(b) The salesman's report about the customer.

(ii) From the Customer

(a) Personal interview with the customer.
(b) Financial statements of the customer submitted by him.

(iii) External Sources

(a) Trade References given by the customer.
(b) Bank References submitted by him.
(c) Information from Trade Associations, Chambers of Commerce, Inquiry Agencies, General Mercantile Agencies, etc.

Trade and Bank References

Trade references are the names of the business firms that

can submit a report on a customer's creditworthiness. Whenever a customer requests for supply of goods on credit, the trader has to obtain necessary information about the four C's of the applicant. For this purpose, the trader asks the applicant to name a few businessmen of his acquaintance to whom he may 'refer' the matter. These businessmen are called references.

Bank reference is the name of the credit-applicant's banker who can supply all necessary information about him to the trader. While it may not hurt the feelings of the party, the seller's letter to his bank must make it clear the seller is seeking this information as a matter of general policy and not because of any doubt about the credit standing of the customer.

Hints for drafting

1. Express your pleasure at the request for credit and thank the party for the order.
2. Explain why you need the credit information.
3. Making a request for specific information: tread reference, bank references, financial statements, or personal interview, etc.
4. Assure that the pieces of information will be kept confidential.
5. Write something to build up goodwill; tell the customer that it will be in his own interest to send promptly the required information, complete in all details, for it will enable you to immediately open his account and dispatch the good to him.

Since it is in the mutual interest of both the trader and the customer, the latter should feel free in giving the necessary information to establish his own credit in the business.

The credit references asked for should be furnished in as simple and polite a fashion as possible, even if the customer thinks them unnecessary.

There should be no room for feeling insulted because the trader requires the information to establish the customer's credit only as a matter of routine.

Example:

M Ranganath & Bros. Bros. (P) Ltd.
26 Anna Salai, Chennai.
Ref. No. . . . . 5th August, 2010

The Credit Manager,
Sudha Radio Corporation,
Bangalore, Karnataka State.

SUBJECT : CONFIDENTIAL

Madam,

In reply to your letter dated 19th September, we vouchsafe the amount of credit you mention. We have had our business relations with this firm for the last seven years and we have found the partners quite enterprising.

However, our experience in the last three years is that the firm has been slow in making payments.

We hope this information will be considered confidential and without any liability or responsibility on our part.

If you need any other information, in confidence, please write to us.

Cordially yours,

For M. Ranganath & Bros. (P) Ltd.
M. Krishnamurthy,
Manager

Bank References

Bank reference is the name of the banker of the credit applicant with whom he maintains his account and through whom he meets or negotiates bills, etc.

The trader should request his own banker to get the necessary credit information from the credit applicant's banker.

Hints for Drafting

1. Mention the credit applicant's name and address and the address of his banker as given by him.
2. State the terms and amount of credit asked for.

3. Make a polite request for providing necessary information after taking up the reference.

Example: Write a letter to your bank asking your bank to get you necessary information about the credit standing of a firm, desirous of operating a credit account with you.

You must mention the business handled by the firm and its full address and the bankers with whom the firm deals.

You may also undertake to keep the information supplied as confidential.

SUDHA RADIO CORPORATION
Veeraraghavan Nagar
Bangalore-5

5th April 2008

Ref. No. . . ..
The Manager,
Canada Bank,
Bangalore-4.

Subject : Credit Information from Bank

Dear Sir,

We have received an order from Messrs. Murali & Co, Radio and Watch Dealers, near Bank of Madera for the supply of radios and transistors worth Rs. 60,000 on 3-month-credit.

We have been referred to their Bankers, Syndicate Bank, Bank Road, Madera, for information on their credit standing.

If you can field out anything about their activities and financial standing in general and their reputation to meet their bills promptly, we shall be very grateful to you. They estimate their quarterly orders at about Rs. 70,000.

You can, of course, rely on us to act discreetly.

Yours faithfully,
For Sudha Radio Corporation,

Miss K. Geetha
Credit (Sales) Manager.

Example: A favourable reply to the letter from Punjab National Bank in response to Enquiry made earlier.

Punjab National Bank
Head Office
Bhikaji Kama Place, New Delhi

Confidential

Ref. No. . . . 6th April, 2008

The Credit Manager,
Salman Electronic Corporation,
New Delhi - 110 089

Subject : Credit Enquiry

Dear Sir,

We have just received credit information about the firm you mentioned in your letter dated 19th March 2008. We can advise you that the firm has a good reputation for its financial standing and have a network of clientele. The recent expansion of the firm, with additional investment by the partners, has met with great success and they have now taken up wholesale distribution of a popular electronic firm.

The firm can be considered quite safe for the credit you mention.

This information is for your use only and is given in confidence and without any liability or responsibility on the part of the bank.

Yours faithfully,
For Punjab National Bank

V.K. Sharma
(Manager)

Example: Unfavourable reply from the bank.

Confidential

Subject : Credit Enquiry

Madam,

Our enquiries about the firm you mentioned in your letter dated April 19 indicate that the firm does not enjoy a good reputation for its financial management and for meeting its liabilities.

We would advise you to follow rather a line of caution.

The information is given in strict confidence and the Bank does not accept any liability or responsibility on its part.

Yours faithfully,
For Punjab National Bank

Kay Cee Krishnan
Manager

Request for Credit from Bank to meet overseas orders, likely to be repeated.

SARASWATI TEXTILES LIMITED
MITHAPURI

Ref. No. .... August 25, 2010

The Manager,
Unco Gabriel Bank,
Mithapuri (India).

Subject : ***Ad hoc*** **Export Credit Limit of Rs. 100 Lac**

Dear Sir,

Our special Marketing Team headed by our newly appointed Executive Director (International Business) had a tour of African countries and have concluded Memorandum of

Understanding with the Public Sector Units in Uganda, Zimbabwe, Tanzania and South Africa for export of acrylic fibres and cotton and acrylic textiles on terms and conditions considered most favourable to our company and the country. The rough estimate of the orders, in the first instance, would be approximately Rs. 5 crore. The supply has to be made within six months.

We have spare machine capacity and, therefore, there will be no difficulty in executing the orders on time schedule.

While we are preparing the proposal for the Export Credit, please let us have your approval, in principle, in the meantime. Awaiting favourable reply.

Yours faithfully,
Director (Finance)

Requesting bankers to examine a proposal for setting up a subsidiary in Canada:

K.C.A. FABS LIMITED
25 Columbus Nagar
Basantpur - 177 009

Ref. No. .... 20th September, 210

The Branch Manager,
Peoples Bank,
Trutnagar

Subject: Setting up a subsidiary in Canada

Dear Sir,

As you know, we have been dealing in handlooms and handicrafts for the last 20 years. We export over 70% of our goods to various countries. Our sales in Canada have jumped up tremendously.

Out of our total exports of Rs. 27 crore, exports to Canada has reached Rs. 12 crore (up from last year's figure of Rs. 6

crore); it is a 100% jump in one year. We have so far received orders, 50% of them repeat orders, to the aggregate figures of Rs. 9 crore.

Unconfirmed orders valued about Rs. 6 crore are being negotiated. We are sure of getting at least Rs. 5 crore out of them. Our marketing executives are still in Canada and we hope to receive at least further confirmed orders of the value of Rs. 4 crore.

All payments will be either in US Dollars or Canadian Dollars. We shall also book forward contracts with you as usual.

We are forwarding a proposal prepared as per your bank's guidelines in the prescribed format. All relevant papers are also attached therewith.

On perusal of our accounts and the financial statements for the past five years, you will not find any weakness on our account. Please go through our proposal and let us know when our Finance Executive may call on you for discussion, if necessary.

Thanking you,

Yours faithfully,
For K.C.A. Fabs Limited

YXYZ
Director (Finance)

Encl.

CHAPTER

8

Claims and Adjustments

As long as men are men and machines are machines, and not infallible, there are bound to be imperfections and mistakes.

It is often supposed that the making of complaints requires no special care, but this supposition is very far from the truth.

If a wrong is to be righted, making a complaint requires tact, carefulness and the art of convincing. Clarity, courteousness and an inoffensive style of writing are extremely important in a letter of claims.

The claim should be made politely but firmly without showing any signs of anger. "A quiet, confident and dignified letter commands respect and gets more attention than an excited, agitated letter".

Example:

Even though you were assured of delivery of goods within 3 weeks of order, it is six weeks from the date of order and you have yet to receive them.

Write a letter to your supplier, pointing out the delay and specifying a date by which you wish to get the goods.

A.A. Maniamma & Sons
Paints and Hardware Merchants
Murugan Road, Salem (Tamilnadu)

10th September, 2009

Ref. No. . . . .

Akshay Steel Industries,
27, Industrial Estate,
Jalandhar (Punjab).

Subject : Our Order No. 2334/09 dated June 1, 2009.

Dear Sirs,

On June 1, we placed our above noted order with you for six dozen, No. 7AX, 16 gauge, steel plates and 200 feet of No. 5BZ steel pipes.

When your representative visited us towards the end of June, he assured us of delivery within three weeks, but it is more than three months since we ordered these goods and we have received neither the consignment nor any intimation about it.

All the steel plates and pipes ordered are required by a customer to complete a shipment of furniture to Amsterdam. Your delay is causing great loss to him and a loss of considerable goodwill to us.

Please expedite the dispatch of goods ensuring that we receive them not later than two weeks from today.

Yours faithfully,
A.A. Verma
Proprietor

Example: Reply to letter.

Akshay Steel Industries,
27, Industrial Estate,
G.T. Road, Jalandhar (Punjab)

Ref. No. . . . .
24th September, 2009

Messrs, A.A. Maniamma and Sons,
Murugan Road,
Salem (Tamilnadu)

Subject : Your Order No. 2334/9 dated June 1, 2009.

Dear Sirs,

With reference to your letter dated the 10th September, 2010, we regret that you had to take the trouble of writing to us. Your letter must have crossed with ours in transit advising you of the dispatch of goods.

Owing to a lightning strike in the factory, the production was held up for two months. With a large number of orders on hand, coupled with unexpected suspension of production, it was inevitable that we fall behind the delivery schedule.

We are extremely sorry about this delay which has caused inconvenience to you and your customer but hope you will realize that it was only due to circumstances beyond our control.

Yours faithfully,
For Akhay Steel Industries,

R.K. Malhotra
Sales Manager

SALES LETTERS

Publicity has a very important role to play in a competitive society. No business can be done successfully without publicity in one or the other form. It is because of this that the art of salesmanship is needed in every business activity. Salesmanship assumes different forms; as we know, publicity and advertising are an impersonal form of salesmanship; and a sales letter is just part of publicity and advertisement.

Advantages of Sales Letter

A sales letter can find way easily and quickly to any person at almost any place. It is not unwelcome; for it does not impose itself. It can quietly wait till the addressee has enough leisure to go through it. Moreover, it is quite cheap.

It can be as brief or as long as may be necessary. It has the advantage of having a personal touch and has far less risk of missing the aim. A general advertisement may fail to attract attention or to impel action. It has also to face competition from other advertisements appearing in the same newspaper or magazine.

It is also likely to appeal to only a few of the large readers. But a sales letter does not suffer from these defects.

Unlike a salesman, the postman always carries the sales letter. Whereas a salesman, and even a pretty sales girl, has to wait for hours to get an appointment with prospects, a sales letter gets a direct and free entry even into the 'No Admission without Permission' room. Thus a sales letter plays quite a significant role in conducting business in general but is particularly useful in direct selling by mail.

Objects of a Sales Letter

As a part of salesmanship, a sales letter has to "educate, persuade, and convince" the customer to buy a particular product or service. Main objects of a sales letter are:

(1) It has the immediate object of promoting the sale of a product, a service or an idea.
(2) It introduces new goods in the market more effectively, quickly, at a lower cost and in a wider area.
(3) It introduces the salesman to the prospects even before the former has called on them, because it reaches them earlier than the salesman and thus keeps them informed.

(4) It widens the market for existing products without much cost.

(5) Repeated appearance of a sales letter has the effect of a reminder. It helps the customer to remember the product or the service of a firm whenever he is in need of it.

(6) It educates the customer in selecting the right type of article and also in better understanding of products and services.

(7) It creates and maintains goodwill among the customers by offering quality products and services.

(8) It is the main source of securing orders for a Mail Order Business House.

(9) It functions as a salesman (with its force of persuasion, education and conviction) wherever a salesman cannot visit the customers.

(10) It also keeps the customer constantly in touch with the company and its products and services.

Three P's that a Sales Correspondent should Know

The three most important factors of which a sales correspondent should have the knowledge are: Prospect (Potential customer), Product (Service or Idea) and Proposition.

To write an effective sales letter, a person must put himself in the readers' place. Then only can he have the understanding of the readers' response to the message carried by the letter. Understanding the prospects is akin to understanding their wants and offering goods, services or propositions from their point of view.

A proposition is an offer of items—prices, discounts, guarantee, money back guarantee, performance, repairs, replacements, services, etc. Every customer studies these terms very carefully and weighs in his mind the comparative advantages of the terms offered by different sellers. Hence, a sales correspondent must study his terms from this angle and make them more attractive and competitive and, ultimately to make them readily acceptable to his customers.

The Functions of a Sales Letter

A sales letter has the following functions to perform:

(1) Attracting attention,
(2) Arousing interest,
(3) Educating and convincing,
(4) Stimulating desire, and
(5) Securing action (sale).

COLLECTION LETTERS

The collection department is entrusted with the job of maintaining accounts of credit customers, preparing periodical statements of accounts to be sent to dealers and collecting the dues promptly. The major problem of this department is how to collect the dues and also retain the customers.

How to Write Effective Collection Letters

The following guidelines may be suggested for drafting collection letters:

(1) The tone should be positive, cheerful and optimistic.
(2) The contents and style of the collection letter should be determined with an eye on the customers' usual conduct and his circumstances.
(3) The "you" attitude should be used to convince the debtor that it is to his own advantage to pay.
(4) An informal and friendly approach helps to "break the ice", the debtor finds it difficult to resist, and he is impelled to respond favourably to the correspondent's letters. So, let not the letters be stiff and lifeless.
(5) Friendliness must be tempered with tact and firmness. The style should be neither blunt and offensive nor unduly soft. Friendliness coupled with firmness allows the debtor to preserve his self-respect but reminds him that he cannot keep the creditors' money.
(6) A collection letter should not be too brief. Too short a collection letter appears to be curt, its abruptness

betrays lack of courtesy and business etiquette on the part of the writer and it offends and embitters the customer.

(7) Before forcing the debtor to pay, an appeal should be made to his fairness, pride, self-interest and the advantage of doing business with the correspondent.

(8) Finally, it must be remembered that the correspondent is not to lose the customer. A wrong approach, a ruthless or inconsiderate policy or ungainly hate may force the customer to stop trading with the correspondent's firm and transfer his dealings to a competitor's firm. This will result in loss of money, goods and the customer's future business.

Collection Series

Collection letters are usually written in a series, each successive letter stronger in tone than its predecessor, and sent out at intervals varying with the type of credit risk involved.

A poor credit risk will be dealt with sooner and more frequently than a good credit risk. A poor credit risk may receive say, four letters over a two month period, a good credit risk five or six letters over a six month span.

The typical unpaid account passes through the following stages of collection correspondence:

(a) Sending statement of account,
(b) Reminders,
(c) Inquiries and discussion stage,
(d) Appeal and urgency, and
(e) Demand and warning.

(a) Sending Statement of Account

The actual collection correspondence starts, in fact, from the stage of sending reminders, because sending statement of account is a duty of the creditors.

The customer is periodically sent a statement of account showing the amount due from him. It does not make any request for payment. It is just a notification to the customer of the value of his purchases and he is expected to remit money according to the terms of payment settled beforehand.

The special collection correspondence starts when the amount due is unpaid even after the usual period of credit has expired.

Hints for drafting series of collection letters

At this stage it may be assumed that the customer's failure to pay is due to forgetfulness or oversight. Therefore, he is only to be reminded that his account is yet to be settled.

(a) Refer to the statement of account already sent and the amount due.
(b) Say that the customer has, perhaps, overlooked the statement.
(c) Request for prompt payment.
(d) Enclose the statement of account again.

(b) Enquiry and Discussion Stage

When reminders do not bring expected response from the delinquent customers, the creditor has to take up a different course to 'break the ice', he writes to the customer to ask him why the payment is being withheld. It is yet too early to give up the hope of collecting the amount due.

Hints for Drafting

(1) Refer to the amount due and the period for which it has been due.
(2) Draw the customer's attention to the reminders that have already been sent.
(3) Mention what you feel to be the reason for delay.
(4) Offer assistance to help him get over his difficulties correction of your mistakes, allowance for wrong goods, extension of credit term, arrangement for instalment payment, etc.
(5) Insist that the customer should write to you or visit your store for explaining his difficulties.

Example: Demand and Warning

JADUNATH & SONS
Kali Ma Road, Saleempur

Ref. No.....
10th April 2008

Subject: Bill No. . . . . dated..... for Rs. . . . ..against 2-month credit unpaid

Dear Sirs,

We would offer sincere regrets having to say "your account has been handed over to our lawyers for legal action", but you have left us with no alternative.

All our efforts to receive a cheque from you against your Feb. 10 account of Rs. 500 now two months and a half past due have failed. Our chief Accountant has already asked the lawyers to move the matter to the Court. But I have specially requested them to wait till April 25.

So, you have 15 more days to help retain your credit with us. Do act now. Send the cheque by return post and save yourself the cost and consequences of legal proceedings.

Assuring you our attention awlays,

Yours sincerely,
Manager (Sales)

CIRCULAR LETTERS

There are four objectives of writing circular letters:

(a) To obtain publicity for a cause, a campaign, or merchandise,
(b) To make the reader interested in their contents,
(c) To impress the reader with facts and information about the firm, its policy and the event which may have necessitated the sending of the circular letters, and

(d) To gain the confidence of the reader.

Situations that need Circular Letters

(1) Opening of a new shop, or a branch, or expansion of the store;
(2) Change in address or premises;
(3) Introducing a new article;
(4) Price reduction and clearance sales;
(5) Obtaining an agency;
(6) Admission of a partner;
(7) Retirement or death of a partner; and
(8) Change in the constitution of the firm.

Important points that each of these letters should contain are given in the following examples:

Opening of a Branch

(1) The name and address of the new branch is, of course, given in the letter head.
(2) Tell something about the development of the business and its popularity elsewhere.
(3) Give the date of the opening of the new branch.
(4) Describe the goods and services offered.
(5) Invite the customer to the store or offer your personal attention to him for proving your claims about goods and services.

Sometimes, the name, qualifications and experience of the manager of new branch are also given.

Change of Business Premises

(1) Give the new address, as far as possible, at the beginning of the body of the letter.
(2) Explain reasons for change mainly the expansion of business requiring more accommodation and lack of it in the old building.
(3) Stress the advantages and convenience of the new location.

(4) Mention the change, if any, in the telephone number.
(5) Point out the additions, if any, made to the stocks.
(6) Make an appeal to the customer to continue extending his patronage to you.

Introducing New Products

(1) Arrest the interest of the reader with some appealing statements.
(2) Briefly outline your progress in general and make a particular reference to the regular improvements made by the firm for the customer's convenience.
(3) Give news of the new product that you have introduced.
(4) Describe the features and utility of new product.
(5) Appreciate the customer's patronage in the past and request that it is also continued in future.
(6) Suggest a trial order to be placed by the customer.

Announcing Reduction Sales

(1) Preferably at the beginning itself, mention the best reduced price of a popular articles and then write about other goods and their reduced prices.
(2) Give the date of commencement of the reduction sale, also mention the period for which the special sale is open.
(3) Mention the reasons for such a reduction sale/ clearance sale, sale of shop—soiled goods, slightly damaged goods, shifting of premises, etc.
(4) Give special timings, if any, for the reduction sale.
(5) Suggest that the customer should pay a visit to the store as early as possible to get the advantage of a wide range of goods available at the beginning of the special sale.

Opening of a new Shop

This letter is written exactly on the same lines as that of opening a new branch:

(1) Mention the date of inauguration of the new shop.
(2) Mention the goods that you are dealing in.
(3) Tell how the business is constituted whether it is a proprietary or partnership concern, the experience, qualifications, etc. of the proprietor or partners.
(4) You may also state that with adequate capital invested, your shop provides a wide variety of goods in sufficient quantity, etc.
(5) Stress the competitive prices, prompt services, etc. that you are offering.
(6) Invite the customer to the store.

Making an Announcement about Getting an Agency

(1) Explain the reasons, if any, that necessitated the taking of agency increasing demand for the goods, etc.
(2) Mention the area of agency operation.
(3) Inform that you can now execute the orders more promptly and are in a position to stock a wide variety of goods.
(4) Explain the quality, utility, durability, popularity, price, advantages, etc. of goods.
(5) Offer special discounts, if any, planned.
(6) It may be notified that the customer should not send his orders directly to the manufacturer but book them with you only.
(7) Appreciate and request the co-operation of the customer.

Admission of a Partner

(1) Mention the reasons for the admission of the partner—expansion of business, additional investment, more efficient management of branches, etc.
(2) Mention the experience and special knowledge of the partner and express the hope of offering still better service to the customers.

(3) Mention the new name of the firm, if there is any change.
(4) Explain that the policy of the firm in serving the customers continues as before.
(5) Solicit the customer's continued patronage.
(6) Give specimen signature of the new partner.

Retirement or Death of Partner

(1) Express your regret at the loss of a retiring or deceased partner.
(2) Make an appreciative reference to his services to the firm.
(3) Say whether the vacancy is being filled by a new partner; explain the quality and experience of the new partner.
(4) Stress that the change in the constitution of the firm does not at all change its relations with its customers or its policy.
(5) Point out that the change has not occasioned any deficiency in capital and hence the firm is capable of maintaining its business on its old scale.
(6) Point out the change, if any, in the name of the firm.
(7) Solicit the customer's patronage.
(8) Give the signature of the new partner, if admitted.

Change in the Constitution of the Firm

(1) Mention that the development of business required additional capital and comprehensive management.
(2) The changed name under which the company will now do its business should be given.
(3) Make some reference to other Management members, i.e. directors, their qualifications, etc.
(4) Assure that the change in the constitution will not change the firm's policy of serving the customers to their satisfaction.
(5) Request the customers to continue extending you their co-operation.

CHAPTER

9

Banking Correspondence

Finance is like lubricating oil, which helps to run the wheels of trade and industry smoothly. The chief object of every business institution is to earn money. But the realization of this object calls for heavy investment in different activities as well as on machinery and other assets. Whenever a business house decides to expand its activities, it again requires investment. And howsoever rich the proprietors or partners, howsoever sound the capital structure of the organization, the expansion programme needs additional funds, which cannot be managed by the owners from within. Sometimes, business houses make it a matter of policy not to disturb the existing capital structure to meet their additional capital requirements and they seek financial assistance elsewhere.

BANKING CORRESPONDENCE

In performing these functions, a bank has to communicate:

(1) With its customers,

(2) With other banks, and
(3) With its Head Office.

Most of this correspondence is of a routine nature and does not call for any special skill in drafting. To facilitate correspondence and to save time and energy, form letters are prepared in advance. These letters have blank spaces to insert the customer's name, address and other relevant particulars. Form letters can be easily designed to carry on the following correspondence:

(a) Application for opening a bank account

  (i) By an individual,
  (ii) By a partnership firm, or
  (iii) By a joint stock company.

(b) Credit or debit advice by the bank to its customers.
(c) Statement of account sent by the bank.
(d) Initiation of non-collection, refusal or dishonour of cheques, bills, etc.

Hints for Drafting

(1) Always address the letter to the 'Manager', or the 'Agent'.
(2) Give particulars of the cheque-number, date on which drawn, payee's name and amount.
(3) Mention the reason for stopping payment (in most cases, instructions are given to stop payment because the cheque has been misplaced).
(4) Request the manager to take necessary steps in the matter.

Example: **Letter from the Head office refusing to sanction the loan.**

Hints for Drafting

(1) Referring to the Branch Manager's letter mention

that the directors do not view with favour the loan case of the party concerned.

(2) Give reasons for the unfavourable view. In most cases, some one of the following reasons will be found appropriate:

  (a) The value of the security offered does not leave a sufficient margin.
  (b) The security is not liquid.
  (c) The value of the security is liable to wide fluctuations.
  (d) The security is overvalued.
  (e) The security is not free from charge, mortgage, or attachment.

(3) The Branch Manager may also be instructed to be more careful in future so that he does not sanction loans without making a thorough investigation of the case.

Example : **Letter from one Bank to another asking for the Credit Repot on a Customer of the latter.**

Hints for Drafting

(1) Mention the words 'Private and Confidential', in the middle of the letter, immediately after the inside address.

(2) Request the Bank to furnish the credit report on the party giving—

  (a) The name and address of the party.
  (b) The business or profession of the party.
  (c) The amount of the loan requested by the party.

(3) Give an assurance that the report will be treated as private and confidential and that you are ready to reciprocate whenever required.

Example : **Reply to the above letter.**

Hints for Drafting

(1) Referring to the above letter mention that you have enclosed the report in strictest confidence and without any responsibility on the part of your bank or its employees.

(2) Mention that the report is sent on the condition that its contents and the name of the bank will not be disclosed when the information is passed on to the customer of the enquiring bank.

(3) Close the letter, as usual, with the complimentary close.

(II) Then give the Report in the following form:

Name of the Bank
Address

Date

Ref. No. . . .

THE REPORT
Private and Confidential

(Mention here the report/opinion of the bank concerning the party in question)

Signature

CHAPTER

10

Insurance Correspondence

Every business activity, like any other human activity, is exposed to many types of risks. The whole process of transfer of goods from producer to consumer takes a considerable time. During this period, many changes may take place in the demand for and supply of goods leading to loss of market or profit. The goods stored, the buildings, or any other property may be destroyed by a fire, storm, flood, civil disturbance, etc. The goods may be destroyed or damaged while in transit, or there may be a shipwreck. All these events, if and when they happen, cause heavy loss to businessmen.

A big businessman may sometimes bear such a loss but for a small business, it may mean ruin. Even for a large business, such a loss would be heavy. Risk is uncertainty with regard to cost, loss or change.

Business is pregnant with uncertainties about the course of future events. The time and place of their occurrence and the impact they will be creating are difficult to predict. But so long as there is uncertainty, there is the need of security. "The drive for security is one of the basic motivating forces determining the human attitudes. Out of the search for security, insurance was born".

TYPES OF INSURANCE

Many types of insurance contracts are effected to cover against various contingencies. But presently, we are going to consider only three types : Fire Insurance, Marine Insurance and Life Assurance.

Fire Insurance

A contract of fire insurance is a contract whereby the insurer, in consideration of a payment called premium, undertakes to indemnity the insured against loss of or damage to property due to fire during a certain period generally a year, agreed upon. The contract can be renewed at the end of the specified period.

Example : **Your consignment of handicrafts to New York has been damaged during a voyage. Submit a claim for compensation from the Insurance Company stating all the necessary facts.**

LUDHIANA HANDICRAFTS
GT Road, Ludhiana

Ref. No. . . . . 10th April 2010

The Manager,
Marine Deptt.
Oriental General Insurance Co. Ltd.
G.T. Road, Ludhiana.

Dear Sir,

Subject : Claim under Marine Policy No. . . . . . dated. . . for the amount of Rs. . . ....

We have just received a Report from our consignees at New York saying that our shipment of handicrafts sent per S.S. Bay of Bengal has reached them in a damaged condition. This shipment was covered by a valued policy No. 111 issued by you on 10th April, 2008, the details of the damage are as under:

Sr. No.	Description	Amount
(1)	7 cases containing embroidered products, found in soaked conditions	Rs. 580.00
(2)	5 boxes of sandalwood products, found broken and damaged	Rs. 1,420.00
		Rs. 2,000.00
	To this must be added 10% of the Invoice price for estimated loss of profit. Rs. 200 Plus Surveyor's Fees	Rs. 50.00
		Rs. 2,050.00

According to the standing instructions, the damage was surveyed by your authorized representative at New York Port, Mr. V.K. Sharma, whose report we are enclosing along with the original Invoice in support of the claim made. The policy and the Cash Receipt for the surveyor's fees are also enclosed.

We now request you to arrange to pass the claim for payment and to send us a cheque for the claim amount at an early date.

Yours faithfully,

Ludhiana Handicrafts,
K.S. Chauhan
Manager

IMPORT-EXPORT CORRESPONDENCE

The Import-Export trade correspondence runs almost on the same lines as the inland trade correspondence. However, the procedure and the formalities involved are somewhat special and require a little special study.

Indent Business

An indent house substantially helps the domestic importers in their purchases from foreign manufacturers.

Indent houses generally have their agents or branches in important foreign countries. They carry a full range of illustrations, catalogues and samples and other details of goods offered by foreign suppliers. They also help the importers to complete the various formalities involved in importing. For all this, they get a commission, normally $2^1/_2\%$ of the invoice value, though the rate may vary from one order to another.

Indent houses generally use printed order forms to be given by the importers. Such an order form is known as an indent. Where goods cannot be obtained at the rate specified in a closed indent, the indent house may have to quote a different rate to the importer. Such a quotation would be a counter offer by the indent house. The original indent can be taken up for further action only when the importer confirms it under the terms of a counter offer. Such an indent is known as Confirmatory Indent.

Terms in Quoting Prices

Following are the special terms used in quoting prices in foreign trade. Expenses included in the price quoted are borne by the seller, while the buyer has himself to take care of the further expenses:

Sr. No.	*Terms*	*What they represent*
1.	F.A.S	Free Alongside Ship cost, carriage to docks and dock charges.
2.	F.O.B.	Free on Board—F.A.S. plus charges for loading the goods on board the ship.
3.	C&F	Cost and Freight—F.O.B. plus freight charges up to the port of the importer.
4.	C.I.F.	Cost, Insurance and Freight—C&F plus marine insurance charges. This is a common method of quotation and the price, (ii) Carriage to the Port, (iii) Port Deck charges, (iv) Loading charges, (v) Export Duty, (vi) Freight, and (vii) Marine Insurance.

5.	Franco, Rendu or Free	C.I.F. plus import duty, port charges at the importer's port and conveyance charges from the port to the buyer's place.
6.	Ex-ship	All charges after the ship reaches the shore are to be paid by the Importer. (It is almost similar to C.I.F. Price)

Bill of Entry (B/E)

It is a form used by the importer to declare the information regarding the goods entering the port. Information in the B/E enables the customs authorities to levy appropriate import duties. Different forms of B/E are used for Free Goods, Dutiable goods and goods to be stored in Bonded Warehouses.

Bill of Loading (B/L)

It is a document of title to the goods that are shipped. It is also an acknowledgement from the shipping company for having received those goods onboard the ship. Further, the B/L is a contact of carriage and includes the terms and conditions on which the shipping company has accepted the goods for transportation. The original of the B/L is enclosed with the bill of exchange sent to the importer.

Insurance Policy

Marine insurance is compulsory in foreign trade. The original document relating to marine insurance is also sent to the importer.

Invoice

This document giving full details of goods being shipped is prepared by the exporter and sent to the importer.

Consular Invoice

Whenever the customs authorities levy import duty on the value of imports, the exporter has to obtain a consular invoice from the concerned officer of the importing country stationed at the exporter's port. This document must be enclosed with the Invoice.

Certificate of Origin

Certain international trade agreements enable the importer to claim reduced rates of import duties for goods imported from specified countries. If this be so, the exporter of such a specified country has to obtain a certificate in respect of the original country of production/manufacture of the goods shipped. This document should be supplied as proof of production/manufacture of the goods shipped. This document should also be sent along with the bill of exchange.

Bill of Exchange

Generally, the exporter secures payment for his shipments through a bill of Exchange drawn on the importer and sent through his (exporter's) bank to importer's bank. With this bill are enclosed, in original, important documents like the B/L, Insurance Policy, invoice, Consular Invoice, Certificate of Origin, etc.

Shipping Advice

After the goods have been shipped, the exporter sends a letter to the importer advising him of the dispatch of the goods, sailing of the ship and forwarding of the documents through the banker. This letter is called shipping advice.

Packing and Marking

Goods exported are generally packed according to the specifications of the importer. To facilitate identification, all the pickings carry particular marks as given by the importer. The exporter has to pay special attention to get these markings on the packing.

Letter of Credit

The importer has generally to obtain a letter of credit from his banker and sends it to the Indent house or the Exporter.

Correspondence

From the correspondence point of view, importing can be divided into two parts:

(a) Direct Importing, and
(b) Importing through Indent houses.

Direct Importing

The intending buyer makes a direct enquiry with the foreign manufacturer, asks for quotations, places orders and obtains the goods.

Example : **Direct Enquiry with the manufacturers.**

Jalandhar Plastics Ltd.
Regd. Office, Unity Building, J.C. Road,
Jalandhar

Ref. No. .... 10th April 2008

Messrs. Kogakusha & Co.
23, Central Street,
Tokyo, Japan.

Dear Sirs,

Subject : Trade Enquiry

We have been manufacturing plastic products of a very wide variety for the last fifteen years. The use of plastic products in our country has been rapidly increasing in the recent past. So, we plan to multiply our production capacity by installing five additional machines.

Your name was suggested to us by the Trade Commissioner of your country during his recent visit to Jalandhar. We have already obtained Import Licence as actual users. Will you please send us an illustrative catalogue of your latest machines for use in the production of plastic material of different types and varieties? We expect a very reasonable quotation from you.

An early reply will be greatly appreciated.

Yours faithfully,
For Jalandhar Plastics Ltd.
M.M. Shukla
Director, Purchases.

AGENCY CORRESPONDENCE

Manufacturers having a wide marking for their goods generally appoint agents for the sail of their goods. Appointment of agents is preferred to opening of branches as the "branches are often luxuries, with a tendency to eat deeply into their revenues. Agents generally handle goods of a number of manufacturers. As such, their overhead expenses are spread over all such products and they prove less expensive than running a branch.

Correspondence

The correspondence between the principals and their agents includes a wide variety of letters on different occasions. But we shall restrict our discussion to the following types of letters only:

(a) Offer of agency by the Principal.
(b) Agent's reply to the above.
(c) Application for agency by a prospective agent.
(d) The manufacturer's reply to this application.
(e) Announcement by the agent regarding obtaining agency.
(f) Cancellation of agency and public notice by the Principal.

Example : **The manufacturer offers an agency.**

Hints for Drafting

(1) Refer to the potential market for your goods.
(2) Explain the merits of your goods: brand name, quality, variety, reasonable price, popularity of the goods elsewhere, etc.
(3) Persuade the addressee to handle your products.
(4) Mention the remuneration and other terms of agency stocking, payment of advance, method of sale of be followed by the agent, remittance, additional commission, area of operation, etc.

Example : **Application for an Agency**

Hints for Drafting

(1) The opinion paragraph depends on how the applicant has taken up to write to the manufacturer for agency:

(a) Application with reference to an advertisement:

(i) Make a reference to the said advertisement of the manufacturer.
(ii) Offer your services and express your willingness to work as an agent.

(b) Application based on information from others:

(i) State the source from where information has been received about the manufacturer's desire to have agents in your market.
(ii) Offer your services and willingness to work as an agent.

(c) Application on own initiative:

(i) Introduce yourself as an agent.
(ii) Explain the potential market for the manufacturer's goods in your area.
(iii) Express your desire to take up the promotion of the sale of his products as an agent.

(2) In the next paragraph, you have to furnish your particulars:

(i) How long you have been in the field, the goodwill you have created.
(ii) Your business contacts.
(iii) Your knowledge of the market conditions, the buyers, the competition, etc.

(iv) Your arrangements for storage, distribution, advertisement, display, show rooms and window dressings, etc.

(3) Next, you have to mention the terms of agency acceptable to you, or, alternatively, you can write to the manufacturer to specify their terms of agency.

(4) It would be of assistance to the manufacturer if you mention a couple of Trade References and your banker. The manufacturer can refer your case to them before taking his decision on the granting of agency.

(5) Confidence your letter with the hope of getting a favourable reply from the manufacturer.

CHAPTER

11

Application Letters

Letters of application are written by those seeking jobs. Such letter is considered to be personal letter incorporating a few features of a business letter. Perhaps this is the most important personal letter for the career because it gets him the job he wants and may well determine his entire career.

Therefore, "when applying for a situation, the applicant should remember that he is attempting to sell something and like a shopkeeper displaying his wares, he would be worker, should display the qualities which he believes will be useful."

The job-application letter is a letter through which the writer tries to sell his services. The principles and technique of writing a Sales Letter should be equally applied here. Of course, it is more difficult for a person to say something about himself than buying some product.

TYPES OF APPLICATION LETTERS

There are two types of application letters:

(1) Application in response to an advertisement, and
(2) An unsolicited letter of application.

In both the cases, in a resume of the writer's education, experience and business background must be given. Such a resume may be a part of the letter itself or it may be written on enclosed separate sheet called 'Personal Record Sheet'.

An application letter and resume should be tailored to the viewpoint of the reader:

The 'you' Attitude

As already noted, the application of the 'you' attitude is very important. Undoubtedly, it is very difficult to incorporate the 'you' attitude in his letter, because the writer is more interested in telling the prospective employer 'what Aim' and 'what Has' in terms of qualifications, experience, etc. Still, it is important to remember that the prospective employer has his self-interest uppermost in his mind and he will select an applicant who is likely to satisfy him most.

The 'you' attitude, therefore, will be found in an application letter when it is written from the perspective found in an application letter.

To achieve this object, the writer of an application letter must ask himself: What have I got that an employer can use profitably? The answer would include the following points:

(1) Personal qualities like intelligence, imagination, ideas, industry, accuracy, speed and enthusiasm.
(2) Personal factors like honesty, loyalty, judgment, initiative and alertness.
(3) Special abilities and interests like supervision, planning, selling, research, accounts, sales promotion, etc.
(4) The knowledge of the prospective employer's traded products or nature of job, state of competitive jobs, business, languages, laws relating to the business, etc.
(5) Other factors such as education, expedience testes and aptitudes, ambitions, etc.

The Personal Record Sheet

A recent tread in writing application letter is to write it in two parts:

(i) the Application Letter itself, containing an appeal to the prospective employer and summary of personal details containing the best of the applicant's qualifications and experience:

(ii) the personal Record Sheet that gives a detailed information about the education, experience, etc. of the applicant.

This form is generally preferred by those who have something worth telling about their qualifications and experience; but those having just a normal or not-so-good a record of education and experience prefer to write everything in the main application itself.

APPLICATION BLANKS

Many of the government or semi-government departments or undertakings have their own prescribed application form which contains varied questions to be answered by the applicant. The completed application form itself becomes an application—a standardized letter.

Sometimes, the advertiser gives the 'form' of the application in the advertisement itself. The applicants will then have to prepare their application letters strictly assorting to that form only.

ON-LINE APPLICATIONS AND INTERVIEWS

The convergence of computer, technology and communication technology has made it possible to transact business with banks (e-Banking), contracting of goods and services through the Internet/Websites (Business to Business), Selling Goods and services through Information Technology (Business to Customer and *vice-versa*). Even global tenders are formalized and the entire process handled through the Internet.

Teleconferencing is the latest trend. Directors may be at different places/cities, they can discuss matters/agenda on video and can even pass resolutions through the conferencing (Video Conferencing), and so on.

Applicants can download applications from the concerned Website, fill up and send electronically. Money can be directly remitted to the beneficiary's banking account and the latter can instantly verify receipt. Interviews for higher jobs can be held through Video Conferencing.

Universities have started examining candidates on-line though the system is still confined to a few IT courses or computer courses.

CHAPTER

12

Office Correspondence

APPOINTMENTS

Appointments are generally made after the candidates have been interviewed by the prospective employers. In certain cases, the interview is preceded by a written test.

The interview may be either specific or general. In private firms where a single vacancy is to be filled in and in the case of an unsolicited application from a candidate, there is usually a specific interview.

But in the case of public institution and in case where applications are received from a large number of candidates (generally in response to a newspaper advertisement), a general interview is conducted for the selection of suitable candidates.

The letter asking the candidates to attend the interview gives the time, date and venue (place) and the name of the authority before whom the candidate has to appear. It also generally intimates the candidate to produce his certificates and testimonials in original at the time of the interview.

Example : **A letter asking the applicant to appear for an**

interview for the post of a steno-typist. A specimen is given for the purpose of guidance.

SHIMLA PLYWOODS (P) LTD.
26/3, The Mall, Shimla - 171 001

Ref. No. ..... 10th April, 2010

Miss Uma Shankar
8-b, Railway Colony
Shimla.

Dear Madam,

Thank you for your application dated 12th November for the post of a Seno-Typist in our Company. I appreciate your interest in joining our Company.

Will you please come over to our office for an interview with me at 2.30 PM on 1st May 2010 with your original testimonials and certificates?

Yours faithfully,
For Shimla Plywoods (P) Ltd.

V.K. Sharma
Managing Director

Example **: A letter asking the candidate to appear for an interview for the post of an Assistant Accountant.**

VIJAYA AUTOMOBILES LTD.
Adm. Office, Utility Building, Annexe,
Chandni Chowk, New Delhi

Ref. No. ..... 11th April 2010

Mr. Rahul Sharma
48-C, Main Cross,
Rohini, Sector 18, Delhi.

Dear Mr. Sharma,

I am pleased to go through your Bio-data that you sent to me on 5th April. It appears that your qualifications and experience are adequate enough for the Assistant Accountant's post in our Company.

We would like to have further discussion with you in the matter. We have, therefore, arranged your interview with our Chief Accountant, Mr. P.R. Joshi. Will you please see him in his office at 10.30 AM on April 25? You will please see me in my office after your meeting with Mr. P.R. Joshi.

You are requested to check in at 10.00 AM on 25th April and produce your testimonials and certificates in original to Mr. R.C. Verma, my assistant, who will at the same time pay your to and fro second class journey fare.

Yours cordially,
For Vijay Automobiles Ltd.

R. Vijay Kumar
Personnel Manager

LETTERS OF APPOINTMENT

These days, a letter of appointment is drafted in a very formal and official style. It is generally brief and simply tells the salary that the employee will get and the time when he has to report to duty. It can in fact be made more pleasing, informative, polite and interesting. The following important points may be covered in a letter of appointment:

(1) Convey the appointment with words of congratulations.
(2) If it is an important vacancy being filled in, tell the appointee what work is expected of him.
(3) Give the date and time of reporting to duty and the name of the person to report to.
(4) Mention whether the appointment is probationary/ permanent or temporary and the period of probation or the expiry date of the temporary vacancy.

(5) Mention the salary, allowances, perquisites and other benefits the appointee is entitled to.
(6) Request the appointee to convey his acceptance.
(7) Express the hope that the appointee shall have a pleasant association with the firm.

BUSINESS MEMORANDA

The literal meaning of the word 'memorandum' is a note to assist the memory. 'Memo' is the short form of 'memorandum'. Both 'memorandums and 'memoranda' are its plural forms.

A memorandum is mainly used for internal communication between executives and subordinates and also between officers of the same level.

The form of a Memo

The Memo differs from letters that are sent out by the firm. Since a memo moves from one department to another or from one employee to another, it is essential to write the name of the person sending the memo and the name of the recipient and the designation or department of both the persons. It must also have reference numbers.

The words 'From' and 'To' are invariably used in a memo. There is no salutation, and the writer's signature is put without writing the superscription or complimentary close.

The memo is properly dated, is written in a direct style, and is as brief as possible.

Specimen form of a Memo

J.L. MORRISSION & SONS LTD.
INTER-OFFICE MEMO

No .... Date: 10th April 2008
From . . . .

To . . . . . .
Sub: . . . .

(1) ____

____

(2) ____

____

(3) ____

Signature

CC: To

1 _______

2 _______

3 _______

Example : **A memo to inform the extension of probationary period of an employee.**

JANATA BANK LTD.
Head Office
Khairatabad (Hyderabad)

MEMO

Ref. No. . . .. 12th April 2010

Ref: BNS: 4382 : S-B

From:

Deputy Gen. Manager,

Proceedings at the office of General Manager

dated: 12-4-2008

Whereas Shri L.R. Sharma (18588), Probationary Clerk, Janata Bank Ltd., Raipur Branch joined the bank on 23-11-2009 and he is to be confirmed in the services of the bank with effect from 23rtd May 2010.

And whereas, his work, progress, etc. were not found satisfactory, it is therefore considered necessary to extend his probationary period by two months so as to provide him an opportunity to overcome the drawbacks pointed out earlier.

Now, therefore, Probationary period of Shri L.R. Sharma (18588), is hereby extended by two months, i.e. till 22nd July 2010.

P.R. Joshi.

To

Shri L.R. Sharma (18588),
Prob. Clerk, Janata Bank Ltd.
Raipur.

Copy to:

The Branch Manager,
Janata Bank Ltd., Raipur

***Example* : A memo intimating the transfer of the employee.**

JANATA BANK LTD.
Head Office, New Delhi

MEMO

20th September, 2010

Ref: BNS: O.T.: 8-27

To

Shri M.M. Menon
Manager, Panipat Branch

From

R.K. Jaryal, Superintendent, Staff Section

Sub : Overtime Allowance Claim

From the Salary bills of your branch for the month of August, it is observed that there has been a claim made for Overtime Allowance on every alternate day for 3 to 4 clerks. This is even when none of the branch staff has availed himself of leave during the entire month of August. This may be viewed as either a wilful action of the staff to 'Go Slow' or lack of supervision. In the circumstances, please explain why the claim for O.T. Allowance should not be disallowed.

Please submit your explanation before the end of September 2010 to facilitate closing the salary Bill file of August 2010.

General Manager
(P.K. Kamath)

Example : **A memo as a circular**

JANATA BANK LIMITED
H.O. Mumbai

MEMO

Ref No. .... 12th August, 2010

To:

All Branch Managers,

Ref: Mr. J.P. Vohra, Internal Auditor.

The bank has relieved Mr. J.P. Vohra of his services as the Internal Auditor from 2nd August, 2010. All Branch Managers are, therefore, to note that no books of accounts shall be made available to Mr. Vohra or his office staff for any audit work.

J.L. Sharma
Dy. General Manager
CC
1.
2.
3.
4.

Example : **Specimen of an official letter**

Office of the Additional Secretary,
Government of India,
Ministry of Food,
Central Secretariat, New Delhi - 110 001

No. . . . Dated July 10, 2010
Shaka Era ....

The Secretary, Government of Maharashtra,
Department of Agriculture,
Civil Secretariat,
Mumbai-400 001

Subject: Sugarcane crushed during 2009-2010 crushing season—Starred Question in the Lok Sabha on July 6, 2010

Dear Sir,

Please refer to the above subject and supply data/ information in the enclosed Proforma to enable this office to reply to the Lok Sabha starred Question by the 20th July, 2010. Please treat the matter as urgent.

Yours faithfully,

(K.C. Deshpande, IAS)
Additional Secretary

Encl.—1 proforma

DEMI-OFFICIAL (DO) LETTER

A Demi-Official letter is written when there is inordinate delay in receipt of information or the subject is so important that it requires personal attention at higher level.

Example : **A specimen of Demi-Official (DO) letter is given below:**

Office of Additional Secretary,
Government of India,
Ministry of Food,
Central Secretariat, New Delhi-110 001

DO No. . . Dated July 21, 2010
Shaka Era...

Dear Mr. Kulkarni,

Subject: Reply to Starred Question in Parliament about Quantity of sugarcane crushed during 2009-10 crushing season in Maharashtra

Please refer to this office letter No. . . dated the 10th July, 2010, to which no reply has come so far from your office. Please collect and collate the data in the manner indicated in the letter referred to herein. For convenience, a copy of the letter along with copy of the Proforma is enclosed. Please treat the matter as most urgent.

With regards,

Yours sincerely,

K.C. Deshpande, IAS

To

Mr. N.R. Kulkarni, IAS
Secretary Agriculture to Government, Maharashtra,
Civil Secretariat, Mumbai.

NOTIFICATION

Office of the Controller of Supplies,
Government of Tamil Nadu,
Civil Secretariat,
Chennai - 500 001

No. . . . . ….. Dated August 14, 2010
Saka . . . .

Subject : Supply of ration to BPL families at subsidized rates at enhanced scale (25% increase)

His Excellency, the Governor of Tamil Nadu, is pleased to grant enhancement of ration of eligible components to the BPL families by 25% with effect from August 15, 2010. Supply may be made accordingly.

By order
Chief Secretary to Government, Tamil Nadu

CC
All Deputy Commissioners
Secretary, Home
Secretary, Civil Supplies

. . . . ….
. . . . ….

All business houses, especially the corporate bodies are required to pass resolutions in the Board to authorize important work by delegation. A specimen of Resolution is given below:

RESOLUTION

All artificial bodies, created under the provisions of law, create record for reference and evidence. It is lawful for the legal entities to pass resolutions authorizing any action, activity or business, etc.

A specimen of a resolution is given below:

"Resolved that Mr. G.S David, Director (Finance) and Mr. M.V.K. Gopalakrishnan, Director (Production) be and are hereby authorized to contract term loan for purchase of machinery from Japan, already recommended by a special committee constituted for the purpose, and to sign all security documents connected therewith at State Bank of India, and to give security as discussed with the bank".

"Resolved further that Shri K. Kannan, Company Secretary, will authenticate the loan documents and other papers in this connection as suggested by the bank by affixing company seal under his signature".

Sd.-
S.V. Bhobe, Chairman

Sd.-
K. Kannan,
Company Secretary

Important developments are notified through the press a specimen of press note is given below:

K.C. ELECTRONICS LIMITED
534, Lane 14/7, Borivli, Mumbai

Press Note

No. Dated August 31, 2010

Mr. Govindan, till now Chief Executive Officer with Frenkystein of Germany, is joining K.C. Electronics, a Joint Venture with Rollance Group, as Managing Director. The company plans to open subsidiaries in Europe, Africa and South America for diversified products using State-of-the-Art technology. Mr. Govindan will look after the expansion plans of the company in electronics and communications. He has excellent knowledge of the markets and is highly qualified and much experienced person.

Public Relations Officer
(M.K. Pradhan)

Covering Letter to the Print Media, a specimen is given below:

Ref No. . . . . . . Dated August 31, 2010

The Editor,
The Statesman,
. . . .

Dear Sir,

Subject : News Item

We enclose a Press Note No. dated August 31, 2010 regarding appointment of Managing Director in this company. The contents are explicit on the subject. Please publish the news item in the fifth column of your reputed daily.

With best wishes,

Yours faithfully,
G.K.S. Rao
Manager (Public Relations)

Encl. : 1

An example of Press Release is given below. The subject-matter is self-explicit:

Press Released

No. . . . . . . Dated . . . . .

Karnatak Chmicals Limited

Public Issue of 2,00,000 Equity shares of Rs. 10 each for cash at premium of Rs. 60 per share aggregating Rs. 1,40,00,000, Karnataka Chemicals Limited, a public sector undertaking (PSU) promoted by the Government of India and National Iranian Fertilizer Company, Iran is entering the capital market with a public issue of 2,00,000 equity shares of Rs. 10 each for cash at a premium of Rs. 60 per share, aggregating Rs. 1,40,00,000 in the second week of August, 2010.

The company has been producing and marketing complex fertilizers and urea under the established brand name, "Vinayaa" for the last 25 years. It is the first PSU to have obtained ISO 9002 accreditation for its commitment to total quality management.

The company has undertaken substantial expansion and modernization of the existing plant at an estimated outlay of Rs. 5 crore with technical know-how from the world-renowned process consultants Haldor. The fully modernised plant is scheduled to become functional by the 31st July, 2010

Secretary

OTHER OFFICE CORRESPONDENCE

Now, we shall deal with the following two types of correspondence:

(a) Correspondence with the Government, and
(b) Office Drafting.

CORRESPONDENCE WITH THE GOVERNMENT

On frequent occasions, a businessman is required to communicate with different departments of the Government—Central, State and also Local Government. Basically, the correspondence is a business communication and has, therefore, to be written on the main principles of a business letter. However, the following points may be considered as especially important in drafting such letters:

(1) The letter must be addressed to the officer concerned with the subject matter dealt with in the letter. The officer should never be addressed by his name, howsoever close or familiar the correspondent may be with the officer.
(2) The best forms of salutation and complimentary close are : "Sir" and "Yours faithfully".
(3) The letter should invariably contain the 'Sub' or 'Re' and the 'Ref', parts for the convenience of the recipient.
(4) The subject matter must be dealt with clearly and completely but always precisely. Unnecessary explanations should always be avoided.
(5) Wherever the letter deals with law and office procedure, the correspondent must strictly adhere to the procedure and law.

It is difficult to deal with office correspondence comprehensively and exhaustively in this book. A few model letters are given below to help grasp the fundamentals of such letters.

Example : **A Letter applying for Import Quota to Ministry of Commerce, Government of India through State Bank of India**

THE VARUNA EXPORT TRADING COMPANY
57, Commercial Street
Ghaziabad

Ref. No. 12th April, 2010

The Controller of Imports,
Govt. of India, Ministry of Commerce,
New Delhi - 110 001.

Dear Sir,

Re: Request for issuing Licence for Imports.

Recently, our firm has successfully concluded negotiations with a few West German buyers for machinery manufactured by us. According to their specifications, we require certain components and accessories that are available from American suppliers. The details of the articles are given in the enclosed prescribed form of application.

We, therefore, request you to issue us an Import Licence as applicable to Actual Users for the current year and also grant foreign exchange worth USD 68,000.

We have also enclosed a statement showing the details of the quantity and the value of various articles imported by us during the past 12 months preceding 1st April 2010.

Yours faithfully,
For The Export Trading Co.

S.N. Rao
General Manager

Encl: Two statements

Example : **A letter requesting for adjustment of excess tax deducted in the earlier assessment year.**

PRAKASH AND COMPANY
26, Grand Building,
G.T. Road, Panipat,

12th April, 2010

The Income Tax Officer,
Third Circle,
New Delhi.

Re: Return of Income for A.Y. 2010-11

Sir,

I have submitted today in your office the return of my income for the financial year ending 31st March, 2010. The following documents are enclosed:

(i) Trading and Profit & Loss Account
(ii) Balance Sheet
(iii) T.D.S. Certificates for Dividends,
(iv) Advance Tax Challans,
(v) Donation Receipts, and
(vi) Letter from DCM Co. Ltd., Delhi.

On my total income, the tax liability amounts to Rs. 2,510. The total of TDS in respect of dividends and advance tax paid amounts to Rs. 2300. For the balance of Rs. 210, I have to request you to kindly adjust the amount against the Refund of TDS on dividends from the DCM Co. Ltd. Delhi for the years 20 ….., 20 ….., 20 ….. and 20 ….. which were not taken into account and claimed in the previous years. In this connection, I am enclosing the copy of a letter from the Secretary. CBDT and the ITO Company Circle III, New Delhi. The refund of TDS in my case, according to these letters, will be Rs. 210 which may please be adjusted against my net tax liability.

Yours faithfully,

P.N. Desai

OFFICE DRAFTING

Office drafting or official correspondence refers to correspondence between different offices, departments and branches of the government. It includes inter-government, state to state and center to state (or *vice-versa*), correspondence also.

Office Notes and Office Orders

Almost all office communications are 'drafted' by subordinates in the office. 'Drafting' here refers to the 'preparation' of the communication for submission to the concerned higher officer for his perusal and 'approval' with or without alternations. The draft, after approval, is re-written in the proper form of communication and is signed by the officer concerned.

Such drafting is based on 'office notes' and 'office orders' that are given by the Heads of departments or other administrative heads.

When the note is to be put up, it is the duty of the assistant or any other person preparing the note—

(1) To see whether all facts, as far as they are open to check, are correct.
(2) To point out any mistakes or mis-statement of facts (in the letter or paper under consideration). To draw attention, where necessary, the statutory or customary procedure and to point out the law and rules with suitable references.
(3) To supply other relevant facts and figures available in the Ministry and to put up precedents or papers containing previous decisions of policy.
(4) To state the question or questions for consideration and to bring out clearly the points requiring decision.
(5) To suggest a course of action, wherever possible (and necessary).

Official Routine

When a letter is received in a government office, it has to pass through different departments and stages before being finally disposed of. This is called official routine. A brief explanation of the official routine is given below.

Opening of the Dak (Post)

All official letters are addressed to the officer by his designation or by name followed by the position held by him. On receipt of such letters, they are opened by the Daftary in the presence of the Head Clerk or Office Superintendent or Registrar's Department. Upon the priority of attention required for their disposal, letters are labeled as Urgent, Immediate, Top Priority, Confidential, etc.

Registration

An Inward Mail Register is maintained for registering the receipt of every letter. All inward letters are serially numbered and dated with the inward date stamp.

The register contains information regarding the name of the sender, the officer to whom the letter is addressed and a brief note of its contents.

Docketing: Letters are then sent to the dealing clerks who write thereon a brief description or summary of the contents of the letter for easy future reference. These clerks are generally called diarists.

Classification and Distribution

The diarist then gives the entire Dak (called post or mail also) to his section officer who deals with it as under:

(a) He goes through all letters and classifies the letters as (i) "Primary" (P)—those letters which provide a starting point for new action, (ii) "Subsidiary" (S)—letters which are the outcome of the work already commenced on earlier 'P' letters and which therefore do not require any new action, and (iii) 'PX'—those Primary letters which require a long time for their disposal.

(b) He arranges for the distribution of the letters among the dealing (concerned) clerks or assistants by putting their initial, generally at the left hand top margin.

(c) He marks those letters that are to be sent to higher officers for their perusal.

(d) He gives all the dak/post back to the diarist.

Diarising

The Diarist then enters all the letters in the Diary. This work is known as diarising. All the entries that are made on the paper from the Inward Register are re-entered in the diary so that each Section will have a copy of the inward letters received by it every day. The diary contains columns for recording the movement of the letter every day until it is finally disposed of.

This enables the office to locate any letter at any time easily and quickly. Letters or files that come from other Departments or Branches, etc. are diarised separately.

After diarising the letters, the Diarist distributes the letters among the dealing clerks and also sends some letters to the higher officers in special pads under the label 'Dak or Post for Perusal'.

Referencing

It is the work of giving a reference number to each letter for the purpose of proper filling along with similar letters received and filed previously. Referencing facilitates back reference of letters.

Noting and Précis

The dealing hands then prepare précis of the letter/s, wherever necessary and then make notes on the letters before sending them to the higher officer.

Drafting

The letters must be drafted on the basis of the notes approved by the officer and also in accordance with the orders passed and instructions given by the officer, and submitted for final approval. The draft must be a faithful representation of the orders passed.

Typing

The finally approved draft is sent to the typist who gets a minimum of two copies of each letter, one for dispatch to the addressee and the other for office file. If copies are to be sent to other departments, etc. the number of copies to be typed is varied accordingly.

Dispatching

Dispatching is the duty of the outward clerk. He has to put a reference number of each of the outgoing letters and enters it in the Outward Register. The dispatch clerk should ensure that the letter is signed and the cover contains all the enclosures referred to in the letter. He has also to write the outside address on the cover clearly and completely.

CHAPTER

13

Types of Official Correspondence

Official letters are written in different forms. The exact form depends upon the purpose and the person to be addressed and the message to be communicated. There are the following types of official correspondence:

(1) Official Letter
(2) Demi-Official Letter
(3) Express Letter
(4) Official Memorandum
(5) Memorandum
(6) Unofficial Memorandum or Note
(7) Endorsement
(8) Notification
(9) Circular
(10) Resolution

(11) Press Communiqué/Note
(12) Telegram or E-mail

THE MEMO FORMAT

The memo format is different from that of a letter. Since a memo moves from one department to another or from one employee to another, it is essential to write the name of the person sending the memo and the name of the recipient and the designation or department of both the persons. It most also have reference numbers.

Example : **A memo to an employee granting permission to join a part time diploma course in marketing.**

VEEKAY EXPORT (P) LTD.

MEMO

No: VKA/83/1999.
Date: July 5, 2009

From: V.B. Agarwal, Marketing Manager

To : Sushant Bashin, Marketing Dept.

Subject : Your application dated 3 July, 2009 seeking permission to join a diploma course in marketing.

The office has no objection to your joining the YMCA to do a part time diploma course in marketing in the evenings. But this must not interfere with your normal office routine. Please note that you will not be allowed to leave the office early to reach the institute in time nor will you be entitled to any special leave to prepare for your examination.

Example : **A memo to an employee informing him of a cut in his salary.**

JANATA BANK LTD.
Raipur

MEMO

Ref: 8.400STF01863 : 2009
Date: 29th August, 1999

To : Mr. N.R. Deshmukh, Clerk

From: R.K. Rama Rao, Manager

You remained away from your duties on the date/s and for the period/s mentioned below. Please note that you have not earned salary and emoluments for the said period.

Date	Period
August 28, 2009	10:30 am to 5.30 pm

This is without prejudice to our right to take disciplinary action against you.

R.K. Rama Rao
Manager
Accounts Department

Copies to:
(1) Staff Section, North Zone,
(2) Salary Section

Example **: A memo declining the grant of deputation to an employee still on probation.**

NEW ERA ELECTRONICS (P) LTD.
Delhi

Office Memorandum

No. Pers/79/03
Date September 8, 2009

To : Ajay Jain, Production Dept.

From: M.V. Tyer, Personnel Manager

Subject : Your application regarding joining JVG on Deputation.
Refer to your letter dated 7th September 2009

Joining JVG on deputation would have given you valuable exposure and experience, and I really wish I could write 'Yes' and sign.

But you are still on probation with us and there is a clearly laid down policy of sending on deputation only permanent employees.

Don't get disheartened, for many more opportunities are sure to come your way.

K.N. Kachroo
Sr. Executive (Research)

Example : **An office memorandum warning an employee against his habit of reading the newspapers and magazines during office hours.**

C.V. KAMATH & SONS (P) LTD.
Pune

Office Memorandum

No. 863/2009
Date: 6th June, 2009

To: J.M. Samtani,
Administration

From: K. Rangachari, D.G.M.

Subject : Reading newspaper and magazines in office hours.

I appreciate your interest in the rapidly changing political scene in the country. But would you please confine your reading of newspapers and magazines to before, or after, office hours sitting in the comfort of your drawing room?

You will agree that maintaining office decorum is of utmost importance for the welfare of the organization.

DGM

Example : **A memorandum warning an employee for his being habitually late.**

MDH LIMITED, NAGPUR
Public Relations

No. DGM 89

To : Amit Basu   Date: April 26, 2010
From: S.K. Seth, DGM

Subject : Late coming to the office

Punctuality and courtesy brighten the image of an organization and earn valuable goodwill. Non-punctuality is a reflection both on the individual and the organization.

Your attendance record shows that during the week ending 26 April, you were late for the office by more than half an hour on three different occasions. This is a serious matter.

Yours is an important seat. This casual attitude of yours often throws all public dealing out of gear and even causes embarrassing situations.

I am also pained to point out that many oral warnings to you have gone utterly unheeded. May I hope that you will be punctual in future and will not force me to take any strict disciplinary action against you?

Signed
(S.K. Seth)

Example : **A memorandum from the Managing Director to the Production Manager about a complaint by a customer for not attending to an urgent communication.**

JETKING MOTORS & PUMPSETS, DELHI

MEMO

No. RNS/83/2010
Date: 7 June, 2010

To: Preetmohan Singh
Production Manager

From: R.N. Sawhneuy, M.D.

Subject: Mr. Madhavan Nair's complaint

Mr. Madhavan Nair, Model Town, Delhi, has just rung me up to say that his letter to you regarding some manufacturing defect in the pumpset he bought from us on 15 May has elicited no response from you. He wrote the letter on 17 May.

Perhaps, the grueling summer months have brought in the usual pressure on you. Still, taking after sales responsibility for a machine is no less important than selling it.

Kindly attend to Mr. Nair's complaint without any further delay. He is also available on 7252503.

Note: In the next few examples, only the message is being given, the top notations are being excluded.

***Example* : An Office memorandum warning an employee for submitting fake medical bills.**

The Accounts Department has drawn my attention to a medical bill submitted by you on 5 November, 2010. You have claimed Rs. 758 as reimbursement for getting yourself treated for viral hepatitis during the third week of October. Your application for three days' leave submitted on October 17 stated that you were suffering from flue.

Obviously, the medical bill submitted by you is not genuine.

I know for certain that the medical bill referred to above does not present an isolated case. Discrepancies noticed in several earlier bills have cast persistent doubts over their genuineness.

Claiming reimbursement against fake medical bills is a serious matter calling for stern action. You are hereby warned that you will not indulge in this unethical practice in future, failing which strict disciplinary action will be initiated against you.

Signed
(MD)

Example : **A memo to an employee asking for explanation for going on leave without prior permission.**

Ref. No. . . . . Dated . . . . . .

MEMO

Sub : Your absence from 16-8-2009 to 20-8-2009
Ref : Your telegram and letters dated 16-8-2010 and 22-8-2010

(1) We note that you sent a telegram from Hubli on 16th August requesting the medical leave from 16-8-2010 to 20-8-2010 and later submitted an application for leave from 16-8-2010 to 20-8-2010 producing a medical certificate from a doctor practicing at Hubli. Please let us know whether you had obtained prior permission to leave station.

(2) In your application, you have stated that you were suffering from cold and fever. But your medical certificate says you had amoebic hepatitis. Will you please explain the discrepancy?

(3) If your reply does not reach us on or before September 13, 2010, your absence will be treated as one without leave and will incur loss of pay.

Example : **A show cause notice to an employee for his gross misbehaviour with his superior.**

It has been reported to me:

No. . . . . Dated . . . . . .

MEMO

(1) That on September 6, 2009, you pressurized the Stores Superintendent, Mr. Imtiaz Ahmad, to sign

certain fake bills regarding purchase of stationery and on his refusal, you physically assaulted him causing bruises and minor cuts on his face and neck.

(2) That you abused and even tried to assault physically your colleague, Mr. Surjit Singh, when he tried to intervene.

(3) That on that day, you had come to the office in a drunken state.

(4) That you often come to the office late and drunk.

(5) That you threatened Mr. Ahmad of dire consequences if he dared lodge a complaint against you to the higher authorities.

Getting fake bills signed and physically assaulting your immediate superior are both actions of gross misconduct. Please explain in writing why disciplinary action under the service rules should not be taken against you.

Your reply should reach me latest by 10 September 2010. In case, no written explanation is received by then, it will be assumed that you have no explanation to offer and disciplinary action will be initiated against you.

Signed
(M.D.)

OFFICE ORDERS

The word 'order' suggests acceptance or compliance. If a message is conveyed as an order, it means that it carries a stamp of authority with it and has to be accepted. Office order is a tool of downward communication; it travels from the higher ups down to the subordinates.

Orders are usually related to posting, promotion, suspension, termination of services, granting/withholding increments, granting/withholding certain privileges, imposing certain restrictions, intimation of disciplinary proceedings, etc.

An office order is a very sensitive form of communication and if it is misunderstood or misinterpreted, it can lead to serious unintended consequences. The following points should be kept in mind while drafting orders:

- Orders must be very concise. They must not contain any unnecessary details.
- The language employed should be absolutely clear. The order should be written in very simple words that can be easily understood by all. Idioms, phrases and slang should be strictly avoided.
- Orders should clearly specify whom they are meant for. Some orders are sent to the concerned individuals with copies to the concerned departments, others may be meant for display on the notice boards.

Example : **An office order posting a new recruit to a department.**

GUEST, KEEN, WILLIAMS
Sansad Marg, New Delhi

Ref: Per/597/22 Date: 4-5-3009

Office Order

Shri Anil Sachdeva has been posted as Sales Executive w.e.f. 5-5-2010. He will be reporting to Shri C.M. Handa, Sales Officer.

Copies to:

(1) Shri Anil Sachedva
(2) Shri C.M. Handa
(3) Accounts Office

Sd/- S.K. Jain
Deputy Manager (Personnel)

Example : **An office order regarding the transfer of an employee from head office to take over the independent charge of a unit.**

NEW TRENDS CASUAL WEARS

12, Lamington Road,
Bangalore.

Ref: SPS/24/973 Date: 5-3-3009

Office Order

Shri Rahul Chaturvedi, Assistant Administrative Officer, is transferred from the Head Office to take independent charge of the production unit at M.G. Industrial Area. He will hand over charge of his duties at the Head Office to the undersigned and take charge of the M.G. Industrial Area unit from Shri Gopal Subramaniam latest by 12-3-2010.

GM (Adm.)

Copies to:

(1) Shri Rahul Chaturvedi
Sd/ V.K. Menon
(2) Shri Gopal
Subramaniam
Deputy General Manager
(3) Accounts Office

Note : In most of the cases of employees, only drafts for the office orders are being given. Students can fill in the other details themselves.

***Example* : An office order regarding the promotion of an employee.**

Ref: Pers/598/03 Date 1-7-2010

Office Order

Ms. Geetika Rastogi, Accounts Assistant, is promoted as Senior Accountant with immediate effect. She will draw the basic pay of Rs. 3200 in the pay scale Rs. 3000-100-3500-125-4500. Other allowances will continue to be admissible as per the Company's Rules.

Manager (Personnel)

To : Ms Geetika Rastogi
Sd. Kanwar Jain Accounts Department
Manager (Personnel)

Example : **An office order granting special increment to an employee.**

No. . . . .
Date: 28-7-2009

Office Order

In appreciation of the excellent performance of Ms. Smitha Ramachandran in the sales promotion campaign during the summer months of June-July 2010, the Management is pleased to grant her a special increment of Rs. 100 effective from 1-8-2010.

Sd. DGM (ADMIN)

Example : **An office order suspending an employee.**

No. . . . . Date 27 September, 2009

Office Order

Shri Jai Pal, Office Assistant, is suspended from the services of the company with immediate effect. He will, however, be allowed to draw subsistence allowance as per the rules of the company.

From today onwards, Shri Jai Pal is not allowed to enter the office premises except for the purpose of attending the disciplinary proceedings before the Enquiry Committee.

GM (Admn.)

To: Shri Jai Pal
Copies to:

(1) Accounts Office
S.P. Chauhan
(2) Notice Boards, All departments
Personnel Manager

***Example* : An office order reinstating a suspended employee.**

Ref: GDB/1198/18 Date: 13 October, 2010

Office Order

The Enquiry Committee constituted under the chairmanship of Shri G.D. Baweja has absolved Shri Som Dutt, Accountant, of charges of financial irregularities. Hence order number GDB.898/5 dated 28th August, 2010 suspending him from service is revoked and he is reinstated in his position as Accountant with immediate effect.

S.P. Chaudhary
Senior Manager (Personnel)

CC
Accounts
Personal File

Office Order

No. . . . . . . Dated . . . .

Pursuant to the report of the enquiry conducted by the Enquiry officer Shri H.R. Khanna, the services of Shri Ajit Miglani, Accounts Clerk, are terminated with immediate effect. The accounts Department is hereby directed to settle the accounts of Shri Ajit Miglani immediately.

To : Shri Ajit Miglani Vivek Navlkar
Senior Manager (Personnel)

Copies to:

(1) Accountants Department
(2) Notice Board, all departments

***Example* : An office order instituting an enquiry against an employee.**

No. . . . . .   Date: 23 February, 2010

Office Order

An Enquiry Committee is appointed to look into charges of misappropriation of cash amounting to Rs. 35000 by Shri Satya Dev, Accountant. The Committee consists of:

(1) Shri S.A. Kidwai, Deputy Manager, Administration, Chairman.
(2) Shri Sudhir Shinde, Deputy Manager, Personnel, Member
(3) Shri H.S. Ahluwalia, Deputy Manager, Accounts, Member.

The Committee is authorized to call any employees of the company as witnesses as it feels necessary for proper conduct of the enquiry.

The committee is hereby directed to complete the enquiry and submit its report to the undersigned latest by April 23, 2010.

K.S. Bajpai, Director (Administration)
Disciplinary Authority

Copies to:
(1) Shri S.A. Kidwai
(2) Shri Sudhir Shinde
Senior Manager
(3) Shri H.S. Ahluwalia
(Administration)
(4) Shri Satya Dev
(5) Personnel Manager

Example : **An office order asking the employees to use the canteen only during the fixed hours.**

Similar orders may be drafted for practice.

No. . . . . . .   Date July 1, 2010

Office Order

All employees are hereby directed to visits the office canteen only during the lunch hours 12:30—1:30 p.m. During the rest of the office hours, if the employees need tea, cold drinks and snacks, they can order the canteen to get them at their seats.

DGM (Admin.)

Copies to:

Notice Board, all departments
Sarvesh Bhosle
Administration Officer

Example : **An office order banning smoking in the office premises.**

No. . . . . Date 16-6-2010

Office Order

All employees of the company are hereby informed that smoking is strictly prohibited in the office premises. A small booth near the stairs can be used occasionally if the urge to smoke is uncontrollable. But the employees should not use it too frequently.

This order comes into force with immediate effect and employees violating it can be subjected to disciplinary action against them.

Administrative Officer (Personnel)

Copies:

Notice Board, All Departments.

Example : **An office order cancelling the weekly holiday of the accounts section in view of income tax deadline.**

No. . . . . Date: 8-9-2010

Office Order

In view of the urgency of completing the accounts of the company and filing the income tax return by the 30th September, the weekly holiday on Sunday is cancelled for all employees of the Accounts Section till the 7th October, 2010. The employees will be duly compensated for working on the holidays as per the company rules.

C.K. Bhardwaj
Personnel Manager

CC
Accounts
Notice Boards

OFFICE CIRCULARS

Office circulars are meant to convey the same information to a large number of people. Such information is usually of general nature and not confidential. Circulars can be used for the following purposes:

- To emphasis certain aspects of office conduct.
- To intimate changes in the working hours of the office, canteen, library, etc.
- To invite applications from employees for promotion tests, etc.
- To inform the employees about changes in medical rules, LFC rules, reimbursement of conveyance expenses, etc.

The subject of the circular must be mentioned at the top.

Circulars are usually put on the notice board. If they contain some information of substantial importance, they can be circulated among the staff and the signatures of the staff members obtained on an employees' list.

Example : **An office circular inviting entries for the news bulletin of the Company.**

Shri Ram Enterprises
New Delhi - 110 050

Date: 2-10-2010

Circular No. 21/20

Subject : Entries for the News Bulletin 'Jyoti'.

- The next issue of the office News Bulletin, 'Jyoti', is proposed to be brought out in the first week of January 2011. Articles, poems, cartoons, stories, news regarding individual achievements/milestones are invited from the employees and the members of their families.
- All entries can be either in English or in Hindi.
- Entries should be preferably typed, on one side of the paper, with at least 1.5 inch margin on both sides.
- Entries should reach the undersigned by the 15th November, 2010.
- Contributors are advised to keep a copy of their contribution with themselves.

C.K. Naidu
(Public Relations Officer)
Editor

***Example* : A circular drawing the attention of the employees to some undesirable aspects of their conduct.**

Circular No. 58/2009

Dated: 6th May, 2010

Sub : Proper conduct of the employees in the office premises.

The management is constrained to draw attention to the

following undesirable aspects of conduct of employees during the working hours:

(1) Some members of staff show scant respect for punctuality. They have a tendency to report for work late and leave early.

(2) The attendance register is not signed at the appropriate time. Some members sign it in advance so that they can report late without getting detected.

(3) Members are often absent from their seats without any convincing reason. This causes great inconvenience to the customers.

(4) Members tend to use office stationery for personal purposes. They not only carry it home but even gift it to the visitors.

(5) The office telephone is kept busy with personal calls. As a result, while some customers fail to get important calls through to the Bank, valuable man-hours are wasted in trivial and inconsequential gossip. Besides, this also has a damaging influence on the general atmosphere in the bank.

The management seeks the cooperation of all members of the staff to improve the working climate in the Branch and to make it one of the most efficiently run branches in the country.

V.K. Agarwal
Branch Manager

Example : **A circular informing the staff that a certain employee has been relieved of his duties.**

Circular No. Pers/2009/15

Dated: 3rd August, 2009

Ref: Mr. J.P. Vohra, Internal Auditor

The bank has relieved Mr. J.P. Vohra of his services as the internal auditor from 2nd August, 2010. All Branch Managers are, therefore, to note that no books of accounts shall be made available to Mr. Vohra or his office staff for any audit work.

P.R. Narayanan
Deputy General Manager

Example : **An office circular drawing attention of class IV employees to attend office in the prescribed uniforms.**

Circular No. Pers/2009/23

Dated: March 23, 2010

Sub: Wearing of office uniform by class IV Employees.

It has been observed that class IV employees who are expected to attend the office in their uniforms have been coming rather casually dressed. This grossly violates the code of conduct prescribed by the company.

All class IV employees are hereby requested to come to the office wearing the uniform prescribed by the Company. It will make them look more respectable, brighten the image of the company and improve the general work environment in the office.

(N. Gopalaswamy)
Director (Personnel)
Kaveri Fertilizers Limited

CC
Notice Boards, Records, All Sections/Departments

Example : **An office circular emphasising the need of minimizing the use of the staff cars.**

Circular No. 58/2009

Dated: 21 November, 2010

Sub: Minimising the use of staff cars.

In view of the recent hike in the petrol and diesel prices, growing air and noise pollution in the city and unusually long traffic jams on the roads at all hours of the day, it has become advisable to minimize the use of staff cars.

The Management at its emergency meeting on 20th November has taken the following decisions in this regard:

(1) Officers of the rank of deputy managers and above can use staff cars to visit the plant or to go to any other place on official work.
(2) Employees below the rank of deputy managers should ordinarily use the battery service operating between the office and the plant at hourly intervals.
(3) If it is unavoidable for an employee to use a staff car, he/she can use it by getting the trip sanctioned by a competent authority of the rank of senior manager and above.
(4) These directions come into force with immediate effect.

It may be pointed out here that staff cars are meant to optimize work efficiency and they should be used by all means. But indiscreet use should certainly be curbed.

The Management solicits the cooperation of the entire staff on this issue.

(Sadhana Srivastava)
Administration Officer

Example : **An office circular informing employees about the decision of the Board to grant them leave travel concession from the current year.**

Circular No. 58/2009

Dated: 7th April, 2009

Sub: Leave Travel Concession.

The Management of the Company is pleased to announce that at the Special Board meeting held on the 5th April, 2010, it was decided to grant our employees leave travel concession facility from the current year.

The Company has decided to adopt the Central Government L.T.C. scheme without any deviation. All employees of the Company can now avail themselves of the L.T.C. facility to visit home-town once in a block of two years and to visit any place in India once in a block of four years. These facilities have to be availed of alternately, for example, if LTC is taken first, then the next facility will be to visit Home. Board of directors may permit employees in the pay scale not lower than Rs. 5500-7500 to travel by air on L.T.C.

The Central Government rules on L.T.C. in their full detail are displayed on the office notice board.

M.M. Lal
General Manager (Personnel)

***Example* : An office circular informing the employees about the change in office timings.**

Circular No. 58/2009

Dated: 27-8-2010

Sub: Change in Office Timings.

Ministry for Surface Transport, Government of India, has suggested vide its Notification No. _____ dated ________ that office timings of various companies should be staggered to ease traffic congestion on the Delhi roads.

Hence from 1st September, 2010 onwards, the office timings will be as follows:

8.30 am to 12.30 pm	Morning Session
12.30 pm to 1.30 pm	Lunch Break
1.30 pm to 5.00 pm	Evening Session

Employees are expected to strictly adhere to these office hours/timings.

B.K. Mittal
Personnel Officer

OFFICE NOTES

Office notes are used for horizontal communication. They are exchanged between departments, or between officers of almost equal rank asking for suggestions or seeking or giving information about some matter concerning their respective departments.

Office notes usually follow the memo format.

Example : **An office note to the head of another department asking some vital information.**

SERAPHIC FOODS
Orchards, Bangalore

No. . . . . . . Date: 15 June, 2010

To : T.N. Muthuswami
Manager, Quality Control

Ref: MNP : TR

From: M.N. Pai
Sales Manager

Orange squash, Batch No. 631/4-2009

(1) Serious complaints have been received about our orange squash bottles released for sale on April 19,

2010 under batch No. 631/4-2010. It has been pointed out that about a week after a bottle is opened, it starts giving out a very unpleasant smell. I would like to know if these bottles were duly inspected and approved before being released for sales.

(2) Please let me know, by 18th June, 2010 if the squash was prepared strictly according to the specified formula and if the raw materials used were subjected to quality test.

(M.B.P. Bagchi)
Sales Manager

Example : **An office note seeking suggestions from an official of equal rank on some important issue.**

KIRAN ELECTRICALS LIMITED
Bhopal

Date: 12 July, 2010

Ref: B.P.B. MK.

To Shri A.K. Khazanchi,
Finance Officer

From: M.B.P. Bagchi
Sales Manager

Sub : Funds for Export.

The newly established Export wing has successfully explored a good number of foreign markets in the Middle East for electronic items. The profit margin in the export sales appears to be very attractive. But we are faced with a serious problem, how to meet the export demand.

We have two options: (1) Increase our production, (2) Divert some supplies earmarked for the home market towards meeting export commitments.

The first alternative is decidedly the better one, for it yields higher profits to the company. But it involves raising production capacity and employment of additional hands both in the production and sales departments. There will be corresponding increase of work for the other departments also. These changes call for additional funds, a subject-matter of your department.

Kindly give your suggestions on how to raise funds, and their costs and returns, along with a fund-flow statement to enable the Board of Directors to take a final decision in the matter. A copy of the statement from the Production Manager and a statement from this department are enclosed for your information.

Kindly send your suggestions to me by 19th July so that I can prepare a consolidated Report and present it at the next Board meeting on 23rd July.

M.B.P. Bagchi
Sales Manager

Copies for information to All Directors.

Secretary to Board for including the subject in Agenda of Nucleus Group for business development.

Example : **An office note seeking the superior's approval for the transfer of an employee**

PROVISIONAL TRANSPORTS (P) LTD.
Pithugaon

No. . . . . Date: 3rd May, 2010

To: Shri K.K. Bagi
Marketing Director

From: S.M. Tayagi
Manager

Sub : Transfer on promotion of Shri A.N. Coorgi, senior clerk to Regional Office, Mysore.

Please refer to letter No. H.O./348/40-2009 from the

Accountant, Regional Office, Mysore for filling up the vacancy of an Assistant Accountant in his office caused by the resignation of the earlier incumbent.

In the light of the latest agreement with the employees, this position is to be filled up on seniority-*cum*-merit basis. Accordingly, seven senior clerks of the company were called for a written test followed by a personal interview.

The written test was conducted under my supervision. The interview was conducted by a panel comprising two directors, Shri M.R. Jogi and Shri R.S. Magi, myself, and the Chief Accountant, Shri M.S. Dasgupta. Shri A.N. Coorgi was unanimously selected by this panel.

I write this to seek your approval to issue to Shri A.N. Coorgi an order of transfer on promotion.

S.N. Tyagi
Chief Manager (Personnel)

Example : **An office note from the stores department to all other departments informing them of the stock-taking.**

SUPER HEALTH PHARMACEUTICALS LIMITED
Lalgarh

Date: 27TH March, 2010

Ref: T/23/10

To: All Departments
From: Stores Departments

Subject : Stock taking for the year ending 31-3-2010.

The stores department will remain occupied on 30th and 31st March, 2010 for stock taking for the purpose of closing the accounts for the year ending 31st March 2010. All the departments are requested to draw their requirements latest by 29th March, 2010. The stores department would not be able to make supplies to the departments on both these days.

(D.P.S. Subramani Iyer)
Stores-in-charge

Example : **An office note from the Production Manager to the Personnel Manager requesting him to take disciplinary action against an employee for gross misconduct.**

OFFICE NOTE

Ref. No. . . . ….. Date: 12 July, 2010

From: P.S. Jaggi, Production Manager,

To: Trilok Singh, Personnel Manager,

Subject : Gross misconduct of Ram Dev Yadav, Foreman

Mr. Ram Dev Yadav, foreman in the production department, has been creating problems for the production unit for the last three months.

He is running his own parallel business and does not conform to our working hours. Since 1st March, he has been absent thrice without any prior notice and any valid reason, causing serious dislocation of production.

When on 15th March, I tried to explain to him the seriousness of the issue, he misbehaved with me in the presence of the rest of the staff. He keeps instigating others in the Department, under the belief that it would keep his position strong.

Yesterday, when I pointed out to Mr. Yadav that he was late for work by more than half an hour, he not only shouted at me but also provoked the labour to suspend work.

This is a serious matter calling for strict disciplinary action.

P.S. Jaggi
(Producton Manager)

FORM MESSAGES

Introduction

Form letters or form memos are used when an identical message is to be sent to large number of people. While Form Letters are used for external communication, Form Memos are used for internal communication.

We can use form letters to:

- Answer often recurring enquiries.
- Acknowledge orders, payments,
- Make simple adjustments,
- Invite candidates for a test/interview
- Make appointments,
- Promote goodwill, and
- Give news to customers, stockholders, suppliers, etc.

Form memos may be used to:

- Give news to employees,
- Deal with disciplinary matters,
- Deal with leave and other service conditions of employees, and
- Simplify office procedures, etc.

ADVANTAGES OF FORM MESSAGES

Form message enjoy certain obvious advantages:

(1) *They save time*: A master draft is prepared and is duplicated at an automatic machine. Within seconds, we get as many copies as needed.

(2) *They save money*: Sending a typewritten message to every individual would prove quite expensive. If we calculate the cost of man-hours saved by sending form messages, we shall discover that form messages are very economical.

(3) *They can be of better quality*: If letters are written by disgruntled, incompetent or overworked

subordinates, they are poor and shabby both in content and appearance. But if competent people are entrusted with the responsibility of preparing and typing the master draft, the form message may turn out to be very impressive.

(4) They facilitate mailing campaigns, it would be impossible to think of a large-scale mailing campaign (where thousands of customers have to be contacted simultaneously), if a personal, separately typed letter were to be sent to each individual.

KINDS OF FORMS

Four kinds of forms are in use:

Complete Form

In a complete form, the messages are identical word by word. If it is a form letter, the general salutation of Dear Student, Dear Customer, Dear Subscriber, etc. is used saving time. But if Form Memo is used, the words to be used will be followed by such terms as all staff members, all employees, the heads of all sections, etc.

Fill-in Form

In this form, messages are prepared in advance to meet specific kinds of situations with blank spaces left for filling in variable information. If the blanks are filled in at the same electronic typewriter or computer on which the original form was prepared the fillings will be hardly noticeable and the addressee will get a personalized letter.

Guide Form

Here, model letters or memos are prepared in advance to meet various kinds of situations. Whenever someone has to write a similar message, he/she can adopt the model to meet the specific situation.

Paragraph Form

A letter containing a number of paragraphs or a booklet of paragraphs to respond to different situations is kept ready.

When a reply is to be sent, relevant paragraph(s) is/are ticked and the letter mailed. Or the communicator marks relevant paragraph(s) in the booklet and dictates a couple of paragraphs to personalize the letter. The typist then types the letter giving a suitable order to the paragraphs. In this way, even lengthy messages are prepared in a short time.

Example : **A form letter inviting a candidate for the interview.**

Dear Sir/Madam,

With reference to your application for the post of ________________, you are required to present yourself for an interview at this office at ________________on ____________

Please note that you will be appearing at the interview at your own expense and no TA or DA is admissible.

Yours faithfully

Manager (Personnel)

Example : **A form letter sent to a referee before giving appointment to a candidate.**

No. . . . . Dated . . . .

To

Dear Sir/Madam,

Mr./Mrs/Miss______________________________ has been selected for appointment to the post of ___________________ in this office. He/she has given your name as a reference.

We shall be grateful if you give your opinion about the applicant in the following format:

(1) How long have you known the applicant? ________

(2) In what capacity? ______________________

(3) Give your appraisal of the applicant in terms of the qualities listed below:

	Out-standing	*Superior*	*Good*	*Average*	*Poor*	*Unable to rate*
Leadership potential						
Commitment to work						
Ability to work with others						
Creativity and originality of thought						
Proficiency in spoken English						
Proficiency in written English						

(4) What in your opinion are the applicant's strong points? ______________________

____

(5) What in your opinion are the applicant's weak points? ______________________

____

(6) Any further comments that could help us in our evaluation of the applicant ______________________

____

(7) What are your overall recommendations with regard to the suitability of the applicant.

Strongly Recommended ☐ Recommended ☐

Recommended with reservation ☐ Not recommended ☐

Place:

Date: Name and signature

N.B. :

We assure you that the information provided by you will be treated as most confidential.

Yours faithfully,
Manager (Personnel)

***Example :* A form memo intimating the Branch Office the confirmation of an employee.**

RAGHUVIR PLACEMENTS
H.O. Hyderabad

Office Memo

No. . . . . Dated . . . .

To

From:

Dear Sir/Madam,

Re: Mr./Mrs. Miss .______________________

We are pleased to inform you that Mr./Mrs./ Miss________________ has been confirmed in his/her existing capacity as ___________________________ with effect from ________________. Consequently, he/she would be eligible to the benefits of Provident Fund as per rules from the said date. He/she has been allotted Provident Fund account No. ____________________

He/she is advised to return the enclosed provident fund forms duly filled in and signed by him/her.

Please inform Mr./Mrs./Miss ______________________ accordingly.

Yours faithfully,
Manager (Personnel)
Encl. : As above

TELEGRAMS AND CABLES

Telegrams and cables are used for quick transmission of messages. In India, telegrams are used for transmission within the country and cables are sent for overseas transmission. Telephone is, of course, quicker than telegram and it (telephone) has the advantage of personal talking. Therefore, in a telephone talk, there is very little possibility of misunderstanding or confusion about any word or any part of the talk.

Telegram, however, enjoys one obvious advantage over telephone: a telegram is a written communication. It can be a permanent record, it can be read and re-read to come to a definite conclusion over a course of action; it can be field for future reference and consultation: it can even be a legal document to bind the sender to the message contained in it.

A very important point to note about telegram is its cost. Every word and every punctuation mark used therein is charged. Therefore, first of all, a telegram must be used only when the transmission of the message is really urgent. Some of the situations requiring a telegraphic message are as follows:

(i) The seller's acceptance of the buyer's order is urgently required by the buyer.
(ii) There is undue delay by the seller in sending goods, which may be causing inconvenience or loss to the buyer.
(iii) The buyer may be requiring quotations very urgently.
(iv) The seller has to send his acceptance of the order or his quotations but the time left is very short.
(v) There is a sudden change in prices, and the new prices must be got accepted by the other party before effecting delivery of goods.
(vi) There is need for inquiring about some missing documents or parcels.
(vii) Delays in shipping or the departure of the ship have to be intimated.
(viii) A report is urgently required on some matter.

In all cases, the sender of a telegram must bear in mind the following two points:

(i) If the time available is short, telegram is the only method of sending a written message, and

(ii) Telegram is one of the most effective means of making the receiver realize the urgency and the need of doing something in regard to some matter.

How to draft a Telegram

Brevity and clarity are the principal features of a telegram. The message must be restricted to the main points only. Any extra word or information is unnecessary, and costly, too. The rules of grammar are forgotten in writing a telegram, the essentials of a letter like attraction, conviction, persuasion, the 'you' attitude, etc. are also set aside.

What a telegram contains is a piece of information, or words of instruction, or both, all in as few words as possible. Many words like 'and', 'that' 'the', 'a', 'but', 'however', 'i', 'you ', etc. are conveniently dropped. Only nouns and verbs are used because they give full meaning for the matter more precisely.

Along with brevity, clarity of expression is equally important. Since elaborate information is not given in a telegram, every word chosen must give the meaning clearly, completely and without ambiguity.

For example, a telegram reading "Dispatching Goods Monday" leaves the reader in doubt as to whether the immediate next Monday or the one after that. Instead, if it says "Dispatching Goods Monday Fifth", it means the Monday that falls on the fifth-day of the month.

Where absolutely necessary, even lengthy telegrams are sent. But it is always preferable to omit the punctuation marks, except the full-stop. For the full-stop, it is not the "." Mark that is used but the word "Stop".

People use many abbreviated forms for two to three words together. There can be no standard abbreviations for all cases.

A few of them are:

(i) REFLECT = please Refer to Letter . . . .
(ii) RYL = Regarding Your Letter
(iii) ROL = Regarding Our Letter
(iv) REFGRAM = Referring to your telegram
(v) REFQUOT = Referring to quotations

Example : **Draft a telegram for the following letter.**

STEEL-AGE (P) LTD.

Mumbai

12th April 2010

Dear Sir,

Many thanks for your letter dated 10th April along with order for 1200 folding chairs and 200 tables. It speaks of your confidence in the quality of our products which brings us repetitive orders from you.

In your order, you have mentioned the cost of chairs as Rs. 50 each and of tables Rs. 85 each, including packing and forwarding, and F.O.R. your place. We have earlier supplied the good at these prices and terms, but that was one year ago and it was F.O.R. our place and not yours. Since then the prices have changed and we regret we cannot accept your offer at these prices, FOR your place. The present Quotation is:

Chairs Rs. 60 each, including Packing and Forwarding
Tables Rs. 90 each. FOR Our place.

Since you wish us to dispatch the goods within a week's time from the date of your order, please let us know whether you can confirm your order immediately at the above rates so that we can proceed in the matter.

We await your early reply.

Yours faithfully,
V.K. Bansal
Manager.

(190 words excluding punctuation marks)

Telegram

Reflect Tenth April stop regret your prices unacceptable stop current quotation chairs rupees Sixty tables Rupees Ninety for Mumbai stop confirm order.

Steelage

(20 words)

Two more points to be observed in connection with the telegrams are:

(i) The message of the telegram should preferably be typed on the telegram form in capital letters. This serves as a precaution against wrong reading of any word/s.
(ii) Every telegram must be confirmed by a follow-up letter. The letter can be elaborate. It must refer to the telegram and must reproduce the message of the telegram.

REPRESENTATIONS

Representation is an act of trying to bring home before an authority certain problems or certain issues or the consequences of a certain rule or law, or act, etc. Representation can also be a remonstrance, i.e. an act of protest against someone or something.

Representation involves two persons: one represents and one representing his case and the other to whom the case is represented. The person representing may be an individual or a group of organized individuals like an Employees' Union/ Association, Employer's Organization, Trade Association, Chamber of Commerce, Citizens' Forum, Consumers' Association, Association of Professionals, etc. The person to whom something is represented may be the highest official like the management, the Minister, the Administrator, the Commissioner, the Vice-Chancellor, the Registrar, or any other such person.

The subject matter of a representation generally consists of two important parts, viz., grievance of the representing party on a particular matter and the demand to get the grievances redressed. The grievances are explained with facts and figures by pointing out defects and limitations, difficulties and impracticalities, existing conditions and problems, etc., and then demands are put forth to solve the problem, or suggestions are made for a definite course of action.

The matter of a representation itself includes a variety of subjects like the pay-scales, better working conditions, retirement benefits or other policies relating to employment, tax-laws, accounting procedures to be followed, restrictions on movement of goods, stringent government policy in the matters of licensing, credit facility and so many other issues that affect a businessman, a policy of the educational authority that is harmful to the existing educational units, and a number of civic problems, etc. It may also include matters relating to privileges, rights, moral principles, religious or political or cultural matters, etc.

A representation may be written in the letter form or in the memorandum style. When the letter form is chosen, the letter-head, inside address, salutation, subject line, body of the letter, complimentary close and subscription, all the useful parts of letter are found in the draft of the representation.

However, when a memorandum is submitted, it generally has at the top, the name of the person or official to whom the representation is submitted, a very formal salutation, 'Sir' or 'Madam', the body of the memorandum, and finally, the name of the association submitting the memorandum. There can, of course, be no such clear-cut distinction between the form of a representation and a memorandum, as a memorandum can also take the full form of a letter with all its usual parts.

Important Points to Note

(1) The representation should preferably be drafted on the letter head, if there is no letter head of the sender, his address must be recorded at the top left or right hand corner.

(2) As in the case of any other communication, the representation must contain date.

(3) The inside address has got to be clearly written and it must have the official designation of the addressee. What is important here is that the representation must be addressed to the correct person/official. If it is addressed to a wrong person, the representation would be a waste or there would be undue delay. It must be addressed to only that person who has the authority to redress the grievances.

(4) The best form of salutation is 'Sir/Madam'.

(5) The subject line is invariably inserted before the main body of the representation.

(6) The body of the representation should now be written in a very appealing, convincing and effective style and tone. Some important hints for writing this main part are given below:

   (i) The subject-matter of the case in question should be thought out clearly before the representation is written.

   (ii) The problem involved must be of common interest to a sufficient number of persons because something that is inconvenient to one or a few selected persons may be beneficial to a larger number of other persons.

   (iii) No complaints should be made on unfounded or unreal grounds or beliefs.

   (iv) The possibility of redress must also be forethought keeping in view the difficulties of the other party who is always bound by certain rules, regulations, laws, principles of natural justice, budgetary provision, temporary difficulties or shortages, extraneous conditions or pressures, etc.

   (v) Once the necessity and propriety of the subject matter have been established, the facts must be arranged logically so as to focus the reader's undivided attention on the whole matter.

(vi) Wherever possible, the statements given in the representation should be substantiated by documents and reports. True copies of these may also be attached to the representation.

(vii) The tone must be persuasive but not irritating, the language should be objective and not unduly strong. However, if the representation contains a demand which is a legal right, the demand can be put forth in strong words.

(viii) It must be very precise, to the point and clear.

(ix) At the end, what is expected from the addressee must be mentioned clearly in the form of demands or suggestions or forceful request.

(7) Wherever necessary, the writer may also request for a personal interview with the addressee. This would give him an opportunity to elaborate the case more efficiently.

(8) Original representations not responded to will have to be flowed up by repeated representations.

Following are a few specimen representations:

Example : **A representation for better water supply and sanitary facilities.**

Mumbai,
12th April 2008

No. . . . .

The Administrator,
G.B.M.C.,
Mumbai - 400 085

Dear Sir,

Sub: Request for better water supply and sanitary facilities.

We, the residents at R.S. No. 446/1+2, in the locality of Fort, Mumbai, wish to respectfully request you to provide the following amenities to our locality:

(1) Laying out a 3″ sub-line for water supply,
(2) Construction of proper roads, and
(3) Provision of sanitary facilities.

Nearly ten months ago, we submitted to you a similar representation. To our regret, no action has been taken till today, nor have we received any reply to our representation. We had the follow-up work in the form of personal meetings with the officers concerned but all we could get was an "assurance for sympathetic consideration".

(1) The existing sub-line for water supply is of just $1^1/_2$ of G.I. Pipe.

The standard minimum size of the pipe everywhere else is of 3″ h. We are, therefore, getting just half the supply in the sub-line itself on which a number of houses depend for their scanty share daily. Added to this, on account of the main line being on a high head, the pressure of supply is also very low. So, as if to add insult to injury, the valve man obliges us with only half-an-hour supply daily as against one full hour's supply in all other areas. We are sure, sir, you can realize how badly affect we must be on account of these inconveniences.

We, therefore, request you to kindly arrange for:

(i) Replacement of the present $1^1/_2$″ G.I. Pipe by the regular 3″ supply pipe line.
(ii) Supply of the water for one hour daily, both the facilities being enjoyed by residents of their localities, and
(iii) Change in the time of supply from 4.00 PM to any other time between 8.00 AM. And 12.00 noon, the time when the pressure in the main pipes is said to be adequate to rise up to the height of our locality.

(2) Regarding the road, Sir, ever since they were laid 3 years ago, no maintenance work has been done. The result is that the roads are now in a very unsatisfactory condition.

(3) Since there is no proper outlet provided in the locality for the flow of waste-water, it gets soaked and accumulates close to our houses providing a good breeding place for mosquitoes.

May we, therefore, request you to kindly arrange the construction of metalled roads and gutters for waste-water outlet. An early action in the matter will help us get out of very unhygienic conditions of living. We shall be grateful for your looking into the problems personally and arranging for their immediate and satisfactory solution.

Thanking you,
We are,
Yours faithfully,
. . . . . .
. . . . . .
(Residents)

Example : **A representation to the management on behalf of the workers asking for a better lunch room and facilities for sports.**

MAZDOOR UNION
METRO MOTOR INDUSTRIES LTD.
Balapore

6th May, 2010

The Chairman, Board of Directors,
Metro Industries Ltd.,
Mumbai - 400 001.

Dear Sir,

On the eve of the fifth Anniversary of the Company, the Mazdoor Union of the Company wishes to convey to you our felicitations and sincere good wishes.

We trust that the Union has been successfully functioning to achieve its objective of promotion of cordial staff-management relations. The Union takes this opportunity to thank Board of Directors for giving consideration to many of the staff suggestions during the Union-Management meetings.

For the last one year, the employees of the Company have been experiencing an urgent need of a well-equipped lunch need of a well-equipped lunch room and a sports room.

There are about 125 employees of the company who are taking their mid-day lunch in the factory. The existing shed is too small to accommodate all these employees simultaneously during lunch hours. Moreover, the furniture provided and drinking water facilities are also inadequate. We, therefore, request you to kindly arrange for the construction of a new lunch room, with attached toilets, with tables and furniture for 150 members. Drinking water facilities should also be improved.

You may be aware that many employees of the company recently participated in the local open tournaments in different games. They have also brought honour to the company by winning many cups and trophies. All these sportsmen have been practicing in private sports clubs and gymnasia. We sincerely feel that there is an urgent need for a sports room-*cum*-gymnasium for the company's employees.

It will also give them a good place and an opportunity for recreation. It will certainly strengthen the cordial relations between the workers and the employees. It will also help them to develop a sense of mutual understanding and co-operation. Moreover, the workers would get themselves refreshed and get free from the physical strain of the day-long work. The development of such mental qualities in the workers will certainly improve the efficiency of their work.

We would suggest that, with some minor alternations, the present lunch room can be converted into such a sports room-*cum*-gymnasium. It may cost about Rs. 12,500 only. To start with, we shall have to purchase sports equipment for about Rs. 15000 and the yearly expenses should not exceed Rs. 5000. Considering the advantages it will have for the Company, the workers in general and the sportsmen workers in particular, it is worth incurring this expenditure. We, therefore, request you to take immediate action in this connection.

Thanking you again,

I remain,

Yours faithfully,
Vinod Dongree
Secretary

LETTERS TO THE EDITOR

Almost all newspapers and magazines have a special column as "Letters to the Editor", or "From Our Readers", or "Readers' views", etc. Through this column, readers can express their views on various matters such as: (a) any news that has been published by the paper, (b) any event in the field of politics, education, administration, labour, management or other social activities, or (c) any defect in the working of any public institution, may it be a library, a sports organization, a charitable institution, a hospital or a Local, State or Central Government Department.

It is through this column that one can draw attention of the public and win its sympathy for a particular issue or cause that requires attention or action of the government or some institutional authorities. Sometimes, this column provides a platform for a 'debate' or 'discussion' on a certain issue which gets invaluable opinions from qualified and experienced persons. Thus it is highly beneficial to many interested readers in general and to the persons responsible for creating the issue, in particular.

How to write letters to the Editor

The following points must be borne in mind in drafting letters to the editor:

(1) *Be Brief:* Very limited space is available in the papers and magazines to publish readers' letters/views. In this space, editors have to publish letters that cover different subjects. They select only those letters, which are short but clear. Hence we must write in brief. Editors do 'edit' the letters before publication and may shorten the matter and may make

necessary alternations too. Still they prefer short letters because they cannot afford to go through lengthy letters as they have very busy schedule of work daily—there are deadlines.

(2) *Be Relevant*: The letter must contain only relevant points about the subject. This aspect is related to the aspect of brevity. Irrelevant and unwanted material makes the letter lengthy and perhaps unintelligent and unwanted material makes the letter lengthy and perhaps uninteresting.

(3) *Be Reasonable*: When something is 'commented' on, there must be some concrete base or reason to say something. We must substantiate our views by giving reasons, facts, consequences, benefits, etc. when a reader expresses 'what' he thinks about a thing, he must say 'why' he thinks so. Then only can his letter have the expected effect on other readers and the concerned authority.

(4) *Arouse Interest*: To bring home the point we are making, we must try, as far as possible, to make the letter bright and amusing. Use of amusing phrases and a light tone will sustain the readers' interest in the letter.

(5) *Be prompt*: If the letter is topical, it must be written at the appropriate time. A stale letter is like stale news, and editors have little interest in either.

Some other hints for drafting a letter to editor are listed below:

(i) It is preferable to choose a daily or a periodical which does not radically disagree with the writer's views.

(ii) A salutation must be used in the letter and the most proper one is, "Sir".

(iii) At the beginning of the letter, a clear reference must be made to the topic or event or the news that occasioned the writing of the letter.

(iv) Letters should not contain any personal message or advertising material. The letter should deal with a subject of common interest to the people belonging to the state as a whole, a locality, a constituency or a trade, employment or section of the society.

(v) Personal attacks as well as insulting and un-parliamentary words must be avoided.

(vi) The appropriate complimentary close to be used is "Yours truly".

(vii) The covering letter should contain the full address of the writer. However, if the writer does not want his name to be published with the letter, alternate phrases used are: "A Reader", "A sufferer", "A Sympathizer", "Interested", "A Traveller", "The Neglected", The Affected", etc.

Example : **A letter to the editor of a newspaper regarding Income Tax Exemption.**

(I—The Covering Letter)

Pune,
No. . . . . . . 12th April 2010.

K.G.S. Nagpal
Goregaon,

The Editor,
The Decann Herald,
Pune.

Sir,

I shall be thankful if you publish early the enclosed letter in the "From Our Readers" column of your popular daily.

Yours faithfully,
K.G.S. Nagpal
Address and Contact Number

(II—The Letter to be published)

Sir,

The tax-pattern has been penalizing to the middle class. A budget, whether from the centre or the state, means a pinch to the pocket of the middle class. This class is neither able to rise to the upper class nor lower its standard of living. The vast majority of middle class comprises workers and small businessmen or professionals who live on hard earned income.

The Bal Thakare Government of Maharashtra has exempted the working class from payment of Income Tax. It is earnestly desired that the Government of India also extends a similar privilege to the working or middle classes of India.

Raising the exemption limit to the level of Rs. 200,000 would help many sections of the middle class. Recent increases in pay scales to match to some extent the steep increase in the cost of living would defeat the very object of increase in wages on account of enlarged scope of income tax which takes away the increased wages.

Yours truly,
A.B.C.

This complimentary close, however, is not published in the paper.

Example : **A letter relating to the take-over of industries.**

Sirs,

This refers to the reported remarks of Dr. H. Swami (ET-Jan 2010) challenging Mr. K.G. Rane as well as Mr Mohan Raj in the context of the take-over of key industries. I congratulate Dr. Swami for his bold and outspoken comments on the government's failure in efficient handling of the public sector. It is needless to emphasize that private entrepreneurs and personal element do play a vital role in any sphere of activity. It would, therefore, be appreciated that the ministers do not deliberately go in for a move resembling nationalization without rhyme or reason.

The remarks of Mr. Tata are also worth noting. The mixed economy concept will be paralysed on account of such moves. The efficiency of the private sector cannot be infused in the public sector. Nationalization would only cause severe drain on the economy, which more often than not shows signs of stagnancy. While nobody disputes that the big houses should be checked regarding their relations with small-scale industries, one would expect a rational approach by the government. It would be wrong to believe that the government can handle more efficiently the business of units, which have already proved their best beyond doubt.

It is indeed heartening to note that the national executive of the ruling party has refrained from making any such move as envisaged by the two ministers and I, among many, endorse my approval in the interest of the nation.

XYZ, Mumbai.

Example : **A letter to the editor of a newspaper regarding LIC Premium.**

Sir,

The government of India, before it decided to nationalize life insurance in 1956, had declared that it planned to reduce premium as longevity has increased. If I recall correctly, the rates of premium were based on an average life span of 32 years at that time.

If the insurance were allowed to be in private sector, the Government would have seen to it that not only the premium were reduced in 1956 or there about but would also have reduced them further periodically.

LIC is but one example of exploitation of people by their own government. Unless policy-holders and people in general demand with one voice and agitate for proper accounting, there is no remedy to have the grievances redressed.

Yours Truly,
B.M. Patel
Vadodara

CHAPTER

14

Correspondence of a Company Secretary

SECRETARY AND HIS DUTIES

The secretary of a company occupies an important position in the administrative work. In olden days, he had to look after the entire correspondence of the organization in which he was employed. The secretary is now-a-days left with the correspondence of a special nature; dealing with directors, members, staff and Registrar of Companies and other government authorities and institutions.

On the administrative side, the secretary is now considered an important link between the directors and shareholders and a responsible officer concerned with the general administration and management. In the words of H. Hughes, "the work of company secretary is exacting but interesting. On the one hand, he is the trusted, confidential servant of the Board, and on the other, an officer of the company responsible for certain statutory and other duties".

CORRESPONDENCE

Secretarial correspondence can be classified into the following categories:

(1) Correspondence with directors.
(2) Correspondence with shareholders.
(3) Correspondence with others.

Correspondence with Directors

Sending notices of Board Meetings and the reports of the proceedings of such meetings, sending periodical reports of the proceedings of such meetings, and periodical reports of the working of the company are the routine course of the Secretarial Section.

The secretary corresponds with the directors on special occasions, for some information, of request for a matter to be taken up for discussion in the Board meeting, or when the chairman wishes to communicate with the directors in connection with the Board meetings, etc.

Being subordinate to the directors, a secretary has to be very tactful and courteous to them while communicating with them. Sometimes, a director may be new to his assignment and may not be fully conversant with the nature of the work or may not be in possession of all the relevant information.

The first person he will then think of getting in touch with will be the secretary. But even in such a situation, the secretary will have to show due deference to the director. A secretary just cannot afford to assume airs.

Example: **A director asks for the details of the previous Board meeting which he could not attend.**

He also requests the secretary to include in the Agenda for the next meeting his suggestion to hold meetings on certain fixed days of the month.

Vishal Mahajan,
102, Verma Hotel,
G.T. Road, Ludhiana.

No. . . . .   10th April 2010

The Secretary,
National Textiles Ltd.,
Mumbai - 400 001.

Dear Sir,

I have been on a business tour of the Punjab for the last 10 days. Hence I could not attend the Board meeting that was scheduled to be held on the 3rd April. I shall be thankful to you if you send me the details of the proceedings of this meeting at the address given above. I shall be staying in Ludhiana up to 5th April and you may send me the Notice of the next Board meeting at the same address.

With regard to the dates of various Board meetings, I wish to suggest to the Chairman to hold the meetings on certain fixed days of each month. This will eliminate clashes between the directors' personal programmes and the Board meetings. The trouble of issuing notices for every Board meeting will also be saved. Will you please include, in consultation with the Chairman, this proposal in the agenda for the next meeting?

Yours sincerely,
Vishal Mahajan

In reply to such a letter, the Secretary will send a copy of the minutes of the Board meeting referred to. But the minutes give a very brief description of the proceedings and just record the resolutions.

So, it is highly desirable that the Secretary includes in his reply relevant details of the discussion on some important aspects. About the proposal to include a certain item in the agenda, a simple answer in 'yes' or 'no' is to be given. If the chairman has not accepted the proposal, a brief explanatory note should be added.

A shareholder asks about the progress of the Company in future with a view to increasing his shareholding.

The letter is as under:

Dear Sir,

A good dividend record in the last five years and a high price of your company's shares in the share market have impressed me very much and, therefore, I want to increase my shareholding in the company. I shall be obliged if you kindly let me know whether the company is contemplating the issue of any rights shares or bonus shares for the expansion of its activities or there is any possibility of increase in the dividend rate this year.

Your advice in the matter will facilitate me greatly.

Yours faithfully,

Reply to the above letter will contain the following points:

1. Appreciation that the shareholder takes interest in the company.
2. As Secretary, I have to maintain secrecy and, therefore, can not disclose all the information asked by you.
3. Giving such information will be prejudicial to the interest of the other shareholders.
4. Reports in the *Economic Times* or *Financial Express* can assist you in the matter of investment.
5. You may contact some Consultancy Firm, if you so desire.

Yours faithfully,

Secretary

CHAPTER

15

Business Reports

INTRODUCTORY

What is a Report?

"A business report is an orderly presentation of facts about specific business activity or programme". C.A. Brown defines a report as "a communication from someone who has some information to someone who wants to use that information".

Thousand of reports, long or short, formal or informal, crucial or ordinary, special or routine, are written everyday. A foreman, at the end of the day, reports to the manager the progress of the work carried on in his supervision.

A publication firm, interested in introducing into the market a new series of paperbacks, has to ask for a report on the nature and variety of the current best sellers.

The Managing Director of a company would like to get a report on the efficacy of the measures introduced by him to promote efficiency among his staff.

A textiles firm may have been using various modes of publicity messages broadcast from the Vividh Bharati, slides flashed on the TV or the cinema screen, hoardings on the roadside, fashion parades in big cities, participation in exhibitions and trade fairs, regular advertisements in newspapers and journals, distribution of leaflets, etc.

The Board of Directors of this firm would definitely like to get a report on the effectiveness of these modes in the light of the expenditure incurred in order to make an optimum use of the funds earmarked for publicity. Reports, thus, play a very significant role in the management of modern business.

Oral and Written Reports

A report may be either oral or written. An oral report is simple and easy to present. It may consist in the communication of an impression or an observation. Sometimes, it may be quite useful. But a written report is always preferred. It enjoys several advantages over the oral one:

(1) As oral report can be denied at any time, a written report is a permanent record. The reporter cannot deny what he has reported once.

(2) An oral report tends to be vague. It may be encumbered by the presence of irrelevant facts while some significant ones may have been overlooked. In a written report, the writer tries to be accurate and precise.

(3) A written report can change hands without any danger of distortion during transmission.

(4) A written report can be referred to again and again.

Informative and Interpretative Reports

If a report merely presents facts pertinent to an issue or a situation, it is informative. On the other hand, if it analyses the facts, draws conclusions and makes recommendations, it may be described as analytical or interpretative.

An informative report on the sale of folding beds will simply record the number of folding beds sold during the various months. But an interpretative report will analyze why and to what extent their sales go up during the summer months of May to July and may make recommendations on the schedule of production.

The Importance of Reports

A report is a 'basic management tool' used in 'decision-making'. Hence it is extremely important. In a one-man business, the functions of reporting and decision-making are combined in one man, the proprietor. He knows his business inside out and is capable of making on the spot decisions. So, he does not need any reports. But in large scale organizations, when engaged in manifold activities, variously entrusted to a large number of employees, reports are just indispensable.

The top executives cannot keep a personal watch over all the activities, so they have to depend upon reports coming from the heads of the various departments. Companies that want to diversity their production, explore new market potentials, set-up new agencies, enter into collaboration projects, have to depend upon relevant reports.

CHARACTERISTICS OF A GOOD REPORT

(1) *Precision:* In a good report, the writer is very clear about the exact purpose of writing it. His investigation, analysis and recommendations are directed by this central purpose. Precision gives a kind of unity and coherence to the report and makes it a valuable document.

(2) *Accuracy of facts:* The scientific accuracy of facts is very essential to a good report. Since reports invariably lead to decision-making, inaccurate facts may lead to disastrous decisions.

(3) *Relevance:* The facts presented in the report should be not only accurate but also relevant. While it is essential that every fact included in a report has a bearing on the central purpose, it is equally essential to see that nothing relevant has escaped inclusion. Irrelevant facts make a report confusing; exclusion of relevant facts renders it incomplete and likely to mislead.

(4) *Reader-orientation:* A good report is always reader-oriented. While drafting a report, it is necessary to keep in mind the person(s) who is (are) going to read it. A report meant for the layman will be different form another meant for technical experts.

(5) *Objectivity of Recommendations*: If recommendations are made at the end of a report, they must be impartial and objective. They should come as a logical conclusion to investigation and analysis. They must not reveal any self-interest on the part of the writer.

(6) *Simple and unambiguous language:* A good report is written in a simple and unambiguous language. It is a kind of scientific document of practical utility; hence it should be free from various forms of poetic embellishment like features of speech.

(7) *Clarity:* A good report is absolutely clear: clarity depends on proper arrangement of facts. The report writer must proceed systematically. He should make his purpose clear, define his sources, divide his report into short paragraphs giving them heading, and insert other suitable sign posts to achieve greater clarity.

(8) *Brevity:* A report should be brief. It is difficult to define brevity in absolute terms. Nor can brevity be laid down as a rule. All that can be said is that a good report should be as brief as possible. Brevity should not be achieved at the cost of clarity. Nor should it be at the cost completeness. Sometimes, the problem being investigated is of such importance that it calls for a detailed discussion of facts. Then this discussion should not be evaded. Brevity in a report is the kind of brevity one recommends for a précis: include everything significant and yet be brief.

(9) *Grammatical Accuracy:* The grammatical accuracy of language, listed under the characteristics of a good report, is of any other piece of composition. Who is going to read a report if its language is faulty?

Besides, faulty construction of sentences makes the meaning obscure and ambiguous.

(10) *Stephen Sweet in his book 'General and Business English' adequately sums up the characteristics of a good business report when he writes*: "The report should be characterized by clear expression and neat display; should be in the nature of an argument, well reasoned and conclusions and recommendations set forth".

TYPES OF BUSINESS REPORTS

We can classify business reports in three different ways:

(a) On the basis of legal formalities to be complied with, we can have two types of reports:

    (1) Formal reports: and
    (2) Informal reports.

(b) On the basis of the number of persons entrusted with the drafting of a report, there can again be two types:

    1. Reports by individuals; and
    2. Reports by committees and sub-committees.

Finally: On the basis of the nature of a report, we can have the following five types:

1. Periodic or recurring reports;
2. Progress reports;
3. Examination reports;
4. Recommendation reports; and
5. Statistical report.

A brief discussion of various kinds of reports is given below:

(a) On the basis of legal formalities to be complied with:

1. Formal Reports

A formal report is one which is prepared in a prescribed form and is presented according to an established procedure to a prescribed authority.

2. Informal Reports

An informal report is usually in the form of a person-to-person communication. It may range from a short, almost fragmentary statement of facts on a single page, to a more developed presentation taking several pages. An informal report is usually submitted in the form of a letter or memorandum.

The formal reports are again of two types:

(i) Statutory reports; and (ii) Non-statutory reports.

(i) Statutory Reports

A report prepared and presented according to the form and procedure laid down by law is called a statutory report. The director and the secretary of a company are required by the Companies Act to prepare and submit statutory reports.

Examples: Report submitted at the statutory meeting of shareholders, Directors' report to the annual general meeting. Annual Return, Auditors' Report, are statutory reports.

(ii) Non-Statutory Reports

Formal reports which are not required under any law but which are prepared to help the management in framing policies or taking other important decisions are called non-statutory reports.

Some of these non-statutory reports are prepared regularly as parts of the routine procedure of business while others are prepared on certain special occasions, or whenever the exigencies of business demand them. These reports may be prepared by the directors, their committees, and the executive heads of departments, the secretary and other officers of the company. These reports may be of the following types:

A. *Report of Directors to the shareholders*

The report submitted by the directors at the Annual General Meeting of a company is a statutory report. But apart from that, the directors may be required to submit occasional non-statutory reports to the shareholders on special problems or special projects undertaken by the company.

Examples: Reports on diversification of production, undertaking a special project, entering into collaboration with another company, holding negotiations with another company for purchasing its business, entering a new line of business, etc.

B. *Reports of Committees of Directors*

The Board of Directors usually appoint standing committees consisting of two or more directors to help the Board of efficiently carrying on their task of management and administration.

Example: Finance committee, share allotment committee, share transfer committee, arbitration committee, etc. are the usual committees which are required to submit their reports to the Board of Directors at regular intervals.

C. *Reports of Special or Ad hoc Committees of Directors*

In addition to standing committees, special or *ad hoc* committees of Directors may be appointed to go into and report on matters of special or current importance. Such *ad hoc* committees may be needed to advise the board on the advisability of setting up a new branch, the methods of raising additional capital, the suitability of a particular site for constructing a new factory building, etc.

D. *Reports of Individual Officers*

Executives in charge of various divisions of a company, viz., sales, purchase, production, accounts, personnel, etc. or departmental managers are required to submit periodical reports on the activities and progress of their respective divisions or departments. Such reports are very useful to the board in planning, controlling and co-coordinating their business operations. Other officers like the secretary, auditor, solicitor, etc. are also required to submit reports on special matters.

E. *Financial Reports*

These reports are prepared by the Manager of the Finance Department or the Controller of Finance. They provide valuable information on the financial structure, effectiveness of the use of capital, the need and ways of reorganizing the available capital resources, etc.

F. *Reports of the Company Secretary*

The secretary is a principal officer of the Joint Stock Company. So, he is frequently asked to submit reports on a variety of subjects like : (i) selecting of a suitable accommodation for the main or branch office, (ii) complaints from branch offices, (iii) suspected irregularities in some departments, (iv) improvement in office organization, (v) grievances of the staff, (vi) causes of discontent among labour and their threats to go on a strike, (vii) improvements in the working conditions in the office or the factory, and (viii) position and prospects of any business proposed to be purchased by the company, etc.

G. *Reports on Meetings*

The secretary is also required to prepare reports on the proceedings of meetings: (a) for the benefit of members who could not attend the meeting, (b) for the filing section for the purpose of record, and (c) for publication in newspapers.

These reports may be verbatim or summarized. The usual practice is to report verbatim the resolution passed at the meeting and to summarise the other proceedings.

Reports on meetings are not to be confused with minutes, which are the official records of the proceedings of a meeting.

(b) On the basis of the number of persons entrusted with the drafting of reports:

(1) Reports by Individuals

Reports submitted by the executive heads of various departments, the company secretary, the auditor, the solicitor, etc. are reports by individuals. These reports are naturally related to the work in their own department. The production manager may be asked to submit a report on a proposed new method of production or the sales manager may be required to submit a report on the declining sales and the means to boost them.

(2) Reports by Committees or sub-Committees

Sometimes, reports are needed on subjects that do not concern any one department, or they are so important that it is thought advisable to associate more than one department, or they are so important that it is thought advisable to associate more than one person with them. In such cases, committees or sub-committees are formed to prepare reports. Reports of committees of directors or of *ad hoc* committees are such reports. These reports are written after a careful and cautious deliberation of the members. They are formal in style and impersonal in tone. They may be signed by the Chairman and the Secretary.

(c) On the basis of the nature of reports—

(1) Periodic or Routine Reports

These reports are prepared and presented at regular, prescribed intervals in the usual routine of business. They may be submitted annually, semi-annually, quarterly, monthly or weekly. Generally, they contain a mere statement of facts, in detail or in summarized form, without any opinion or recommendation. So, they are mainly informational reports. They present a chronological record of events.

Examples: Reports of Directors to the Annual General Meeting of a Company, Auditor's Reports, Administrative Reports of Government departments, municipal bodies, semi-government undertakings, universities, chambers of commerce, Trade Associations, etc.

Details Covered: The main purpose of this type of report is to present a correct and coherent picture of the working of the firm or the department concerned during the period covered by the report. It should cover the following details:

(i) A brief summary of the important events of the period under review in their chronological order;

(ii) A brief summary of the turnover;
(iii) A brief account of production;
(iv) Financial statements showing gross and net profits, assets and liabilities, dividend declared, transfer to reserve fund, provision made for contingencies; etc.
(v) A reference to the condition of the plant, machinery, equipment, if desirable;
(vi) A reference to important changes in the administration; and
(vii) A comparative study of the current period along with relevant previous periods.

(2) Progress Report

These reports are meant to describe and assess progress made during a particular period. They present an account of the work already done, work in progress with other relevant facts, and details of the work yet to be completed.

Examples: Progress reports are needed when a company undertakes the construction of a factory or the modernization of a plant, or a research project, or say a dam or a water supply scheme is undertaken by a Government or Semi-government body.

Details covered: The progress report should include the following details:

(i) A brief introduction to the nature of the project being covered by the report.
(ii) A brief account of the work completed in an earlier period.
(iii) An account of the work-in-progress during the period under review, assessment of the work done during this period, comparison of this work with the work during earlier periods in order to ascertain if the progress has been satisfactory.
(iv) An account of any special problems that had to be faced and the solutions of those problems
(v) Important aspects of the work yet to be completed.
(vi) Any obstructions or hindrances that might slow down the work, any other relevant information that might be of help in the completion of the project.

(3) Examination Reports

These reports are specially commissioned to cover important aspects or events. They are prepared after thorough investigation. Old files are studied. Personal interviews are held, questionnaires are circulated among people, surveys are conducted, relevant literature is studied, the important facts are compiled and analysed and certain conclusions arrived at. These reports may or may not contain recommendations but the findings or conclusions of those who have prepared them definitely influence the final decisions.

Examples: Reports to assess the effectiveness of a new device introduced in the factory, a report on a fire accident causing substantial financial loss, a report on declining sales or increasing cost of production, a report on unsatisfactory functioning of a branch office, a report on the need of mechanizing the accounts department, credit report submitted by the manager of a branch of a bank to the head office to enable the latter to take a decision on a loan application, etc.

Details Covered: Examination reports usually cover the followings details:

(i) The aim and scope of the report,

(ii) A brief account of the methods adopted for the collection of the data, inspection of site, records in the old files of the company, personal interviews with the employees as well as customers, questionnaires circulated among people, study of relevant literature, etc.

(iii) Analysis of the data so collected,

(iv) Findings, and

(v) Recommendations, if asked for.

(4) Recommendation Reports

In nature, these reports are not very different from examination reports. Only, these reports must end with specific recommendations. In such reports, the data is analysed in such a manner that the analysis inevitably leads to the recommendation being made at the end. These reports are argumentative and persuasive in tone. They are very useful to large business houses.

Details Covered: Recommendation reports are expected to cover the following details:

(i) Aim and scope of the report,
(ii) Methods adopted for the collection of data,
(iii) Analysis of data,
(iv) Findings, and
(v) Recommendations for a definite programme of action.

(5) Statistical Reports

As the name suggests, these reports are largely made up of financial data, mathematical charts, tabular columns of figures, etc. Although statistical data may be introduced into other types of reports to corroborate facts and facilitate recommendations, if a report consists mainly of such data, there should be some justification in describing it as a statistical report.

Example: A report submitted by the costing department of a company is basically a statistical report.

Setting a suitable type of report

Before a writer undertakes to prepare a report, he must consider the following points:

(i) What kind of report is requested or expected?
(ii) How much time has been allowed to prepare the report?
(iii) What is the purpose of the report?
(iv) What exactly is to be examined?
(v) What facts are to be furnished?
(vi) For whom is the report meant? Of, who is going to read the report?

(i) The reporter may have been instructed to prepare a specific kind of report or there may be precedents to follow. But in majority of the instances, he will have to decide for himself whether he is to prepare an informal report, whether it is a statutory or non-statutory report. It is important that a reporter, right in the beginning, is clear about the lines along which he is to plan the content, form and style of the report.

(ii) The length of time the writer has been allowed to prepare the report can give him valuable guidance on the type of report expected. An informal report highlighting some important aspect of the problem may be acceptable if the time is short. But if there is sufficient time to make a thorough study of the problem and to conduct some research if needed, the reporter will have to prepare a formal report with definite conclusion, perhaps even specific recommendations. A salesman's weekly or bi-weekly reports to his main office can be short, informal reports. The secretary, who has been asked to prepare a report on the unsatisfactory functioning of a branch and has been allowed a week to study the problem in depth, will have to be formal and specific about his findings and recommendations.

(iii) The purpose of a report is perhaps the most important factor to bear in mind before deciding the type of report needed. If the writer has been asked to prepare a report on whether his company should set-up a new branch that involves considerable initial expenditure or on the advisability of merging into or collaborating with another company, these are matters of vital importance and they need very carefully written formal reports. Probably a number of people would be associated with writing such reports. But if the purpose of a report is simply to find out the incidence of late arrivals in the office, it is a simple affair and does not need much research.

(iv) Just as it is important to keep in mind the purpose of the report, it is also important to be constantly aware of what exactly is to be examined, to be studied. Such an awareness will eliminate much redundant labour; at the same time, it will help in the inclusion of all that is pertinent to a problem and will help in making the report a document complete in all respects.

Let us suppose the Development Manager of a bank has been asked to report on the feasibility of setting up a branch of the bank in a new colony. Exactly, what is to be examined: (i) What type of colony is this—residential, commercial or industrial? (ii) If it is primarily an industrial or commercial complex, what is the number and size of industrial complex, what is the number and size of industries or business houses? (iii) If it is a residential area, what is its population, what is the general standard of the residents, and what could be their saving capacity? Will the study of these facts suffice? Or has something of crucial importance been overlooked? A careful look at the three facts listed above will immediately reveal that something of vital importance has been left out: how many branches of other commercial banks are operating in this colony? Is not this really important? And if the report-writer is alert, he will have to examine the availability of suitable premises and make a rough estimate of the initial expenditure to be incurred and the amount of business expected.

Sometimes, a report of a very general nature involves considerable research. In such cases, it is advisable to find out if somebody else has earlier done some similar research. B. Maude, in his book, "Practical Communication for Managers" mentions the case of a friend who was asked to report on "the growth of nodules in pipes carrying fluids which contained copper". He spent several months and finally submitted his report to the Plant Superintendent. A few days later, he was shown another report, forwarded from another mine in the group, which covered the same ground and reached precisely the same conclusions. Obviously, if this friend had done some preliminary research on relevant literature available, his labour could have been saved.

(v) While studying the old files of the company or conducting a market survey, the reporter is likely to come across a number of interesting facts that appear to be relevant but in reality are not. The temptation to include them in the report will have to be resisted. A medley of facts is likely to preclude the central purpose and lead to confusion. So, it is very important to be clear about the facts that are to be included.

(vi) The last point to be kept in mind is: who is going to read the report? If the report is going to the Research Director, it ought to contain a detailed, step by step account of the investigations carried out along with detailed, minutely described findings. On the other hand, if your report is going to the Managing Director, who, you know, has implicit faith in you and is more interested in your recommendation, it is these recommendations which will have to be emphasized both in the beginning and at the end. This point is beautifully made by B. Maude:

> "Be reader-oriented. Don't include any information, which is surplus to the reader's requirements. If all he wants is a guideline to help him reach a particular decision, don't offer him a mass of tests and results and pages of statistics. If the report is to be considered by a committee of laymen, include adequate background information, avoid jargon, and stress your conclusions and recommendations".

Preparing the Report

Once you are clear about the purpose of writing a report, the persons for whom it is meant, the facts to be examined and the facts to be included, and the time at your disposal, and you know what type of report you are going to write, it is time to start the work. To write better, speak better, the following five steps are suggested to write a report:

(1) Investigating the sources of information,
(2) Taking notes,
(3) Analyzing the data,
(4) Making an outline, and
(5) Writing the report.

(1) Investigating the Sources of Information

Investigating the sources of information is a kind of spadework. It is to be done right in the beginning. The extent of investigation will, of course, depend on the length and importance of the report. Major sources of information are: company files, personal observation, interviews, letters, questionnaires, library research.

(a) Most of the relevant information is already contained in the old files of the company. Something is there like precedents and old findings and recommendations which may be of considerable help. So, it is very important to go through the old files of the company. Declining sales or rising costs of production are recurring phenomena. And their causes are also usually similar. In these cases, old files may be containing some valuable information.

(b) In reports on a fire accident or on the progress of a project, personal observation will be of greater help. It needs on the spot enquiry to ascertain the cause of fire or to find out why the work of installing a new plant is going on rather slowly.

(c) Complaints from customers about unsatisfactory services being provided by a branch might necessitate interviews. Interviews with the members of the staff may also be of some help. These interviews should be carefully recorded, clearly indicating the persons interviewed and the time and place of the interviews, letters may be written to different people.

(d) When a large number of people are to be contacted, the only practical method is to make use of a questionnaire. Such questionnaires are often prepared by large business houses to ascertain the popularity of their products or to find out the possibility of introducing some new products into the market. Questionnaires should never be lengthily. Questions should be prepared in such a way that they do not call for writing lengthily answers. Questions that just require ticking-off one of the many alternatives suggested are the best. If the results of questionnaires are incorporated in a report, a copy of the questionnaire should also be included.

(e) In reports on subjects of general nature, library research may be found useful. This includes reference to standard reference books and past as well as current issues of newspapers, trade publications and magazines.

(2) Taking Notes

In the course of investigations, the writer keeps on taking notes of anything that appears to be related to the subject. Then there is no time to analyse them and determine how they will be of help in the final report. But as the writer keeps turning them in his mind over and over again, a kind of pattern starts emerging and he begins to be clear about what is relevant and what is not. It is a very general kind of pattern but it gives the writer at least a starting point.

(3) Analyzing the Data

Now is the time to analyze the collected data in the light of the pattern that has evolved. A lot of data will have to be rejected while a need might be felt to collect more data. The final pattern will emerge at this stage. The writer should never hurry through this stage, since this is the most important stage in writing a report.

(4) Making an Outline

Once the final pattern of the report has taken shape in the writer's mind, he should prepare an outline to write the report. In this outline, the problem is stated, the facts are recorded, they are briefly analyzed, and the logical conclusions are arrived at. And outline is not essential, but it should be found extremely helpful in writing a systematic report.

(5) Writing the Report

The last stage is that of writing the report. It will need a constant shuttling between the outline and the notes. First a rough draft of the report is prepared. Then it is revised, pruned and polished. If the writer has some more time at this disposal, he will find it advantageous to come back to his rough draft after, say, a couple of days. This short interval will make his revision work really meaningful. The writer should also be careful that the language of the report is simple, unambiguous and free from grammatical errors. It is now time to type it out in a proper form and submit it.

ORGANIZATION OF A REPORT

There are three ways in which a report can be organized:

(1) Letter form

(2) Memorandum form
(3) Letter-text combination form

(1) Letter Form

In the case of brief, informal reports, the arrangement followed in business letters is adopted. Its main parts are: the heading or the title, date, address, salutation, the body, complimentary close and signature. It is usually written in the first person—I or we.

The body of the letter can be further divided into the following parts:

(a) *Introduction:* The introductory paragraphs present the terms of reference and the subject of study. Here, the writer states the problem confronting him in the light of the terms of reference and the relevant circumstances.
(b) *Findings:* The next few paragraphs present the findings of the investigation.
(c) *Recommendations:* Adopting the memorandum form is a simpler way of presenting the report, since here the formalities of the letter form are done away with. The title of the subject is stated on the top. This is followed by the name of the writer of the report, the date, the actual text and the conclusion. As in the letterform, the text of the report is divided into paragraphs with headings and sub-headings.

(2) Memorandum Form

Adopting the memorandum form is a simpler way of presenting the report, since there the formalities of the letter form are done away with. The title of the subject is stated on the top. This is followed by the name of the writer of the report, the date, the actual text and the conclusion. As in the letter form, the text of the report is divided into paragraphs with headings and sub-headings.

Large business houses have different types of printed forms to send reports. This simplifies the procedure and ensures uniformity of style.

(3) Letter-Text Combination Form

Long reports are usually written in the letter-text combination form: A complete report in this form includes three major parts:

1. Introductory material
2. The body of the report
3. Addenda.

The complete outline of such a report is as follows:

(I) Introductory parts:

- A. Letter of Transmittal or Letter of Presentation
- B. Title page
- C. Contents page
- D. Summary

(II) Body of the report

- A. Definition of problem
- B. Method or procedure
- C. Finding
- D. Conclusions and recommendations

(III) Addenda

- A. Bibliography
- B. Appendix
- C. Index

It is not essential that a report contains all these parts.

Long Reports containing most of these parts are generally submitted in a book form.

Letter of Transmittal or Letter of Presentation: A letter of transmittal is a routine letter written to transmit the report from the writer to the reader. It performs several important functions: (i) it provides a permanent record of transfer; (ii) it shows the date on which the report was submitted; (iii) it states the name and position of the writer of the report; (iv) it also states when and by whom the report was authorized; and (v) it may invite the reader's comments and suggestions.

A letter of presentation is slightly different from a letter of transmittal. In addition to giving the information contained in the letter of transmittal, it usually states the purpose and scope of the report, refers to the writer's sources of information, and highlights special features.

If a letter of transmittal is written, the additional matter put in the letter of presentation is included in the first part of the body under the heading 'Definition of the problem'.

Title Page: The title page gives the title or heading of the report, the person(s) to whom it is submitted, the date of submission and the name of the writer(s).

Contents Page: This page gives the title and the page number of each chapter. If the report contains illustrations, the contents page may also contain a table of illustrations with their page numbers.

Summary: In case the report is very lengthy, it is advisable to include a summary or synopsis of the report for ready reference.

Definition of Problem: This is the first part of the body of the report. Here, the terms of reference, the subject of study and its importance and scope are stated.

Method or Procedure: It explains how the investigations were made and what the sources of information were.

Findings: This is the main part of the report. It contains the facts found out by the writer along with his comments. It may include charts, graphs, statistical tables and even excerpts from other published reports. These may either be incorporated in this part of the report, or if they are unwieldy and likely to distract, they are put in the end in the form of an appendix.

Conclusions and Recommendations: On the basis of the facts and data presented under the heading 'findings', the writer draws some definite conclusions. Then, he puts forward some concrete suggestions or recommendations. If the report is prepared by a committee or sub-committee to be presented at a meeting of the general body for adoption, the recommendations are put in the form of 'motion' or 'resolutions'.

Bibliography: If the report is based on extensive research, it is customary to add a list of references and bibliography to indicate the sources the writer consulted to draw his material.

Appendix: Statistical data, charts and diagrams that are not incorporated in the main body of the report in order to keep the main line of argument un-entangled, are put at the end in the form of an appendix.

Index: In case of lengthy reports, an index of the contents of the report may be included.

Signature: A report must be dated and signed by the persons(s) who has (have) submitted it. In the case of a report prepared by a committee or a sub-committee, if it is very important, all the members may sign it, otherwise the signature of the chairman will suffice. If the report is not unanimous, it may be signed only by the assenting members. The dissenting members may submit a separate minority report or they may sign the majority report with a note of dissent.

REPORTS BY INDIVIDUALS

The managers, secretaries, accountants, chief executives and experts in certain fields are often required to submit reports on certain important issues like decline in sales, the suitability of some premises, the reorganization of office, the changes on diversification, exports promotion, the desirability of setting up a new branch, etc.

Some of these reports do call for technical knowledge and acquaintance with business subtleties and intricacies. Low output of a plant, for example, needs technical expertise. But most of the problems are usually general. Apply your general knowledge and concentrate on the proper arrangement and organization of the material at your command. Sometimes, imagination can be of greater help than actual knowledge.

Note: Carefully go through the model reports in the following pages and try to grasp the essential features. An effort has been made to make them free from technical encumbrances so that the general essentials are easier to assimilate.

Reports by Managerial Personnel and Executives

(1) Report of a Manager on the Suitability of some Premises

Comments: Large business houses, banks, insurance companies, etc. are often required to set-up new branches. When business expands, the accommodation already occupied appears to be inadequate and new premises have to be searched for. Industrial houses have also to look out for new sites for their diversification activities.

In such cases, it is usual to depute an executive who goes about inspecting various sites or buildings, offices, shops or godowns available and submits a report on their suitability. While drafting such a report, the following points should be taken care of:

(a) Refer to the resolution or order authorizing you to submit this report.

(b) A brief reference may be made to the growing requirements of the company, bank or factory because of which it has been felt desirable to look for new premises.

(c) Consider the suitability of a few premises available.

(d) Suggest the best one among them. Refer to its advantages: suitable location, modern construction, spacious rooms, the possibility of having good show cases, good storing capacity, the availability of other facilities, etc.

(e) Mention some of the drawbacks and disadvantages. It may be situated in a very congested area with a lot of noise around or some other important facilities may not be available. Explain how these drawbacks can be overcome or how its advantages overweigh the disadvantages. Make your report look impartial lest it should give the impression that you are personally interested that the premises is acquired by the company.

(f) Clearly specify the terms on which the building can be rented or purchased.

(g) Give your recommendations in clear terms, without either looking over-enthusiastic or over-cautions. Remember that report should always look factual and disinterested.

REPORT

THE SERVEALL BANK,
BANK STREET
KIRATPUR.

Ref. No. 18th August, 2010

The General Manager,
The Serveall Bank,
Delhi.

Dear Sir,

Sub: Report on suitable premises for shifting the Kiratpur branch of the Serveall bank.

In accordance with your instructions, I visited our Kiratpur branch and carefully studied the business transactions being carried out here. I do find that Mr. R.L. Raina, our branch manager, is quite justified in desiring a shift to better premises.

This branch of our Bank was opened at Kiratpur in 1965 when Kiratpur was a small town with a population of about fifty thousand. Ever since, it has fast developed into an industrial city. Kiratpur Fertilizers, a public sector undertaking, and a unit of the Delhi Chemicals Limited, have started functioning here. With this industrial unit and a large number of other furniture making units firmly established, making this city as the industrial nucleus, a whole industrial complex has come into existence with huge potentialities for banking business. The population of the town has now gone up to three lakh.

The business of this branch has been steadily growing. It is a fact that it is one of the most profitably running branches of the Serveall Bank. Although the present premises of the bank are ideally situated yet these are being found highly inadequate. Every inch of the space available here has been pushed into service, with the result that the whole atmosphere appears to be heavily congested. During the peak business hours, the bank presents an unnerving sight. Such an atmosphere can be hardly considered conducive to efficient business transactions. Besides, with such discouraging looks, the Bank can neither attract nor cope with any new customers. Mr. Raina is right in his observation if we continue to function here, our further progress will be definitely jeopardized.

Since it is undesirable to move to a distant place, I have concentrated all my efforts on finding out some building suitable for our growing requirements in this very locality. The Bank Street is one of the biggest shopping complexes of Kiratpur and it is not easy to find any suitable building here. But fortunately, a building just in our neighborhood, double the size of the one we are now occupying and spacious enough to meet our requirements of coming ten years is falling vacant next month. Its biggest advantage is its close proximity to our present premises, so that if we shift there, none of our customers will be inconvenienced.

It is double storeyed building with a large hall nearly 20 metre x 12 metre and two rooms 4.5 metre x 4 metre each on the ground floor and identical accommodation on the first floor. The large hall on the ground floor can provide enough space to set-up all the counters needed. One of the rooms can be converted into the branch manager's office while the other can be converted into the store room. The loans and advances section can be accommodated on the first floor. A part of the hall on the first floor can be changed into a room for lockers. The other two rooms can be used for keeping records and storing stationery. Of course, we shall have to bear ourselves the cost of constructing the strong room and the safe deposit vault as well as effecting any other changes we deem suitable.

I have already had preliminary negotiations with Mr. Sharukh Wajid, the owner of the building. He is also a valued customer of ours. It appears that he should be willing to rent out the building to us at a monthly rent of Rs. 52,000 a month. It will be initially leased out to us for a period of five years with option in our favour to renew lease for two further periods of five years each.

The rent of this building appears to be a little on the higher side, but in view of its strategic location, I have no hesitation in recommending that this building should immediately be rented.

I have verified from the property dealers that this building is free from all encumbrances. Estimates for the proposed alterations are enclosed. A letter of consent from Mr. Sharukh Wajid offering the building on a rental basis for a period of five years will be obtained and sent to you after we receive your approval 'in principle' to this change.

Yours faithfully,
F.A. Kulkarni
Development Manager.

(2) Report of a company secretary on general inefficiency and negligence of duty by the staff in a branch office

Comments: Company secretaries and executives are often required to visit the branch offices and report on general complaints of inefficiency. While drafting such a report, take care of the following points.

(a) Refer to the resolution or order authorizing you to visit the branch office and submit the report.

(b) Spell out the kind of inefficiency and negligence of duty you were required to investigate. It could include: (i) Lack of punctuality, (ii) Lack of prompt service to customers, (iii) Lack of prompt after sales service in case of refrigerators, TVs, etc.; (d) Inefficiency in the maintenance of records; (v) Inefficiency in prompt handling of correspondence; (vi) Inefficiency in prompt execution of orders; and (vii) Carelessness in execution of orders so that customers do not always get what they have ordered.

(c) Explain what you did to ascertain the truth about these complaints (*modus operandi*): (i) You talked to the branch manager, employees or workers, (ii) You went through the files and looked into the written complaints of the customers, checked the dates on which the orders were received and executed, etc., (iii) You had a direct talk with the customers, and (iv) You paid a surprise visit to the office or the factory to see whether punctuality was being observed.

(d) List your findings: (i) The staff might be inefficient on account of the inefficiency of the branch manager, (ii) The staff might be feeling bitter against the branch manager because of his generally rude or partial treatment, (iii) Engineers engaged to give after sales service might not be properly qualified, (iv) Careless maintenance of office records might be responsible for inefficient handling of correspondence.

(e) Now clearly give your recommendations. The recommendations will, of course, depend upon the nature of findings. You might recommend the transfer of the branch manager or the dismissal of inadequately qualified engineers or you might recommend the introduction of some different system. Perhaps inefficiency was due to overwork. Then you would naturally recommend the recruitment of additional staff.

REPORT

TELECRAFT ELECTRONICS LIMITED

12, Model Town,
Amritsar City

Ref. No. .... 14th April 2008

The managing Director,
Telecraft Electronics Limited,
Industrial Area,
Chandigarh.

Dear Sir,

Sub : General inefficiency and negligence of duty by the staff in our Amritsar branch.

In accordance with your instructions contained in your letter dated 14th March 2010, I personally came down to Amritsar to visit our Amritsar branch and look into it functioning. I have made some investigations and submit my report as hereunder:

Complaints

A number of customers who had purchased our Telecraft Deluxe or Telecraft Super TV sets had complained to the Head Office of poor after sales service being provided to them. All the complaints, directed to the Head Office out of sheer disgust, carried virtually the same refrain. In spite of their persistent telephone calls and even written reminders, no mechanics attended to their TV sets, and if, perchance, they did, they betrayed such abject incompetence that the complaints had to be renewed the very next day. Apart from this complaint, our sales record for the first two quarters of 2009 shows a steep decline of sales at our Amritsar branch.

Investigations

(1) I reached Amirtsar on 30th March 2010 and paid a surprise visit to the office at 11 A.M. I was shocked to find that more than half the members of the staff including Mr. D.K. Khera, our Branch manager, had not by then reported for work. A brief talk with some old, trusted members sent to Amritsar from the Head Office, revealed that very few members bothered to observe punctuality; reaching the office later than 11 A.M. was a usual practice. Mr. Khera actually arrived at 11.15 A.M.

(2) After Mr. Khera's arrival, I went through the complaints file. What a pathetic negligence of duty it was! Complaints lodged three days before had yet to be looked into. One particular customer complained

thrice between 12th March and 26th March that the picture on his TV set was blurred and flickering. His last complaint was dated 27th March but nobody had visited him.

(3) Our Telecraft Deluxe model enjoys enviable popularity in every northern state and was in great demand in the Amritsar zone till December 2010. The sales records show that against an average sale of twenty-five pieces per day during 2009, as few as fourteen pieces per day have been sold during 2010; this decline in sales is really alarming.

(4) I could notice general apathy and carelessness almost in every department. Incoming letters are not sorted in time, papers ready for filing lie piled up in heaps and even important cases are not disposed of in time.

Findings

(1) I have come to the conclusion that the present atmosphere in the office is least conducive to business and the responsibility for its deterioration lies squarely on the branch manager, Mr. Khera. One of the reliable workers has disclosed to me in confidence that one of Mr. Khera's brother has set-up a small factory to manufacture clinical thermometers and Mr. Khera, in all probability, has joined him as a partner. He is trying to promote his own interest at the cost of our work.

(2) Our Amritsar branch has two mechanics to take care of after sales service. Both of them were appointed by Mr. Khera and neither of them is well qualified. They hold diplomas from little known institutes. One of them is also related to Mr. Khera. I do not think they are competent enough to satisfy the customers and I would not be surprised if they have spoiled a number of sets through their mishandling.

(3) In my opinion, prospective customers of TV sets largely depend upon the recommendations of the present owners. If one customer gets dissatisfied, he

can discourage at least three others. I attribute our poor sales in the current year to the dissatisfaction of our patrons.

(4) The casualness with which the office work is being conducted is also to be attributed to the indifferent attitude of Mr. Khera. Since he is very scantily to be seen in the office, a sense of unconcern has gripped the entire staff.

Recommendations

(1) I have no hesitation in recommending that Mr. Khera may be served with a notice and a really efficient man may be sent here from the Head Office so that the functioning of the branch is again streamlined. We shall have to take extra pains to re-establish the reputation we have lost and to extricate the staff from their present state of lethargy. Hence a really experienced officer should be sent here to take charge of this branch.

(2) The services of the two mechanics, still on probation, should be terminated, and some experienced engineers should be sent from the Head Office.

(3) Some more transfers may be desirable, but it would be advisable to effect them in consultation with the new Branch Manager.

Yours faithfully,
S.N. Mehra
Secretary

(3) A Sales Manager's report on increasing competition from rival enterprises and suggestions to overcome it.

Comments

(a) Refer to the letter assigning you the task of submitting this report.

(b) You can briefly mention that the sales have gone down owing to competition from rival enterprises. You can refer to the sales report already submitted to indicate the extent of decline, but there is no need to mention these details here.

(c) Analyze all the probable causes responsible for fall in sales. Explain the type of competition being offered by the rival enterprises, whether they have better quality to offer, their sales organization is better, or their publicity campaign is more effective.

(d) Give your recommendations in the light of this analysis.

REPORT

SWASTIK SOAP MILLS LIMITED
10, Mahatma Gandhi Marg,
Kanpur (U.P).

18th August, 2009

Ref. No.
The Managing Director,
Swastik Soap Mills Limited,
Kanpur

Dear Sir,

Sub: Declining sales owing to competition from rival enterprises

In accordance with your letter No. SSM/Sales/26 dated 8th August, 2009, assigning me the task of finding out why the sale of Swastik Soaps and detergent powders has considerably gone down during the last six months, I wish to report as under:

During the last six months, there has been a spurt of new brands of soaps and detergent powders in the market. Two of them have been marketed by establishments of great repute. New entrants who have started manufacturing them on a small scale, with an eye mainly on the local markets, are quite numerous, and what is more alarming, their number is multiplying quite fast. Together, they have made a considerable dent into our sales.

(1) In order to capture the market, our competitors are selling their products at rates much lower than ours.

(2) Their *modus operandi* is door-to-door publicity and sales. This method enjoys several advantages:

   (a) From April to July, young boys and girls are available to sell these products at very convenient rates of commission.

   (b) People often buy things from these boys and girls in order to encourage them.

   (c) Girls willingly demonstrate the good quality of the soaps and powders. They are out to sell and disarm their more fussy and fastidious customers. Even otherwise, their manners are winsome and persuasive.

   (d) These offers are often accompanied with bonus or gifts offers. Small packs are offered at attractive discounts. Free gifts are given with economy packs; finally, bonus coupons are left with the customers entitling them to get three packs for the cost of only two up to a certain date. Thus they not only affect our immediate sales but also considerably darken our future prospects.

   (e) If we are still able to hold our own in the market, it is mainly because of our reputation as producers of high quality soaps and detergent powders. Some of our customers refuse to be tempted by cheap offers and prefer to buy the standard products we offer. But the competition is very keen if we do not immediately take remedial steps, we shall be in the danger of being undersold.

Recommendations

(1) Although our products compare favourably with any

other quality products available in our country yet I think there is still some possibility of improvement. I understand that our research department has discovered a new chemical compound that fights direct more effectively and is also economical. We should introduce a new, improved product in the market and build up a massive publicity campaign around it.

(2) Our packing also needs improvement. It is time we give our old products some kind of face lift, some new image that may be more in tune with the spirit of the modern times.

(3) We should make special arrangements with the Vividh Bharati and the Doordarshan to advertise our products. Brief messages can also be printed on post cards and inland letters. Regular advertisements preferably in dailies and film magazines can also prove useful.

(4) It is high time we also undertook door-to-door sales. Now that the vacations are over and schools and colleges have re-opened, our rival enterprises will be forced to slow down. So, we can exploit the situation and boost our sales.

(5) We should also offer some gifts along with our products. To offer an attractive and sturdy washing brush with every economy pack of detergent powder and a small tin of Ranipal S with six cakes of washing soap would be a really good idea. Bonus coupons may also be tried.

If we try the methods I have recommended, I have no doubt that we shall soon be able to overcome the challenge of our competitors and recapture the market.

Yours faithfully,

G.S. Mirchandani,
Sales Manager

(4) Report of sales manager on the prospects of setting up a new branch

How to go about it?

(a) Refer to the letter assigning you the task of submitting the report.
(b) Mention the type of study undertaken and the investigations carried out.
(c) Systematically put down your findings, (i) The potential of the market, (ii) The existing units engaged in similar business, and (iii) Why it should be advisable to open a branch there rather than give an agency to somebody.
(d) If you have come across suitable accommodation to house the proposed branch, give its details.
(e) Now give your recommendations.

Report

TOPAZ INDIA LIMITED
12, Nehru Nagar, Jalandhar

Ref. No. . . . . 25th August, 2010

The Directors,
Topaz India Limited,
Jalandhar

Gentlemen,

Sub : A new branch proposed to be set-up at Bhatinda, a town in the Punjab

As instructed in your letter No. TIL/be/77/23 dated 31st March, assigning me the task of exploring the possibilities of setting up a branch office of Topaz India Limited at Bhatinda and finding out suitable premises there, I wish to submit as under:

Bhatinda, a sleepy town in a remote corner of the Punjab, has suddenly stirred into activity with the Government decision to expand and further develop the cantonment area there. The M.E.S. offices have already been shifted there and a bigger cantonment is coming up very fast.

A thermal plant, a unit for the manufacture of fertilizers, and a huge dairy project have also been set-up at Bhatinda. Oil refinery is also coming up. The produce of the white gold (cotton) on large area has made the farmers' purses heavy. An Engineering College is already ten years old. With a constant inflow of government employees as well as workers in other industrial undertakings, the population of this town is fast multiplying. The population has swelled to five lac souls. A vast commercial complex is also under development. The original inhabitants of Bhatinda as well as the neighbouring areas, with their newly acquired riches, have suddenly become conscious of their living standards. Jakhal, a town in the neighbourhood, is a famous wheat market. A string of small towns between these two are also prospering.

Thus I feel that there are very good prospects of selling our Topaz Refrigerators here. At present, there are two shops in Bhatinda dealing in all brands of refrigerators including ours. Apart from refrigerators, they also stock washing machines, stereo systems, tape recorders, mixers, and other electrical gadgets. It is not possible for them to look after the sales of our refrigerators. They operate on a small scale, their methods of dealing are orthodox and old fashioned, their after sales service is inadequate and display facilities are virtually non-existent.

Close to the main kikar bazaar where these two shops are situated, a modern shopping complex (Raunak Mall) is being developed. Here, I have come across a spacious showroom, situated in the heart of the market with storage facilities in the basement, available for immediate occupation. Mr. Ram Singh, the owner of the shop, is willing to rent it out to us at a monthly rent of Rs. 60,000, initially for five years. A letter from Mr. Singh indicating his willingness to lease out his shop to us along with an estimate showing in detail the amount of money required to set-up and run the branch is enclosed.

I strongly recommend that this soap may be occupied at the initial lease offer of five years. The landlord can be persuaded to give us two options of five years each.

We should send our assistant sales manager to take charge of this branch. While experienced mechanics to give efficient and expert after sales service may also be sent from Delhi, the other subordinate staff can be locally employed. Their knowledge of the local market can be of use to us in the beginning.

We should immediately undertake the furnishing and decoration of the show room and arrange for publicity. We can select really prominent sites to put up our hoardings.

If we can start functioning here by 15th March, we can have a busy and prosperous summer season because in April, there is harvesting season and the farmers will have surplus with them.

Yours faithfully,

P.K. Manchanda
Sales Manager

(5) A Company secretary's report on a proposal for the Reorganization of the Office

A specimen is given below:

Comments

As a company expands its activities, the volume of work commensurately increases. This increase is never proportionately distributed over the various sections. While the pressure increases on the accounts, correspondence and records departments, the work in the shares transfer department is usually lightened. This necessitates occasional reorganization of the office.

(1) Clearly mention your views on the imbalance, dealing in detail with the various departments.
(2) If some alterations in the building can offer additional accommodation, they may also be suggested.

(3) The re-organization proposals should be put forward in such a manner that the concerned departmental heads are neither inconvenienced nor offended. In fact, it would be better to consult them before making the suggestions to the board of directors.

Report

ALLIED SALES LIMITED
12, Indira Gandhi Nagar
Shimla (H.P.).

Ref. No. . . . . 25th August, 2009.

The Board of Directors
Allied Sales Limited
Shimla.

Sub : Proposed re-organization of the Office.

Dear Sirs,

In accordance with the instructions given to me by the board of directors at their meeting held on 25th March 2008, I have thoroughly examined the proposal made by the Office Superintendent for the reorganization of the Company's office and would like to report as under:

The Company started functioning in 2002, nearly eight years ago. During this short period, it has made tremendous progress, particularly since it undertook export of Indian handicrafts and readymade garments. At present, the company's business has grown six times what it was in the first few years, after its inception. Work has enormously increased in the Accounts, Correspondence and Records Departments. The Share Transfer Department is overstaffed. The Public Relations Department has also got two surplus members. Besides, while every inch of space in the Accounts Department has been pressed into service causing congestion and a general atmosphere of suffocation has been generated, the Share Transfer Department has plenty of free space. The following suggestions for the re-organization of the office may, therefore, be considered to streamline its functioning.

The Accountant Department should be shifted to Room No. 21, at present occupied by the Share Transfer Department. This is the biggest room in the building and is the only room to adequately house the ever-increasing Accounts Department. The Share Transfer Department can be given Room No. 16, at present with the Accounts Department. Besides, two clerks, Shri P.K. Pahwa and Shri R.K. Bhakshi working in the Share Transfer Department should also be transferred to the Accounts Department.

The Correspondence Department also requires some assistance as its workload has considerably increased during the last a few months. Shri S.A. Salaria, a clerk in the Public Relations Department, may be transferred to the Correspondence Department; Shri Salaria has some experience of handling correspondence also.

In view of the recent rise in the volume of records, I feel that the Records Department is also understaffed. The Public Relation Department could, perhaps, also spare the services of Shri Jodha Singh, a senior clerk, to be posted to Records Department

I would like to add that I have already talked over these proposals to the concerned departmental heads and they have assured me of their full-co-operation.

I am sure that after these changes are effected, the office will be able to function more efficiently.

Yours faithfully,

H.N. Rathi
Secretary

REPORTS BY COMMITTEES

(1) Report of a sub-committee of directors on declining sales with suggestions to promote them.

Comments

(a) It is a formal report and has to be carefully prepared

since the future policy of the Company will largely depend on it.

(b) Refer to the resolution of the Board of Directors according to which the sub-committee has been appointed.

(c) Make a mention of the work done, scrutiny of the sales reports and other important files, personal interviews with important customers, detailed study of the markets.

(d) Enlist the causes responsible for the decline in sales in a systematic manner. Devote a separate paragraph to every cause like general depression in the market, competition of the rival enterprises, decline in the quality of the goods of the company, lack of proper sales organization, inefficient publicity, etc.

(e) Now give your recommendations, again in a systematic manner.

(f) If desirable, a covering letter can be written.

Report

NEW LOOK COSMETICS LIMITED

20, Tower Clock
New Railways Crossing
Kanpur.

24th August, 2009

Ref. No. ....
The Directors,
New Look Cosmetics Limited,
Kanpur

Sub: Report on the declining sales of our cosmetics.

Gentlemen,

We have carefully examined the various causes of steep decline in the sales of our cosmetics as desired by you in the resolution passed at the Board meeting held on 10th March 2010. A brief report of our investigations into causes, and recommendations are being sent herewith. We hope that a quick action will be taken on these recommendations so that any further decline is arrested.

Yours faithfully,
U.S. Sahani
Chairman
V.K. Chaudhari
Secretary

Encl: Report on the declining sales of our cosmetics.

Report of the Sub-committee of the directors of New Look Cosmetics Limited on the declining sales of the cosmetics

Terms of Reference

The members of the sub-committee were appointed in accordance with the following resolutions adopted by the Board of Directors in the Board meeting held on 19th March, 2010:

(a) That a sub-committee be appointed to study the causes of declining sales of the cosmetics produced by the company and to make recommendations for the promotion of sales.

(b) That the sub-committee may consist of Shri U.S. Sahani, Chairman and Shri V.K. Choudhary, Secretary.

Work Done (Investigations)

(1) The Sub-committee scrutinized the sales reports for different quarters of 2009-10 and compared them with the sales reports for the previous years.

(2) The sub-committee made a careful study of the cosmetics market in order to ascertain whether there had been a general slump in the market or the decline had been peculiar to our company alone.

(3) The sub-committee interviewed the wholesale

dealers stocking the cosmetics of our company as well as the retailers and a large number of actual consumers.

(4) The sub-committee actually circulated a questionnaire among nearly one thousand actual users of the company's products to ascertain their views.

(5) The sub-committee had the cold cream, the compact, the hair cream, the talcum powder, the shampoos, the lip-sticks and the nail enamels carefully analyzed by some chemists of repute in order to ascertain their quality.

Findings

(1) The sub-committee found that there had been a steep decline in the company's sales during the year 2008, that this trend roughly started during Nov. 2007 and continues till today. During this period, the sales have come down to nearly half of the sales in 2007 and 2008. It was also found that this decline was peculiar to the products of the New Look Cosmetics Limited and there had been no general slump in the market.

(2) The questionnaire reveals that the consumers are not stratified with the quality of our products. Some of them have clearly stated that there has been a deterioration of quality. Our luster-crème shampoo leaves the hair dry and rough. The ladies using cosmopolitan compact report that after a little while, it starts looking caky or masky. The antiseptic Talcum powder does not act as an effective deodorant. The chemists' reports also point to the unsatisfactory quality of our cosmetics.

(3) Our publicity also leaves much to be desired. We are still following the old modes of publicity like sending long wordy insertions in the dailies. Our

publicity department has not cared to exploit the more effective media like the radio and the television. Our insertions also are not attractive. They are not designed to appeal to the consumer psychology.

(4) During the last two years, some rival enterprises have entered the market in a big way. They offer more attractive terms to their dealers. They have also undertaken door-to-door publicity and sales of their products.

Recommendations

(1) The first thing to be done is, obviously, to take care of the quality of our products. It appears that we shall have to appoint better qualified chemists and subject our cosmetics to strict quality control system.

(2) We should give a new look to our products and build a massive publicity campaign to boost their sales.

(3) We should revise the terms of sale on the basis of market information relating to credit and discount rates.

(4) We should also undertake door-to-door publicity and sales and offer attractive gifts and bonus coupons.

(5) We should make a review of the sales promotion schemes every three months during the next year.

A copy of the questionnaire circulated among the consumers and the chemists' reports on the quality of our products are enclosed for your reference.

U.S. Sahani
Chairman,
V.K. Choudhary
Secretary.
Kanpur
14th April 2010

(2) Report by a sub-committee of directors to enquire into the possibilities of setting up a new cold storage accompanied by a note of dissent.

Comments

(a) Give the terms of reference.
(b) Explain why setting up a cold storage at this place will be a profitable proposition.
(c) If a suitable site is available, give its details.
(d) Give your recommendations.
(e) The dissenting member records his note of dissent separately. He does not sign the main report. He signs only his note of dissent. The note of dissent by no means indicates that the main report will be rejected, it simply means that the dissenting member desires to be free from any responsibility in the decision taken on the basis of this report.

Report

SINGH AND BHATIA LIMITED
5, Indira Gandhi Marg,
Jaipur (Rajasthan)

Ref No. ..... 24th August, 2010.

The Directors,
Singh and Bhatia Limited,
Jaipur (Rajasthan).

Sub : Report on the proposed new cold storage in the Chaura Bazar Area.

Gentlemen,

In accordance with the resolution passed at the Board meeting held on 15th January 2010, instructing us to submit a report on the possibilities of setting up a cold storage in the Chaura Bazar area, we have just completed preliminary enquiries and wish to submit the report enclosed herewith.

Yours faithfully,

S.S. Bhatia (Chairman)
V.K. Chopra (Director)
Narinder Pawar (Director)
Ravi Jaryal (Secretary)

Encl: Report

Report of the sub-committee on the proposed new cold storage in the Chaura Bazar Area.

The members of the sub-committee were appointed in accordance with the following resolutions adopted by the Board of Directors at the Board of meeting of 15th January 2010.

(1) That a sub-committee be appointed to consider the possibilities of setting up a cold storage in the Chaura Bazar Area on the Lake road, Jaipur.
(2) That the sub-committee would consist of Shri S.S. Bhatia, Chairman, Shri V.K. Chopra and Shri Narinder Pawar, Directors and Shri Ravi Jaryal, Secretary (and convener).

Work Done (Investigation)

(1) The sub-committee visited Chaura Bazar Area, Lake Road to study its suitability for setting up a cold storage.
(2) The sub-committee met a number of property dealers operating in this locality to find out if a suitable site could be made available.
(3) The sub-committee met five times between 16th January and 23rd January to discuss the findings and formulate concrete suggestions.

Findings

(1) Chaura Bazar Area is a very suitable place for a cold

storage. It is only 2 km away from the main vegetable and fruit market of Jaipur, situated on Lake Road itself.

(2) This area is also connected with Jaipur Railway station.

(3) The Jaipur Development Authority is planning a big station for road carriers at the junction of Pink GT Road and Lake Road, nearly three kilometers away from Chaura Bazar Area. Thus this area will be a very convenient place from all points of view.

(4) At present, there are only two cold storages near the market and they cannot provide adequate space to store huge bulks of vegetables and fruit pouring day in and day out into the market.

(5) Some dealers have to store their goods in cold storages situated far away from the market, incurring unnecessary expenditure on transport and facing a good deal of inconvenience, too.

(6) A very suitable site on the main Lake Road has been found available. The site is big enough to construct a cold storage and to set-up small office. The complete plan of the area giving a correct picture of the location of this site is enclosed.

(7) The Government is giving all kinds of facilities to develop this industrial area. The facilities include steady supply of electricity and loans to construct the building.

Recommendations

The sub-committee, with the exception of Shri Narinder Pawar, make the following recommendations:

(1) The proposed site should be immediately taken up and necessary arrangements made for the construction of the building.

(2) Orders should be placed for the purchase of the cold storage plant.

(3) The entire project should be put under the charge of Shri M.K. Mahindru, the Development Manager.

Dated at Jaipur, on January 23, 2010

S.S. Bhatia (Chairman)
V.K. Bhatia (Director)
S.N. Malhotra (Secretary)

Encls:

(1) The plan of the Chaura Bazar Area showing the exact situation of the proposed site for the cold storage.
(2) Note of Dissent by Shri Narinder Pawar, Director.

Note of Dissent

Since I disagree with the other members of the sub-committee on the issue of setting up a cold storage in the Chaura Bazar Area, I herewith append my note of dissent and disclaim all responsibility from the above report.

My views on this issue are as follows:

(1) The vegetables market of Jaipur depends more on the fresh supplies arriving daily from the neighbouring areas. Not many dealers make use of the cold storage facilities.
(2) Even assuming that there will be dealers desirous of such facilities, with two cold storages already functioning and another two fast coming up, there will not be much scope for additional business. My impression formed as a result of a careful study of this market is that it cannot feed more than three, or at the most, four cold storages.
(3) The initial expenditure of constructing the building and purchasing the plant and running expenditure will be utterly out of proportion to profits made.
(4) There is acute shortage of power in this region. Hence most of the factories can not run at their optimum. Since a constant supply of power is very essential for a cold storage, we shall need our own generator. I do not think it will ultimately prove to be an economically viable proposition to set up a cold storage here.

I would, therefore, suggest that the company should consider other, more profitable, avenues of expansion and investment.

Narinder Pawar
Dissenting member of the Sub-Committee

Dated at. . . . . , this . . . ... day of August, 2010

CHAPTER

16

Non-verbal Communication

Present day communication is the extension of human communication. Human beings alone have evolved the language of words to convey their thoughts in a structured manner. We tend to share our feelings and emotions of joy, love, anger and hatred by smiling, patting, shouting, frowning or using other wordless clues. We know now perfectly well that such a non-verbal expression of feelings comes spontaneously. At times, we deliberately lace our words with expressive tones, gestures and facial expressions to heighten and modify the meaning of our words.

Unworded messages are transmitted by non-verbal clues and signs (bodily movements and gestures). They (the unworded messages) exist in the forms of meta communications and kinesics communications (body talk). Our response to them influences our interpretation of message received through words.

META-COMMUNICATION

A Meta-communication is an implied meaning conveyed by the choice of words, tones of voice, fumbling, silence or omission. It is a message communicated not through words, but along with words.

KINESICS COMMUNICATION

Kinesics communication is a message conveyed through non-verbal acts.

Non-verbal acts in the forms of body movements, such as gestures, winking, smiling, postures, or style of dressing and grooming send out a message that supports or contradicts the verbal message.

Kinesics communication is also known as body language or body talk. It includes the entire non-verbal behaviour of the communicator. A non-verbal act is usually unconscious. It transmits the unstated feelings, attitudes and hidden intentions of the speaker.

Paralanguage includes pitch, loudness of voice, and speech breakers such as 'er', 'ah', 'uh' or hesitations.

Leakage: A non-verbal message conveyed through bodily movements is known as 'leakage'. A successful receiver is able to observe and interpret the 'leakage'.

CHARACTERISTICS OF NON-VERBAL COMMUNICATION

Verbal and non-verbal communications co-exist. Words literally mean what they say. But those who are keen in observing how the words are written or spoken, find something additional in their meanings. A writer's style or a speaker's tone or voice or facial expressions or movements indicate the attitude and feelings in addition to what is being expressed through words.

Non-verbal act	*Possible unworded Idea*
A senior looks at his/her watch while you are taking.	"Your time is over, go away".
A person winks after saying	"Do not believe what I just said".
	"I am always very busy".

a thing.	
An executive is always late for the meeting.	"I don't bother about your time".
A speaker prefers to speak from the floor, not the dais.	"I want to show my sense of equality with (you) audience".

Instrumental Body Movements

When we move our hands to perform some work, such as wash our face, it is an instrumental movement and not a symbolic clue. All body movements, with the exception of instrumental movements, are meaningful communication.

Communicative movements act as non-verbal clues. For example, wiping one's mouth when confronted by a superior person communicates nervousness. The movement of hand to signal goodbye communicates courtesy and friendship.

Conscious or Unconscious

Non-verbal clues reveal the state of mind, the inner feelings and emotions which may be real or just affected. Trained actors and orators intentionally use gestures, facial expressions, bodily movements and postures to create the intended impact on the listeners/audience. Effective writers use stylistic devices to convey hidden feelings and attitudes.

But in real-life situations, generally, we betray our inner thoughts and feelings through unconscious signs. The speaker may not realise that he/she is conveying these feelings.

The interpretation of non-verbal clues differs from person to person. For example, if the listener keeps on listening to you with continuous eye-contact, you may take it as a sign of effective attention and full acceptance, but to someone else, it could be a sign of the listener's helplessness.

The same gesture may be interpreted differently. For example, two colleagues are good friends. One of them pats the other endearingly. The pat will be taken as a loving gesture.

Body movements and facial expressions often occur spontaneously. They can support or contradict the verbal message. For example, the trembling feet of a speaker indicate nervousness even though the speaker says, "I feel encouraged and inspired to stand before such a learned audience."

The dress or language used will reveal the communicator's status or education.

Similarly, pleasant words exchanged between two hostile parties would show their intention to put their differences aside.

CLASSIFICATION OF NON-VERBAL COMMUNICATION

Exchange of message sans words (feelings and ideas), which take place between two parties, fall within the category of non-verbal communication.

Body movements and facial expressions often occur spontaneously. They can support or contradict the verbal message.

Non-verbal forms of communication include—Paralanguage, Meta-communication, Kinesics, Grooming, Proxemics, Time, Language, and Physical Surroundings.

Symbols of Body Language

When you move different parts of your body such as hands, feet, head (nodding), shoulders (shrugging), eyes (blinking), or stand, sit or walk (postures), you are expressing your feelings and emotions involuntarily along with words. All bodily movements act as symbols (signs), which contribute to the meaning of the message received and interpreted by the listener.

Let us consider Ekman's classification of communicative movements into five types.

Emblems

When the movement of body parts represents ideas as icons or images, the communicative act is emblematic. In other words, the communication represents icons or images. It pictures the meaning non-verbally through a physical image. For instance, a circle made with the thumb and index finger, and the rest of the fingers stretched out straight acts as an emblem for the American sign for "OK". This OK sign is meaningful for those cultures that use the English alphabet. The circle is an image of the letter 'O'.

But in a different culture, the same circle 'O' can represent a coin, just as it does in Japan.

The emblem does indicate a clear meaning, but this meaning is based on culture. For instance, take an arbitrary gesture of holding up the thumb, which in Japan means "boss", and in India "perfect". Thus, same gesture has different meanings in different cultures.

Illustrators

Illustrators are movements of hands and arms for representing size, shape, frequency or speed of something. For instance, widely stretched arms show the enormous size, say of a serpent.

According to Ekman, a speaker uses illustrators when he or she is enthusiastic or fully involved in the subject being discussed. In such a state, the speaker involuntarily dramatizes ideas by using the movements of arms to focus on an idea or an event.

Body Manipulators

These are acts of touching one's own body or an object for no reason. It involves fidgeting with jewellery or touching one's buttons, these are unintentional acts. However, some consider them as clues of nervousness, anxiety or boredom.

Facial Expressions

The most expressive part of our body is our face. Our face reflects our thoughts and feelings. Smile, frown, blush, paleness, reveal our positive, and negative feelings. These are emotional expressions of the face. Our most fundamental emotions of happiness, sadness, anger, disgust, surprise, and fear are involuntarily marked on our face.

Regulators—Eye Movements

The eye movements such a squinting, winking, staring are called regulators. Eye contact, a smile or a frown are strong message of an interest, involvement, acceptance, rejection, or annoyance.

Facial Expressions, especially eyes, draw immediate attention to the unstated part of the message that goes with words to communicate the total meaning of what is being conveyed.

Develop the skill of creating a favourable impact on the other people by using eye contact. Your facial expressions and eye movements should be natural. Your smile should not be artificial; rather it should be a natural reflection of the pleasant state of your mind.

Face facts: In conversation, a smile shows that the interaction has been pleasant for both parties. Even in telephonic conversation, one is able to feel the impact of a smiling voice.

Make conscious efforts to create a positive image by positive body movements and gestures. Avoid negative 'leakage'. Learn to look confident, assertive, and positive. Avoid appearing nervous, aggressive, rude, pompous, indifferent or overbearing and superior.

As discussed earlier, we are not often aware of our bodily message given out to others—the body leakage. Therefore, develop awareness about various bodily movements and gestures and their possible message to those who observe us. Practice them to create a favourable and positive attitude and a good relationship for successful exchange of ideas.

The associated message of some significant bodily movements and gestures are given below—

Positive Gestures

When we speak, our hands move freely to indicate the meaning of our words. Such gestures are natural. They cannot be avoided. They give strength to our words.

Positive gestures are body signals which make you look relaxed, confident and polite.

Positive listening gestures include leaning a little towards the speaker, tilting the head, eye contact and gently nodding the head as the sign of agreement with what is said. Such gestures encourage the speaker to a great extent.

Good speaking gestures include keeping your hands open. Avoid clutching them or folding them across the chest. Avoid putting both your hands in your pockets. If you put one hand in your pocket, it shows arrogance. If you put both, it shows nervousness.

However, if you want to thrust your hands in pockets, then keep the thumb out, so that you do not fully insert your hands inside the pockets.

Impressive moving gestures include walking with your head upright. Hands should swing freely on our sides. Eyes should look straight in front. Steps should be well measured and steady.

We usually carry books, files and documents clutching them against the chest. The proper way is to carry them on one side.

Again, you can politely ask others not to interrupt you when you are busy speaking to someone else, just by showing up your palm to remain quiet for a while.

Gestures are adequate substitutes for words. We should develop the skills of using them effectively. Equally important is that we recognize our negative gestures and learn to hide them.

Negative Gestures

Negative gestures involve body movements, postures, gestures or non-verbal activities, such as shaking, tapping, looking at the watch. You should take note of the following clues.

Signs of Nervousness

Hands in the pockets; Covering the mouth with your hand while speaking; Scratching; Biting nails; Glancing sideways; Drumming fingers; Tapping your foot; Wringing hands; Crossing arms or legs; A slumped postures; Sitting on the edge of the chair; Rocking our legs; Looking at the ceiling; Straightening the tie; Setting the hair with hands; Speaking too fast or too haltingly.

The loudest gestures of your nervousness when you are:

Adjusting your glasses up your nose; Blinking a lot;

Playing with jewellery, watches or cufflinks; Clicking pens; Frequently sipping/drinking water; Starting to smoke.

Gestures Showing Aggressiveness

Staring; Pointing at someone; Showing a fist; Folding both arms; Bending over someone.

Gestures Showing Rudeness

Your behaviour becomes rude if you act in any of the following ways—

Shake hands too hard; Give a limp hand shake; Stand too close; Whisper at a social gathering; Work while someone talks to you; Yawn; Smirk; Look at your watch frequently or during the conversation; Puff; Tut-tut; Groom, specially setting your hair when listening or speaking; Start gathering and folding papers before the meeting is over.

Gestures Showing Self-Importance

Eyes closed while talking; Head bent backwards while talking; Looking at the tip of the nose while talking; Pursed mouth; Steeping the fingers; Peering over the top of the glasses; Waving glasses or key ring while talking; Such acts, which signal our importance, should be carefully avoided in situations that demand solution and negotiated settlements.

Gestures Showing Lack of Good Sense

Banging the table instead of laughing at a joke; Chewing paans; Air quoting, when you want to say something or making air; when you want to say tea; Waving hands around you while talking; Wringing hands; Opening or closing buttons or setting our watch strap as you talk; Wiping hands across face; Touching nose time and again.

Gestures Showing Superiority of Position

Some seniors, without saying anything, make you feel subordinate to them by behaving in the following ways. Creating such feelings of subordination adversely affects good working relationships. Others feel uncomfortable in your presence. Therefore, avoid such power-posturing acts.

Not responding or acknowledging others' greeting; Staring; Shouting orders; Standing too close, or leaning or sitting on someone's desk standing behind someone's desk; Standing behind someone's seat and watching over his/her shoulder as he/she keeps writing/working; Smoking in someone's space; Attending meeting with your cell phones on; Any unwanted or unwarranted touch; Continuing to work as others speak to you; Crushing hand shake or keeping the hand held too long under your hand; Reclining in the chair with your hands folded behind your head.

Lateral Gestures

There are other wordless signs of power, position, taste and culture. The examples are: decoration and size of the office, dress, grooming and so on. They are called lateral gestures and include the following broad categories—

Physical Setting

Dress—Clothes and shoes; Personal Space.

Physical Setting

An executive's position of power is generally seen from the size of his office room, kind of furnishing of the room, the height of his/her chair, the size of the office table. The number of telephone sets and their quality add to the impression created by the size and setting of the room. The floor carpet tells us the status of the executive we are going to meet.

In an office, the executive's table is usually placed a few steps away from the entry door. It is to make a visitor or a subordinate walk up to him/her and feel his/her presence. Space is one of the factors involved in indicating the proximity of relationship.

Dress

Clothes often proclaim a person. It is one of the first things others notice about you. Your clothes, their texture, colour, design, style and stitching speak about your taste and aesthetic sense. Pay attention to your clothes, especially when you need to impress people at an interview or presentation.

Look impressive, not gorgeous. Never be over-dressed for the occasion. Do not go for high fashion and trendy designs and styles of suiting. Business executives look elegant in conventional styles. Your clothes should not distract attention from what you talk.

Wear neither too loose nor tight clothes. Select your clothes according to the mature of your job.

It is necessary that you feel comfortable in your clothes, particularly when you are to attend an interview or make a presentation. Never try a new set of clothes for such occasions. You may feel out of form, if you are putting on a brand new suit at the time of interview or making a public appearance. New clothes may not fit comfortably on you, and they may draw away your attention from time to time. So, the first rule of clothes is the principle of comfort. If you are getting your suit stitched, customize it according to your comfort. And try to wear the customized suit on special occasions.

Your shoes should be formal and in keeping with the colour of the suit.

Business bag, or briefcase or portfolio which you carry also indicates the level of formality, informality, intimacy or distance between them.

Demarcation of Zones

The limits of different zones are set as the invisible space between the two parties. There are five distinct zones—

- Public zone
- Social zone
- Friendly zone
- Intimate zone

A public zone is the widest territory between the speaker and audience. A public speaker addresses a large gathering of persons. He/she needs to speak from a raised platform at a distance of 10 to 15 feet from the audience. The distance and elevation of the speaker provide visibility and sense of security and elevation to the speaker. A social zone is the space maintained between people who are known to each other in a formal way. All business transactions are to be treated as social interactions. Note that as an executive, you should keep a distance of 4-10 feet between you and your audience. This space will ensure the comfort of your customers or clients. At this distance, you can watch the body language and facial expressions of the other party closely. The social zone will be applicable to new colleagues at work, new acquaintances, and small groups during training.

The friendly zone is the distance we observe at business parties, seminars and other informal business gatherings and get-togethers. We remain close but not close enough to jostle against each other. The gap we keep between us is nearly 1½ to 4 feet. We are able to comfortably chat, laugh and joke with each other in his/her own individual space.

The intimate zone or the closest zone is the distance or nearness between you and the person you love or your close relatives and members of family. In this zone, persons tend to be together even at whispering distance. This nearness signals closeness among persons involved in communication. The gap is nearly of 6 inches to 18 inches.

Within the intimate zone or the closest zone is the distance or nearness between you and the person you love or your close relatives and members of your family. In this zone, persons tend to be together even at whispering distance. This nearness signals closeness among persons involved in communication. The gap is nearly of 6 inches to 18 inches.

Within this intimate zone, there are further zones/bands of intimacy according to the level of our intimacy. They are—

Near Intimate sphere—(Up to 6 inches).
Lovers; Partners; Children; Family.
Distant intimate sphere (6 inches to 18 inches).
Close friends: Close colleagues: Relatives.

Both these spheres are sensitive. Our difficulty arises because we often do not know how close is too close.

When our intimate zone is intruded upon by someone, we feel embarrassed and, at times, threatened by the unwarranted approach, response is that of "fight" or "flight".

ADVANTAGES OF LEARNING NON-VERBAL COMMUNICATION SKILLS

Knowledge of non-verbal skills strengthens your communicative competence as a professional.

Body language is not the science of mind reading. The body language is a sudden flashing revelation from one sub-conscious mind to another sub-conscious mind. There is no deliberate attempt to give or receive non-verbal messages. It all happens spontaneously (without effort).

Ability to act as a Victim of Power Posturing

In the presence of power posturing superiors or colleagues, you must have felt a strange sense of being subordinated or over-dominated, suddenly.

In such a state of nervousness, you should learn to manage your body talk. Do not allow your nervousness to be leaked out. If you exhibit nervousness, it would mean you were doing something wrong.

Reassuring Actions and Gestures

Do not feel hurt. The other person is trying to bully you into such a state of mind.

Avoid nervous gestures. Do not leak any signs of nervousness by wiping your mouth or biting your nails or looking lost in thoughts.

Avoid the Double Cross

You are sitting when invaded by power posturing; do not sit at the edge of the seat. Sitting like that will make you look nervous and ready to run away. For the sake of comfort, cross your legs but do not fold your arms at the same time. That will make you look very defensive.

Use Comfort Gestures Skillfully

There are comforting body gestures such as touching earlobes or back of the neck or stroking hair. These acts restore confidence.

Reassuring Standing Postures

If you are invaded by power posturing when you are standing, try to keep nervousness away by standing up in an easy form, with your arms down by your sides, and your feet apart by 9 to 10 inches. This posture will give you firm balanced footing.

Be assertive: We tend to respond to an adverse situation by either fighting or fleeing, or learning to develop an alternative way of responding to unpleasant behaviour or negative situations by being assertive.

Assertiveness should not be taken to mean imposing your own will on others. It means that you try to understand the point of view of others; and put your own viewpoint objectively.

Assertion is a positive way of saying what we want to say. It is a response and not a reaction to a situation.

Hence, the proper way to respond is to say what you want to say. And say it with firm conviction of being right.

Developing Non-Verbal Communication Skills

Watch and Read the Non-verbal Clues

Interpret non-verbal clues in relation to the situation and culture accurately.

Be careful about false non-verbal clues deliberately given to deceive you.

Consider the non-verbal message, along with what the speaker's words say, to know the total message.

Respond, but do not react, to non-verbal signals with self-control.

Know Your Body Language in Action

Develop self-awareness by visualizing yourself as others see you by interpreting your body movements and gestures.

Try to develop positive gestures and expressions to present yourself as you wish to be seen by others—confident, pleasing, and a well-meaning team-worker.

Do not give conflicting non-verbal cues.

Convey sincerity through your tone of voice and facial expressions.

Use Symbols, non-verbal cues (gestures, posture, and so on), intonation (for example, volume, pace of delivery and pronunciation), expressions and so on, to reinforce and clarity the meaning of message. Maintain eye contact with your audience. Smile genuinely to reflect your feelings of delight. Avoid power posturing signals.

Remember that the first impression is the last impression. If not the last, it is certainly a lasting impression. Hence, present yourself well to make a lasting good impression.

Body Language Across Cultures

Body language is a universal phenomenon. Its meaning differs culturally. Culture, like language, lays down rules for accepted social behaviour of people sharing a set of knowledge, beliefs, practices and ideas. In the present day multicultural work-places, communicating between persons of different nations requires knowledge of the meaning of non-verbal acts such as eye contact, touch and time sense in respective cultures. Non-verbal clues are taken as true indicators of the speaker's sub-conscious mind. They are considered more reliable than words. Be careful not to use non-verbal clues that violate cultural norms of other countries.

Touching and Its Context

Touching has a limited communicative symbolism. It primarily conveys intimacy and closeness and also love. But the act of touching has its meaning in relation to its context. For instance, in cricket, some players pat the bottom of their team mates to convey admiration. But they cannot do it with any one of their teammates out in the club. That would give wrong clues to their sexual drive.

It is the context in which touching is done which determines its implied sense. Take for instance, the case of a doctor. The doctor can touch any part of body of his female patients. The patients do not object to his touching. The patient's thoughts are influenced by his ailment. But the doctor's attention is directed by the investigations to be made or the surgery to be performed. In this context, his body movements, touching and so on are instrumental acts, performing certain tasks. They are not communicative body movements reflecting the doctor's state of mind, emotions or attitude. The context characterizes the nature of a body movement and determines it as communicative or instrumental message.

Touch is the mode of communicating intimacy. But which part of the body can be touched by whom and when depends upon the culture of the people of a country or a particular region. As a broad gesture of patronizing, a superior in position or age or status can touch by patting the back of a worker, both male and female, in western countries, but in Asian countries like India, patting a lady on the back is not socially liked.

Among lovers, parents, family members and very close friends, touching is a normal gesture and goes unnoticed, but between strangers, it is at once marked and may also be objected to. But even among those who share the zone of intimacy, only they can be touched while communicating.

Different parts of the body are viewed as centers of intimate relationship, bordering sensuality. The forearm of a woman can be touched by a man while communicating, without offending the concerned lady, but not the upper part of the arm. The two parts represent two different zones of sensibility. Touching the upper part of women's arm is indicative of sensuality.

In the West, men and women can, in public, walk freely holding each other's hand. But in India, Pakistan and other Asian countries, men and women generally do not do so in public view.

Again, in Asian countries such as Nepal, Pakistan and India, it is normal for two males to move around holding each other's hand, whereas in America, such males might be considered gay (homosexuals).

To identify himself as an individual while speaking to someone, an American places one of his hands on his chest, whereas Japanese places one of his fingers on his nose. But some western psychologists consider nose touching to be a Freudian symbol of sexuality.

Like all other emblematic body movements, eye contact is also decoded culturally, in different ways. Eye contact is an important clue of attentive listening. In most western countries, it is considered polite to speak one to one by maintaining eye contact. But in Japan and India, subordinates do not makes eye contact, when speaking and listening to their superiors. It is possible that an American may consider a Japanese to be impolite if he/she keeps the eyes lowered during the conversation. In India, this speaks of humility, not shame. A newly wed Indian bride with her eyes turned downwards, while talking, moving or sitting with others, acts as an emblem of humility and respect.

Similarly, silence is communicative; but it may say different things to people of different cultures. For instance, during discussions between an American and a Japanese, the Japanese may prefer to remain silent if he/she thinks he/she does know much about the matter. An Indian in that situation may keep silent, if he/she agrees with what is being said. But an American would take silence both of the Japanese and the Indian as a sign of withdrawal and non-participation. An American looks for involvement and participation through raising questions or doubts.

For people in the East, silence is a sign of wisdom. But for westerners, it is indicative of lack of understanding.

None can make an exhaustive study of all possible cultural variations to interpret body movements. However, an attempt has been to make you understand the influence of context of cultures on interpretation of body movements and gestures.

Communication Breakdown

We are aware that in life and business dealings, many a time communication breaks down. It happens when we are very keen to talk about our own point of view. We go on, and do not consider whether the other person understands what is said. Sometimes, our discussions become heated and we reach no satisfactory end of our meeting. You may feel bored because the same point is being repeated by the speaker without involving other members in the discussion. Such communication break-downs do happen.

In the heart of hearts, no one wants the discussion to fail. But, often, we fail to realise that it is going to fail. Communication often fails because of two reasons—

(a) We do not keep our own natural pace of speaking;
(b) We do not consider the other person's body language.

Both reasons can be avoided on getting thorough knowledge and skills of oral communication.

Lack of Rapport

The objective of all communication is that it should be useful and harmonious. Harmony is the key word in personal and business communication. Harmony between ideas of speaker and listener is the final aim of communication. The first step is to establish required rapport between the non-verbal languages of the speaker and listeners' understanding: the pacing. For fruitful discussion or dialogue, both speaker and listener should be on the same wave-length. What does the wave-length mean in our communication? It means that the two persons (speaker and the other person) should use similar body language, especially speed, tone of voice, pitch, words, gestures, eye contact and time. The non-verbal language used by speaker should reflect the body language of the other person. You may notice that the word listener is being avoided in this context of rapport. It is being replaced by the phrase 'the other person'. It is a significant substitution. Communication usually fails because the speaker treats the other person a listener. Therefore, he/she keeps on using non-verbal communication during most of the time of speaking. The other person is forced to just listen and have little opportunity to speak. A proper time sharing between speaking and listening should be—

Speaking—30%
Listening—70%

When we devote 70 percent of conversation time to listening, during the moments of silence, we can study the body language of the other person and observe his/her state of mind, feelings and the true response to what we are saying-our point of view. And to make him/her know his/her response as perceived by us, our body language should hold a mirror to his non-verbal language. It does not mean our body language should be imitative. It means that our behaviour, verbal and non-verbal, should reflect the ideas and feelings of the other person. The two behaviours should be in unison.

Suppose, two of us speak at different speeds, pitch and volumes; neither of us would be able to keep pace with the other. Conflicts arise, when expressions of our ideas and feelings differ.

Consider the following example—

> Sonali, a senior HR executive sat sunk in her chair, disappointed. She had come to office very happy. She had prepared a long document on how to reduce cost to the company without cutting down the present number of employees working in core departments of organization. She had gone to General Manager to discuss with him her proposed plan, before formally submitting it for the management's consideration.

Sonali entered the General Manager's Officc and from the door asked him, "Can I discuss something with you? I have very exciting plan to show you. Hope you will like it. We can reduce cost without cutting down number of employees."

The General Manager did not look towards her. Instead, he kept on writing. After a few minutes of silence, without turning his gaze from the paper, he said, "I have to finish this report first. We may discuss later."

Communication in this case definitely breaks down. There is no rapport between Sonali and the General Manager. Sonali is frustrated.

Now, suppose the General Manager responds to Sonali as follows—

> The General Manager stops writing. Turns towards Sonali. Makes eye contact and exultingly says, "Wonderful! Let me first finish this report. We can meet in an hour. I will ring you as soon as I am free. Will that be fine?" Sonali would feel very happy.

The GM responds to her enthusiasm with matching enthusiasm. This exchange satisfies both the parties. The GM gets time to complete his report undisturbed and Sonali's enthusiasm is kept up. What is significant in this communication is that the GM appreciates Sonali's enthusiasm and her keenness to discuss her plan with him. He uses the word 'wonderful', to communicate his own excitement to know about Sonali's new plan. He fixes a time to discuss it. He also lets Sonali know that the plan should be discussed without any disturbance, when both are free.

This exchange is based on rapport between Sonali and the GM. There has been a pacing between the non-verbal languages of both Sonali and the GM.

The communication in the latter instance is fruitful, because the GM is able to make Sonali feel that he values her ideas and through his non-verbal language validates their worth as a colleague.

A simple non-verbal act in everyday life may make you feel unhappy. For instance, you may ring up your boss on his mobile twice. Both the times, he does not respond. You feel cut down. You feel small and unwanted. He knows your mobile number, but does not respond to your call. The lack of rapport frustrates you until he speaks to you next.

Some Steps to Establish Rapport

Develop the habit of talking less and listening and observing others more.

Do not dominate the discussion.

Keep your natural pace of conversation.

Recognise the place of others.

Let your pace and the others' be nearly the same.

Try to establish rapport between you and other person during the first few minutes of your conversation.

Do not introduce any controversial issue before you have been able to create rapport through pacing.

Avoid harsh criticism. Try to see reason for difference of opinion.

Be tolerant of differences.

Focus on Similarities of Ideas

The above steps will gradually overcome differences. Conflicting opinions will find resolution in common understanding gained by both—you and the other person.

In life, as in business, it is necessary that you focus on those aspects of your communication, verbal and non-verbal, that you share with others.

BODY LANGUAGE IN DIFFERENT COUNTRIES

In the United Kingdom (England, Scotland and Wales)

In the European continent, handshaking is done when meeting and departing, day in and day out and even with the same assortment of acquaintances. In these three countries, it is done less frequently.

Summon waiters at restaurants by raising the hand. To signal that you would like to check (called "the bill" there), make a motion with both hands as if you were signing your name on paper.

Loud conversations and any form of boisterousness in public places should be avoided.

Avoid staring at someone in public. Privacy is highly valued and respected in those countries.

In Wales, when addressing a group, speakers should avoid rubbing their noses, standing with hands in pockets, or shuffling the feet.

In England, holding the nose and then pulling on an imaginary chain is a signal for "It stinks", and is something of an insult.

If you smoke, it is the custom to offer cigarettes to others in your conversational group before lighting up.

Other Common Practices

When yawning, cover the mouth; use handkerchief discreetly; remove hats when entering a building; men should cross their legs at the knees rather than placing one ankle cross the other knee; woman usually cross them at the ankle—in fact, watch for news photos of the Queen or other prominent women there are, you'll note that when seated, they usually use the prim, Victorian manner of crossing them at the ankles.

France

The mode of handshaking is usually as follows: a light,

quick, single handshake, which is done with a great frequently (arrivals, departures, each and every day). A strong, pumping handshake is considered uncultured. Also, when entering a room, greet each person in a room.

A French woman offers her hand first.

Close friends and young people often kiss on either cheeck (but it is really touching cheeks and "kissing the air").

Be certain to carry a good supply of business cards, since they are exchanged often.

Some common actions and gestures to be avoided:

Resting the feet on tables or chairs
Using tooth-picks, nail clippers or combs in public
Conversing with hands in pockets
Chewing gum in public
Yawning or scratching in public
Loud conversations in public
Snapping the fingers of both hands, slapping an open palm over the closed fist—both have vulgar meanings.

Some unique gestures in France:

Forming a circle with your thumb and forefinger and placing it over your nose, and then twisting; this signals that "someone is drunk".
The "O.K." sign (thumb and forefinger forming circle) in some parts of France signifies "zero" or "worthless".
Here the "V" for victory signal is done with palm either forward or backward; both mean "peace" or "victory" (in England, the "V" is only done when the palm is outward; if the palm faces inward, it is an obscene gesture).
Playing an imaginary flute is a way of signaling that someone is talking on and becoming tiresome.
On French highways, if another driver raises his hand in the air, fingers up, and rotates it back and forth, it means he is not happy with your driving.

When dining, the French use "Continental" style, with fork on table, and do not put their hand in their lap. Other dining practices:

Bread or rolls are broken and eaten with fingers and placed next to your dinner plate, usually directly on the table- cloth.

Fruit is peeled with a knife and eaten with a fork.

Lettuce and other leaf vegetables are not cut with a knife but, instead, folded into small pieces and eaten with a fork.

Never use bread to wipe up sauces except, perhaps, at family dinners.

The French find it strange to pick up sandwiches and other such foods with a finger. It is more common to cut them with a knife and fork.

When you have finished eating, place the knife and fork side-by-side across your plate with the fork-lines up.

Author and Harvard professor, Laurence Wylie, also offers these important hand singularly Gallic gestures:

Pointing to the eye means "You can't fool me".

To say "How dull", flick the fingers across the cheek.

Using the index and middle fingers to push the nose upward signals "It's so easy, I could do it with my fingers up my nose".

And when the French issue their famous shrug with the shoulders, palms extended, it means "It doesn't worry me."

But if the palms are raised chest high, it becomes "What do you expect me to do about it"?

As a final word on actions and physical behaviour in France, just remember that the word "etiquette" is derived from French.

Germany

A fairly firm handshake is the custom among men, often

with just one or two "pumps". Children and women will often offer their hand in greeting too. Cheek-kissing is rare.

Shaking hands with the other hand in a pocket is considered impolite. For this reason, small children are chastised for putting their hands in their pockets because it is considered disrespectable.

Men rise when a woman enters the room, or when conversing with a woman. On the other hand, woman may remain seated.

Never open a closed door without knocking first.

During operas or concerts, it is important to remain quiet and still. Coughing or restlessness is considered rude.

Never place your foot or feet on furniture.

At dinner parties, don't drink until your host begins. When toasting, clink glasses only for special occasions, like a birthday. Men toast, women never *vice versa*.

When eating: the fork is held in the left hand: don't cut potatoes, pancakes, or dumpling with a knife; smoke between courses only if you see others doing so.

Chewing gum while conversing with another person is considered extremely impolite. As one German remarked, "To German, it looks like a cow chewing on a cud."

To beckon a waiter, raise the hand with index finger extended.

Four special gestures in Germany are:

To signal "one" hold the thumb upright.

On Germany's famous autobahns (highways), if one driver is unhappy with the driving of another, he may point the index finger to the temple and make a twisting or screwing motion.

This is considered very rude, and means, in effect, "You are crazy!"

To signal "good luck", Germans make two fists with thumbs tucked inside the other fingers and then make a motion like they are pounding lightly on a surface.

In some parts of Germany, when people arrive at a large dinner table and it is awkward to reach across and shake hands, they will simply rap their knuckles slightly on the table as a form of greeting to the others. The same gesture may apply when leaving the table ahead of the other guests. It is also used in university-classrooms for students' greeting professors.

Russia (erstwhile Soviet Union)

A good firm handshake along with direct eye contact is the customary greeting. In many parts of Russia, among close friends, the "Russian bear hug" is common and is often accompanied by two or three quick kisses on alternate cheeks—even among men—and sometimes with one kiss directly on the lips. There are exceptions to this practice, however. For example, in our survey of the Uzbekistan

Republic, the reply was as brief as it was clear: "No kisses."

Bear in mind that the U.S.S.R. (now Russia) was composed of 15 very diverse republics with strong cultural differences. As a result, certain gestures and body language may have local flavours and meanings.

Shaking the raised fist shows disagreement and anger. The "thumbs up" sign signifies approval.

When dining, the Russians keep the fork in the left hand and the knife in the right. Also, keep your hands out of the lap while eating; instead, rest the wrists lightly on the table.

However, research indicates this might be considered an "old-fashioned" practice in some parts.

To beckon a waiter in a restaurant, a slight nod of the head should do the job; if not just raise the hand and finger.

Iran

Handshaking is the customary form of greeting. Like most of the Arab nations, however, it may be done with a lighter grip.

Good friends may greet each other with a slight embrace and a gesture of cheek kissing.

People of the same sex will tend to stand close together when meeting and conversing.

Shaking hands with a child shows respect for his parents.

When entering homes, especially rooms with carpets, it may be the custom to remove one's shoes first. Always remove your shoes before entering a mosque.

The "thrum's up" gesture is considered vulgar.

To signal "no", move the head up and back sharply. To signal "yes", dip the head downward with a slight twist.

Avoid blowing your nose in public. Refrain from sloughing in a chair or stretching your legs out in front of you. Also, watch where you point the sole of your shoe, which is considered offensive to any one seeing it.

Nigeria

Because of diverse cultures in Nigeria, it is difficult to generalize about proper greetings. However, those who travel there as tourists or on business will probably find that the local people they deal with know and use Western conventions.

Nigerians try very hard to please guests. They are congenial and hospitable and respect the Western regard for punctuality.

Avoid pointing the sole of the shoe or foot at a person.

Use only the right hand for eating finer foods.

Saudi Arabia

Men will greet each other with a light but sincere handshake, sometimes with the left hand touching the forearm, the elbow, or even the shoulder of the other person.

Among Saudi males, an embrace and cheek kissing may be added to their greeting.

As in other parts of the Middle East, among the elderly and more traditional folk, the salaam greeting may be observed.

This is done by using the right hand to touch the heart and then the forehead in one upward sweep. It is accompanied by saying salaam alaykum or "peace be with you"

Saudis may signal "yes" by swinging the head form side-to-side. "No" is indicated by tipping the head backward and clicking the tongue.

Space relationships are smaller by Western standards.

People of the same sex will stand closer together than North Americans or Europeans.

Avoid excessive amounts of pointing or signaling with the hands.

Avoid showing the bottom of your sole to another person, which is considered rude.

The Arabic language is considered by some a dramatic and emotional language, and conversation is often vigorous and enthusiastic.

Australia

A firm, friendly handshake is the customary greeting here. It's not necessary, though, to offer to shake hands with a woman unless she offers her hand first. Women first may kiss when greeting each other. When greeting someone at a distance, a wave is customary but yelling is not.

Be prepared to exchange business cards, but this practice is not as rigid as in, say, Japan or some European Countries.

In business meeting, eye contact is important.

When addressing audience, use erect posture and modest gestures.

Australians may not consider it good form to show much emotion, so good friends may pat one another on thc back, but there is not much physical expressiveness of emotion beyond that. It is considered unmanly.

Even if you are friends, winking at a woman is considered rude.

Like the British, respect is given for queues, or lines of people. Never barge on jump into a line; always go politely to the end and wait for your turn.

Sportsmanlike gestures (e.g., being a good winner, or loser; congratulating a good performance) of kind are liked and appreciated because good sportsmanship is highly respected.

Australians are known to be warm, friendly, and informal and dislike overly expressive or "gushy" behaviour in any form.

India

The traditional greeting in India is namaste, where the palms of the hands are pressed together in a praying position and held about chest high, then accompanied with a slight bow forward. Westerners can use the namaste as a greeting, and such a show of knowledge about Inidan customs will be appreciated. The namaste is too used when bidding goodbye.

Men customarily do not touch women in either formal or informal situations.

Indian businessmen may indulge in warm and even enthusiastic back-patting and slapping. This is merely a sign of cordiality and friendship.

Carry and be prepared to exchange business cards.

When walking the streets, try not to stare, especially at the impoverished; that is considered a way to humiliate them.

Showing anger is usually the worst way to accomplish almost anything.

Ask permission before you smoke cigarettes, pipes or cigars.

Whistling in public is considered very impolite.

If an Indian smiles and jerks his head backward, it could signal "yes". However, in the south if a person moves his head quickly back and forth, it signals "Yes, I understand what you are saying."

As in the Middle East, where the feet and soles of the shoes are considered the lowest and dirtiest part of body, the same is true in India. Therefore, try not to touch anyone or point at anyone with your shoes or their soles.

When you wish to point, use your chin, the full hand or may be the thumb, but not a single finger. Pointing with a single finger is used only with inferiors. The chin is not used to point to people who are considered superiors. The best way to signal attention towards something or someone is with the full hand.

The standard way of beckoning another person is with the arm extended, palm down and with a scratching motion inward with the fingers.

Whereas Europeans might wave "good-bye" by using the hand and arm in an up-and-down motion; this will probably be interpreted in India as signaling "come-here".

The left hand should be used sparingly; pass gifts or other articles with the right hand, eat with the right hand, and point with the right hand.

Japan

As most visitors already know, the graceful act of bowing is the traditional greeting for the Japanese. However, the Japanese have also adopted the Western practice of shaking hands, albeit with a light grip and perhaps with eyes averted. The reasons are that a firm grip to them suggests aggression and direct eye contact is considered slightly intimidating. It should be added, however, that many well-travelled Japanese are carefully studying Western ways and, therefore, may surprise you with a firm grip and direct eye contact.

The seemingly simple act of exchanging business cards is more complex in Japan because the business card represents not only one's identity but one's station in life.

Here are some tips on what you may encounter:

The business card is held with both hands, grasped between the thumb and forefinger.

It is extended forward in a respectful gesture with the printing pointing considerately toward the other person. A slight bow is made at the same time.

The Japanese will take the card, again with both hands and a reciprocal bow and then read the card carefully. This may be followed by another slight bow.

After this sequence, the Western handshake may occur. (or in deference to the Westerner, the greeting may begin with handshaking and then evolve to bowing and the above ritual of exchanging business cards).

When Westerners take the business card from Japanese, they should avoid examining it casually and quickly tucking into a coat or shirt pocket; instead, examine it carefully, then place it on the table in front of you for further reference.

Avoid scribbling notes on the back of the card. This shows certain measure of disrespect for something that represents a person's identity.

Avoid clapping Japanese on the back, standing very close, any form of public kissing or any prolonged physical contact. On crowded public transportation, however, it is a different matter. People are accustomed to being jammed into tight spaces, as epitomized by the transit employees whose jobs consist of packing people into the public trains before the door close.

When meeting, periods of silence may occur. This is perfectly acceptable and customary. During these periods, the Japanese may even raise their eyes to look over the heads of others while contemplating.

Because of the high regard for graciousness and restraint, one should not shout, raise the voice in anger, or exhibit any excessively demonstrative behaviour.

Displaying an open mouth is considered rude in Japan. That is one reason why Japanese, especially the women, cover their mouths when giggling or laughing.

Correct posture is important in Japan, especially when seated. Consequently, avoid slouching or putting your feet on a table or stool. Balance in life is a basic Japanese principle, so a square, solid posture when seated or walking is practiced (for example both feet squarely on the ground, arms in the lap or on the armrests). Any slouching or leaning back in a tipped chair can be interpreted as showing an "I don't care" attitude.

Listening in Japan is considered not only polite but also regarded as a valuable business skill. Americans and other Westerners tend to interrupt. In fact, author, John C. Condon, writes that the three top complaints the Japanese have about Americans are: they talk too much; they interrupt; and then don't listen.

Crossing the legs at the knees or ankles is the preferred form rather than with one ankle over the other knee.

To get the attention of the waiter, catch his eye, and dip your head downward.

To beckon someone, put your arm out, palm down and make scratching motion with the fingers.

It is considered insulting to point to someone with four fingers extended and the thumb folded into the palm.

The "OK" gesture in Japan may be interpreted as the signal for "money", probably because the circular shape formed by the index finger and thumb suggests the shape of a coin. For example, Japanese may make a purchase of food at the counter and then flash this gesture to signal "Give me my change in coins."

Blowing your nose in public is considered rude. In Japan, the handkerchief is used primarily for wiping the mouth or drying the hands when leaving the washroom. Paper tissues are used for blowing the nose and then discarded.

Present a gift with both hands, as with business cards. This is viewed as a gesture of humility and humility is important in Japan. It is a nice touch to bow slightly while doing either act. Also, when receiving a gift, you are not expected to open it right then and there. Wait until later, in private.

Avoid standing with your hand or hands in pockets, especially when greeting someone or when addressing a group of people.

When eating, pick up dishes on your left side with your right hand and vice versa.

At public restaurants or private homes, it is often the custom to remove your shoes before entering. You'll either see a line-up of other shoes from other restaurant patrons at the doorstep or just follow the actions of your host. Shoes are usually placed with the toes pointing towards the exit.

A formal Japanese tea ceremony is just that—a ceremony. It is graceful, expressive and artistic. Watch your host for the proper procedure.

United States

A firm handshake, accompanied by direct eye contact, is the standard greeting in the United States. Occasionally, among very good friends who have not seen each other for long intervals, women may briefly hug other women, and men may quickly kiss the cheek of women. Males rarely hug each other. However, occasionally, men may shake hand or with lightly gripping the forearm. This represents a higher degree warmth and friendship, and politicians may be seen using this technique when campaigning.

According to anthropologists, Americans tend to stand just about arm's length away from each other while conversing or standing in public. It's called "the comfort zone."

Speaking of exceptions, because the United States has much ethnic diversity, visitors may also occasionally observe people greeting each other with hugs and cheek-kissing.

Certain nationalities have brought these customs to the United States and continue to practice them, but they are not in wide use.

Direct eye contact in both social and business situations is very important. Not doing so implies boredom or disinterest.

There are two well-known rude and insulting gestures in the United States. Both are recognised in all parts of America. They are:

- The middle finger thrust.
- The forearm jerk.

Waving "hello" or "good bye" is done by extending the arm, palm facing down and waving the hand up and down at the wrist joint. Another variation is to raise the arm, palm outward and move the whole arm and hand back and forth like an upside down pendulum, This is important to know because in many other countries, this is a signal for "no".

Many Americans become uncomfortable with periods of silence. Therefore, in business or social situations, if a gap occurs, they will quickly try to fill in with conversation.

Beckoning can be done either by raising the index finger and repeatedly curling it in and out or by raising the hand (palm facing inward) and waggling the fingers back toward the body. Either is acceptable.

To call a waiter, just raise one hand to head level or above. To signal that you want the 'check', make a writing motion with two hands (one hand representing the paper, the other making a writing motion).

It is considered impolite to use toothpicks in front of other people.

Using the hand and index finger to point at objects or to point directions is perfectly common and acceptable.

If an American is seen pointing both hands to the throat, this is the signal for "I am choking". It might be seen, for instance, in sporting events as a sarcastic signal that someone is showing tension and playing poorly. But it can be used in a far more serious situation. Health experts in the United States are urging people to use—and to recognise—this gesture if and when a person is choking on a piece of food. In such a situation, the person cannot talk and is signalling "Help!"

(Adapted and edited from Roger E. Astell, Gesture: the Do's and Taboo of Body Language Around World, John Wiley & Sons, New York, 1991).

CHAPTER

17

Strategies for Success at Interviews

Interview is an opportunity for engaging and advancing in career. Your success in using interview opportunity for a job offer depends solely on you; on how well you have prepared yourself for the interview. Most candidates falter during an interview only because they do not know enough about themselves, about company they are applying for, and about their job profile. The secret of our success for clearing the interview lies in preparing your game plan, a strategy for what the specific organizations look for, like—

Specific Personality traits: are you motivated, mature, ambitious, and trustworthy?

Competence and realistic job expectations—you can impress the prospective employers only when you prove that you know about the industry or the job you aspire to join.

As a practical step, you should equip yourself with the

following information and knowledge before you face an interview.

Know yourself
Know the company
Know your Job Profile

ANSWERS TO SOME QUESTIONS GENERALLY ASKED

It has been seen that most of the interviewers usually move form simple personal questions to general and then to technical questions. The questions put to new graduates focus more on their education and short work experience, current issues, and hobbies. Their areas examined are education and personality. In the case of candidates with experience, the focus is on their recent project, achievements, and what new thing they can do for organization.

MODEL QUESTIONS AND ANSWERS

Q. Tell us about yourself?

A. Born at Pilani (Rajasthan) of an educational family, I did my entire education there. After schooling from Birla Public School, I attended Birla Institute of Technology and Science and obtained my dual degree in MMS and Mathematics. I did my summer project at DCM, Kota and six months' practice at school at USHA International, Delhi, Marketing Division, prompting a product line similar to your household durables. I believe I am motivated and capable of doing hard work.

Q. What are your strengths?

A. I am an intelligent, young, hard-working person who likes to take initiative and shoulder responsibility and complete his tasks to everyone's satisfaction.

Q. What are your weaknesses?

A. I, sometimes, become too impatient and unable to put up with delay in working on targets.

Q. Why do you wish to work in our organization?

A. I know a number of persons working in this organization.

I appreciate its work culture and concern for each individual employed in it. I like its systems flexibility that allows its people to move from one area to another.

Q. Why have you been changing jobs?

A. It is generally believed if you want to grow, don't work at one position for more than four years.
(Then you discuss how your past experience has helped you in developing your skills which will be useful in new job).

Q. Tell us how you can contribute to our company?
(Without claiming too much, tell us in specific terms what you are capable of doing for the company.)

A. I shall bring my experience to bear upon my job in your company. I shall study the system and procedure and, if necessary, suggest changes. Otherwise, I shall adapt myself to the systems and procedures here. I know I can influence others and get their co-operation in doing my work better.

Q. The company can secure the National Highway Golden Triangle Project Construction, if you can bribe the concerned CEO. Will you do it?

A. (The question is asked to judge your personal sense of morality. Straightway say no. And give your moral reasons by praising the organization's reputation for upholding ethical values and moral practices in all spheres.)

Q. Could you tell us something about your current responsibilities?

A. Describe those areas of work which show your initiative and organizing ability.
Be factual, but project your own skills in handling the present assignments of duties/jobs/or projects.

Q. What are your salary expectations?

A. Justify your expectations in terms of your present package. The challenge of the new jobs is your attraction, not a better salary alone.

The questions given here are basically suggestive of the types of questions you can expect at the interview. One cannot possibly list questions exhaustively.

The secret of facing interviews successfully lies in thorough preparation. Bring into play your full understanding, and power of personality while facing the interviewers and their questions.

Aim at making a good first impression. Remember that you have just three to five seconds to do so. Ninety percent of people form a judgment on someone they meet at a job interview in just that time only, according to a report in the German journal MM Wissen. In seventy percent of cases, these first impressions prove to be right.

Decisive factors in making an impression are body language, clothes, status symbols, scent, and the sound of your voice. The content of the conversation plays hardly much role.

PARTICIPATING IN A GROUP DISCUSSION (GD)

The group discussion is a personality test most popular with public/private sector undertakings, government departments, commercial firms, IIMs, Universities and other educational organizations. They use this technique to screen candidates, after the written test.

What does GD evaluate? A group discussion primarily evaluates your ability to interact in a group on a given topic. Your group behaviour means so much for your success as a manager or an executive responsible for co-ordination and organization of activities of groups of individuals. The GD evaluators, therefore, focus on group dynamics rather than the content of your views.

Technique

The group usually consists of 8 to 10 candidates. No one is nominated as leader, coordinator or chairman to conduct the discussion. Normally, 20 to 30 minutes are given as time to complete the discussion. Each candidate is indicated by his/her roll number and is to be addressed accordingly. For easy recognition, the roll number is prominently displayed on the candidate's front and back. The seating is arranged in a circle and the candidates are seated according to the ascending order of roll numbers.

Emerging Leadership

A group discussion starts without a leader. It is conducted in an atmosphere of free and equal chance for all candidates to express their views on the topic. It is during the course of discussion that a leader emerges gradually. No candidate should try to dominate the group to become a leader. Such an attempt is self-defeating, as in GD all are equal as participants. No one is officially chosen as leader. But a candidate by his/her initiative/ability to join in the discussion, maturity and clarity of ideas and understanding of group dynamics gradually begins to direct the course of discussion and mediates between the opposing views to evolve the comprehensive view of the whole group. Such a candidate is implicitly recognized by all other candidates as the leader of discussion group.

GD Protocol Group Discussions are formally informal. There are rules of conduct to be observed by the participants. Some of these rules are discussed here for your guidance.

Norms to be Observed

How to address other members of the group?

Sir/Madam	-	too formal
Mr./Ms.	-	Colloquial
Excuse Me	-	(a bit rude)
Numbers	-	Funny
First Name	-	Ideal

But the problem is that you may not be able to know or remember the names of your fellow participants in such a short time that you might have had to meet them all before the GD.

Then, the best way is to address the whole group, instead of an individual.

(By referring to individual members, we create sub-groups)

Do not create sub-groups

Our tendency is to speak to the person sitting next to us. That creates sub-groups which act against the cohesive team-spirit of the group.

Strategy

To gain entire group's attention.

To begin, speak to the person sitting diagonally opposite you.

Or begin speaking to the person who has just finished talking.

Use opportunity to take discussion forward. Do not let an opportunity pass over without your participating in the discussion.

Make friends by speaking to those who have been ignored by the rest of the group.

Should you invite somebody who has been keeping quiet to participate?

No, unless you have formal authority to do so.

Everybody is equal in a group discussion.

Your objective is—

Getting the group's attention is the first thing. Having got it, use it to make point most effectively.

Language: Formal; Simple, correct spoken English; Not Colloquial English; Not literary English.

Dress: Formal; Men in Business Suits; Ladies in sarees/ formal salwar kameez.

Body Language: Posture; Formal (straight back; hands together in the front/on the edge of the table); Must reflect enthusiasm.

Gestures and body movements: Shouldn't be threatening of restricting other members; Avoid excessive use of hand; Be natural.

Eye contact: Establish eye contact with as many as you can while speaking;

Points to remember

Don't attempt to be a leader by trying to sum up or conclude when the group has not clearly reached any conclusion yet.

Remember that a GD is to assess your ability to interact in a group effectively.

Discussion Techniques

GD is not a debate in which you either oppose or support the topic. There are no clear-cut positions or stands to be taken. GD is continuous discussion. A live interaction in which you examine a subject/problem form different angles and view- points. And as a participant, you may disagree with or support other's point view or bring in a new point of view. But you should do it by showing respect for the other person even if you do not accept his/her point of view as correct. Courtesy in discussions indicates our level of culture and sophistication. Here are guidelines for all GD participants.

How to Join the Discussion ?

I'd like to raise the subject of...
What I think is. . . . .
I think it's important to consider the question of . . .
If I could say a word about. . . ..
May I take a point about. . . ...

To support what some other participant has said.

Remember that you should not say that you support so and so or I agree with him/her. You should support the views of the person, not the person.

I would like to support Miss Renuka's point of view. . .

I agree fully with what Mr. Rahul has just said. I am in complete agreement with fee slashing.

To Support Disagreement

Again, remember that you are opposed to the idea, and not the person who holds it. You can disagree by using polite expressions, instead of curt expressions such as "You are wrong", "you can say".

Please allow me to differ—

I would like to differ.
I think differently on this issue.
I do not agree in my opinion. . . ....

To make a Point Very Strongly

I am convicted that . . . ..
You can't deny that. . . ....
Anybody can see that. . . .
It is quite clear to me. . .

To bring a Discussion back to the Point

That's very interesting, but I don't think it is indeed to the point.

Perhaps, we could go back to the point

Could we stick to the subject, please?

I am afraid we are drifting from the point.

Use such cue phrases and expressions to exhibit your group-culture.

Your analytical ability and your being critical of arguments, assessment and your verbal and non-verbal skills of communication give you competitive edge over others.

Listening

Know that in GD, listening too is a participative act. Listen to know what others have to say. Do not listen with the desire to contradict or refute.

Listen to assimilate and analyze. Then speak to express your thoughts in the light of thoughts of others.

Do not interrupt. But try to join in the discussion tactfully.

Finally, if you really want to stand out, do not try to dominate by demolishing other participants.

RESUME WRITING

Either during interview or at the time applying for a post, a Resume is written and submitted. The focus is specifically made on those particulars which the employer needs as per job requirements. A specimen of Resume is appended:

Example of a Graduate's resume.

AKSHITA MEHRA
21/A, AMRITA SHERGIL MARG, NEW DELHI-110 003
Phone (011) 24620980/24692993, 9810455654.
Email : akshita81@yahoo.com

Job Objective:

Initially, I want to work as a management trainee in an industry where my education in management, with a major in marketing, may be developed. My ultimate goal is to be a senior executive in marketing.

Personal Profile:

Date of Birth	7th June 1981
Martial Status	Single
Health	Robust, physically and mentally alert

Specialization

Marketing and sales Major)

Human Resource Management (Minor)

Education

Post Graduate Diploma in Business Management from Amity Business School, Noida—2004

Bachelor of Arts—Sociology Honors, Lady Shri Ram College (LSR), New Delhi—2002

Senior Secondary (XII) CBSE—Humanities, Sardar Patel Vidyalaya, New Delhi—1999

Higher Secondary (X) CBSE—Sardar Patel Vidyalaya, New Delhi—1997

Scholarships/Awards

Shri Ram Swaroop Ahuja Award for Outstanding Performance in sports—1998

Shri Jaswant S. Pandaya Award for Outstanding Performance in Athletics- 1996

Govt. of India Sports Talent Search Scholarship scheme—1994-1995

Interests and Achievements

President of National Sports Organization

2001-02 at Lady Shri Ram College.

Awarded certificate of merit for Contribution to Sports.

1st Degree International Black Belt in Tae-Known-Do (Korean Martial Art)

Won 62 Gold Medals in Domestic Championships and 4 Bonze Medals as an international player

Held Merit Positions in Basketball, Volleyball, badminton, Table Tennis and Judo

Organized sponsorships worth Rs. 1 Lakh for LSR Sports Festival—2001

Organised a Cross-Country run for "Green & Clean Delhi" on Aug 24th, 2001, LSR and other events in capacity as the President

Participant and member of Organising committee of Sangathan 2003 (Amity Inter-Institute Annual Sports Meet)

Won 9 medals including 7 GOLD

Master of Ceremony for the following events organized by Amity Business School

Alumni Meet

Mentor Meet

Corporate Meet

Acumen 2003, Organised by Business Today

Personal Objective

My desire is to create a truly competitive arena wherever I work. I want to bring my enthusiasm and sense of confidence to the organization and to the people I work with. My involvement in various areas of activities at college had taught me crucial lessions on leadership and teamwork.

Strengths

Team Player

Self-confident and Goal-oriented

Work Experience

Worked as a Trainee in Enterprise Nexus, Ad Agency in the Research and Planning Department.

Conducted research for General Motors undertaken by Enterprise Nexus.

REFERENCE (Available on request).

CHAPTER

18

Presentations and Interviews

PRESENTATIONS : DEFINITION AND OCCASIONS

In preference to 'public speaking', the term 'presentation' is now being used in industry and commerce. The reason, perhaps, is that the purpose of a presentation is more precisely and more concretely defined. In the present status of economy in which the process of globalization has been going on for integration of the world through economic activities, marketing concept has taken the centre-stage. In marketing, the products and services are displayed and described with focus on their characteristics. It may be due to this fact that the person speaking presents products or services or views. There are many occasions for a presentation such as—

(i) Launching a new product or service.
(ii) Starting a training course/session.
(iii) Presenting a new business plan.
(iv) Making a marketing/sales proposal.
(v) Making a contribution to a conference/seminar.
(vi) Diversification of a business.
(vii) Emphasising community service concepts.

For any body, speaking before an audience on any of the occasions stated above, or on a similar occasion, is a serious matter. It requires careful preparation that can not be done satisfactorily by one person alone. It is this reason why a presentation has been defined as "a formal or set-piece occasion with two usual hallmarks: the use of audio-visual aids, (and) team work." (Adair)

In view of the foregoing, particularly the given definition of Adair, a presentation stands out as a speech made with the help of at least one teammate on the basis of sufficient material/information gathered and processed for a significant business occasion and delivered with the help of audio-visual aids to make a positive impact on the audience. For making a successful presentation, the following steps are taken:

(a) Be Clear What the Occasion is about

The person proposing to make a presentation must know his proper sphere and the purpose he wants to fulfil through his presentation. The question arises whether the proposed presentation would be for a seminar or a conference, or the occasion is launching an exciting new product. He has to consider whether there is sufficient time for the presentation and discussion thereafter. It is also very important to know what would be happening till the time the presentation took place. Without this information, the speaker will not understand the context. If, for example, the presentation is going to be made on an inaugural occasion, it is definitely the exciting time to put your best foot forward. On the other hand, if the organization has been facing some financial problems and the audience has to be apprized of the situation, the presentation has to focus on 'vital statistics', inferences drawn from them, and positive suggestions to overcome or remedy the situation.

(b) Make an Analysis of Audience

It is of utmost importance to understand for whom it is meant before making a presentation. Granted that an audience is gathering of individuals at one place, but it has also a collective personality of its own. The data of audience like age, sex, educational background, experience, nationality or nationalities of audience have great relevance to the presentation. Just imagine how important it is to know whether one is going to make a presentation before an all-male, all female or mixed audience. It will influence our choice of words, tones, need for details and appropriate illustrations and so on. It will also give us an idea of their expectations and their likely reactions to what we are planning to say. If we know any one or more of them personally, it will make the presentation more effective. Therefore, it is quite advisable to try to meet the audience before the presentation. At least, get such information from the organizers or sponsors before making rather preparing presentation.

The analysis of audience should continue during the presentation. The reaction of the audience is writ large on their faces as we speak and illustrate. Their body language immediately gives us the much needed feedback. For this purpose, we have to keep our own eyes and ears open. Their smiles, stares—whether blank or excited, silence or whispers or lip movements give us ample idea of their reactions, and guide us through our speech.

(c) Visit to have an Idea of the Location

The location/venue of the presentation should be visited before the event, if possible. There is no wisdom in taking the location for granted. Regarding location, much depends on the size of the room, seating arrangements, room temperature, lighting controls, public address equipments, audio-visual equipment, and acoustics, etc. For example, if the room echoes or resounds with the words we speak, much of the presentation will be spoilt. Similarly, if the audience is huddled in a cramped space and feels uncomfortable in a hot Indian summer afternoon, the whole event will be a waste of time. If the audience is large and the public address arrangements are not satisfactory—as is often the case—both the audience and the person making the presentation become irritated/bored.

(d) Plan Out the Presentation

The next step is perhaps the most important step towards making a presentation and that is to plan it out in writing in detail or at least in outline showing exactly what you would say in the beginning, the middle and the end. A rough plan for any presentation may be made as follows:

Beginning

(i) Introductory remarks.
(ii) Statement of the objective, giving reasons why you are making this presentation.
(iii) Draw the outlines of the presentation.

Middle

(i) Break the main body of the presentation into short, clearly stated units/sections. Not more than five or six sections can be managed.
(ii) Illustrate the points with examples.
(iii) Put a time limit on each point.
(iv) Prioritize the time limit. Certain points may need more time than others.

End

(i) Give the summary of the whole.
(ii) If need be, refer to the points made in the beginning or in the middle for the sake of emphasis.
(iii) Make final remarks and end on a positive note.

At this stage, it is advisable to consult the sponsors of the event, and be in constant touch with the co-presenter. As it is a team work, several minds are better than one.

(e) Decide upon the Method of Presentation

The method of presentation is the next step after having planned out the presentation. There are three most popular methods of presentations, which have been followed and practiced.

Reading

It has been found that many speakers write out their entire speeches and read them out before audience. The greatest advantage of this method is that accuracy is best maintained in it. Sir Winston Churchill is known for having used a written script. As he was a master orator, he would frequently glance up from the script and maintain eye contact with his audience. But not many speakers can do that. In fact, most of us do not read aloud well. Most readers sink into dull monotones, miss punctuation marks and fumble for words. So, this method has more disadvantages than advantages.

Memorized Presentation

Many speakers are known to write and memorize their entire speeches. They have good memory power to remember even the pauses. It is a sad story that very few have been able to do so effectively. The greatest disadvantage of this method is that the speaker may forget some important point/part of the script. Trying to locate it in the script if it is with the speaker at the moment, spoils the entire effect of the presentation. That is why most such speakers memorize key parts and use notes to help them during the presentation.

Extemporaneous Presentation

This is the most popular method used by really effective speakers. They have carefully planned their speeches, but then they speak as if they were getting the ideas, coherently arranged, on the spur of the moment. Whenever they need any help, they look into their notes that they keep handy. They don't waste time in memorizing the speech as it is a strenuous exercise. On the other hand, looking into the notes, serially arranged, seems quite natural and the speech delivered in this way also sounds spontaneous.

(f) Rehearse the Presentations

As a necessary part of preparation, rehearsal is very important. It is a private practice session to gain confidence and work towards self-improvement. But it is best to rehearse as part of a team (not alone as many suggest) and invite suggestions for improvement. The best part of team rehearsal is mutual constructive criticism and gives the speaker an advantage of feedback. This way, it goes a long way in training the speaker to be an effective communicator.

Rehearsing the speech part of the presentation is not all. It also gives the speaker a clear idea of where, when and how to introduce/bring in visual aids to support his presentation. Only a rehearsal can ensure coordination of effort. Moreover, the team can also check the location, seating arrangements, lighting and acoustics, the working of the electronic equipment and so on.

(g) Consider Personal Aspects

Style is the man. So, it is absolutely necessary to analyze oneself before going on to make a presentation. As has been said so succinctly, the speaker himself is essentially a part of the message. The audience first sees the speaker, then listens to the spoken words: first dress and then address. Hence, the importance of a presentable appearance cannot be over-emphasized. A presentation is a formal occasion; the speaker must be formally dressed, but certainly not overdressed. Special caution for ladies please. If the speaker is well prepared and properly dressed for the occasion, he will not only look but also feel confident. Confidence really is the primary characteristic of effective oral reporting/presentation.

Confidence of speaker is clearly reflected in a clear, strong and well modulated voice: voice is virtue, sometimes enchanting. The confidence building for presentation may require endless hours of preparation. But usually two or three rehearsals are enough to gain confidence while working as part of a team. While rehearsing alone, the best way is to look at oneself in the mirror.

For improving body language, rehearsing in front of full length mirror is of immense help. One can always train oneself in establishing effective/appealing eye contact, acquiring the correct and confident posture, and learning meaningful gestures. None can claim to be ideally perfect. There is immense scope for improvement in facial expression and manner of walking. The way the speaker walks before his/her audience at once conveys an impression—that of confidence or otherwise. Similarly, thoroughness in the subject of the presentation as well as sincerity and friendliness towards the audience are indispensable. It is not only the question of the speaker's confidence in him, but also the audience should have confidence in the speaker. Hence, these qualities must be carefully cultivated, day after day, and in every possible way. In a presentation, one has to 'win' the audience. Every effective presentation is by itself an event of triumph.

(h) Overcoming Nervousness

While everyone is not born confident speaker, he does run the risk of becoming nervous when asked to face an audience. The very consciousness of being asked to speak before an audience, especially a select and well-informed audience, makes many a speaker nervous. There are numberless examples of great speakers who, after one or two initial stages of nervousness, trained themselves to overcome this state. Feeling self-conscious even in the face of audience known to us, having a dry mouth and sweaty palms, breathlessness and palpitation, experiencing difficulty in finding the right word, forgetting what we really want to say, of feeling that the mind is going blank, fumbling for words or playing with a button—all these are well known signs of nervousness. There are methods to overcome them: they can be easily overcome by: (a) repeated rehearsals of a thoroughly prepared speech, (b) breathing deeply, (c) looking straight at the audience seated all over the place, (d) breathing deeply again, (e) talking slowly, giving yourself as well as the audience time to relax, (f) moving about slowly and gracefully in front of the audience, and (g) referring to/pointing at the visual aids whenever reference is needed to make rather reinforce a point.

(i) Using Visual Aids

A presentation is made, and is meant primarily, to convey information, and that is the first and foremost function of communication. To make this function effective, the communicators or speakers making presentations have to rely on visual aids like charts, chalk boards, film slides, transparencies, diagrams, maps, pictures, etc. There is quite a large range of visual aids in use. They can also be devised according to the need/purpose of the message. So, it must be clear that there is no one visual aid suiting all purposes. That is why we should have flexible attitude towards visual aids. The visual aid used in the presentation may be of any kind. It should be positioned in such a way that it is easily visible to the audience. It should also be made sure that the speaker, while speaking and moving, does not obstruct the view of the audience.

A suitable position can be selected for this purpose. It may be like the model shown below:

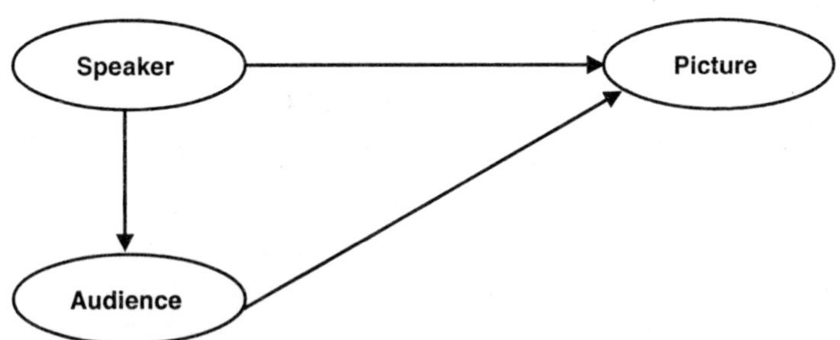

GUIDELINES FOR THE USE OF VISUAL AIDS

Use the visual aids to convey the key part of the message. It means that they are meant to emphasize the most vital points of the presentation. As every presentation is a unique communication event, no hard and fast rules can be laid down for the use of visual aids in all presentations. It depends very much on the individual's choice. Even so, some instructions in this regard can serve well for all speakers.

(i) It has to be ensured that everyone in the audience is able to see the visual aid.
(ii) The speaker must explain the visual aid if there is any likelihood that the audience may not immediately understand it.
(iii) The visual aids must be fitted well into the presentation. They must be an essential part of the plan of the presentation.
(iv) Proper emphasis must be laid on the visual aid. The speaker must point to it with bodily action and with words.
(v) Sometimes, a long stick or pointer is used to draw the attention of the audience to a serial number or a

chart, or a city/location on a map. So, a pointer must be kept handy.

(vi) The speaker must look at the audience more than at the visual aid.

(vii) If the speaker is using slides he must make sure that they are clearly numbered in the correct sequence and are kept right way up. Any confusion in their order/arrangement will simply damage the presenter's image.

(viii) No visual aid should be kept on for too long.

(ix) The speaker should use pictures, drawings and colours for interest. One must remember the Chinese saying that "A picture is worth a thousand words".

(x) A slide should carry only essential information, no extraneous matter.

(xi) The content of the information on the slide should be kept limited to twenty-five words or he equivalent in figures.

Presentation is not only presentation. There is more to it. A presentation has the potential to open up unlimited possibilities for the organization. For example, if a new product is to be launched, the best visual aid will be either to display the product itself or a replica of the product as is sometimes done by motor/engineering/aircraft companies. They either hold exhibitions backed up by presentation or display replicas of their products at selected places. Screening of films on their products also attracts audience who is, then, got engaged in presentation/question-answer sessions. Presentation made in this way serves the purpose to inform-charm-convince-persuade-ask for further information—act for the organization to decide how best to make their presentation 'deliver' their goods.

Speeches: Prepared *vs.* Impromptu

Irrespective of the kind of the occasion, a speech has to be delivered. It may be prepared or impromptu. But one thing is certain—every speech has a certain plan or pattern or structure. In this connection, it is worthwhile remembering the following oft-quoted words of Rudyard Kipling:

"I Keep six honest serving—men
(They taught me all I knew):
Their names are what and why and when
and how and where and who".

GUIDELINES FOR PREPARING A SPEECH

(i) Take care of the six cardinal questions of Kipling. The stanza given above poses the six cardinal questions. Every one proposing to make a speech must ask him those questions. Once he is clear in his mind about the answers to these questions, he will be able to have the desired effect. Given below are these cardinal questions that give rise to many other implied questions:

Cardinal Questions	*Implied Questions*
(a) What?	What do I wish to communicate? Have I thought about the content of my message? What facts and figures should I put forth?
(b) Why?	Why should the audience listen to me? Why have I chosen to speak to them?
(c) When?	Have I taken care of the timing of my speech? When are the listeners most likely to be interested? At what point of time should I say what would they be really interested in?
(d) How?	How can I best convey my message? Have I taken care to couch my message in the most persuasive language? Have I planned the beginning, middle and end of my speech? Do I need any audio-visual aids to make my speech effective?
(e) Where?	Where have I to speak? Or, in other words, what is the physical context of my communication? Will the audience be comfortable at the venue announced? Is the hall/room well lighted and fitted with adequate sound systems?

(f)	Who?	Who am I going to speak to? Do I have to speak to an individual or several persons, or a large audience? What are the interests and expectations of the audience?

(ii) Be Clear and Organized

Once the questions and their implications stated above have been taken care of, the speech automatically turns out to be clear and effective. After all, clarity is the very essence of all speech and writing. Moreover, it is also to be always kept in mind that no listener/reader likes to be caught up in a jumble or confused thinking. It is, basically a question of mental training and logical thinking that come from all good education. Especially, in the world of business, clarity of thought is the greatest asset. All powerful speakers religiously stick to the principle—'Be Clear'.

(iii) Be Simple

It is a fact that from clarity of thought simplicity emerges. The simpler the language the greater is the appeal. A really effective speaker is one who can explain the most difficult or complex matter in the simplest language to the laymen. Every educated person studies some subject in detail; likewise every worker having sufficiently long hands-on experience in a particular area becomes a kind of specialist. As a result, both the scholar and the worker pick up a special variety of language known as jargon. No audience likes to listen to jargon. They can be patient only with the simplest language. Otherwise, they are likely to be bored, distracted or rendered not interested.

(iv) Furnish Concrete Details

Beware of using jargon or talking in abstractions or marshalling platitudes. An effective speaker makes his speech vivid by furnishing details and actual experiences to capture the attention of the audience. Such attention to speech to make it 'full of life' that is the literal meaning of the word 'vivid'. It is, therefore, very important for a speaker to make his speech lively and brilliant with eye-catching details, humorous anecdotes, relevant examples and enthusiastic eye-to-eye contact with the audience.

(v) Cultivate Effortless Grace and Naturalness

"Many things", says C.S. Lewis "such as loving, going to sleep or behaving unaffectedly—are done worst when we try hardest to do them". Perhaps every body reading this book knows that a cultured person moves and speaks with grace and sounds natural. But then, there are circumstances in which it is really hard to act/speak naturally. When we are face to face with a large selected audience, and have to make an important speech, it is quite natural to be conscious, perhaps over-conscious, and, for the moment, to find it difficult to be natural. We have to devise our own ways to look, move and speak with grace. Practicing to speak in front of a mirror is a very common advice. Another method is to find a popular television anchor/personality and emulate his/her ways.

(vi) Enrich Your Mental Equipment

A speaker must be able to create effect. We know that every effective speaker is a learned/well informed person. As the old Greek proverb says, "Out of nothing, nothing comes". So, we must remember that for every occasion, and for every kind of speech, the best arrangement is as well as stocked mind—a mind stocked or equipped with all kinds of information/facts/figures/general awareness/readings in literature and philosophy, current affairs, economic and political developments, new advancements in science and technology, emergence of new business organizations and so on. Having the right kind of information for the right moment is an essential condition of speaking effectively.

(vii) Be Brief

The speaker may have a lot of information; it does not mean that he can go on rambling or into unnecessary details. It means that one has to take care not only of the quantity of information but also of the quality of speech. As Benjamin Franklin has said, 'time is money'. All that superfluous must be cut to make the speech concise. Every word we speak is valuable, and there are no words to waste.

(viii) Be Informal

Being informal is an art. The occasion may be formal but the speaker must strive to give his speech a personal touch; that is being informal. That is the only way to establish rapport with the audience and to crate an impression that will last. Informality creates nearness.

(ix) Be Enthusiastic

Bear in mind that making an effective speech is not just a matter of doing a duty willy-nilly or performing a ritual. One has to get into spirit of the occasion with enthusiasm and keen interest; constipated look is never welcome. Only then will the speaker and the audience be able to empathise with each other. No one likes to listen to a dull or monotonous speaker. But an enthusiastic speaker does get an immediate response. Enthusiasm is contagious.

(x) Mind Your Non-vernal Language

Note that effective use of gestures is a necessary component of a speech whether prepared or impromptu. Pope John Paul is known for his excellent use of arms while addressing the congregation. In the same way, good eye contact is indispensable.

(xi) Remember that the Facts and the Figures are not Enough

If facts and figures had been enough, there would have been no speeches. Anybody could have access to facts and figures. They can just be circulated or blandly stated. But a speech puts life into the dry bones of the facts and figures, which otherwise, are just like a repelling skeleton. It is the imaginative and effective use of language in a speech/writing that breathes life into that skeleton and supplies it with flesh and blood. Many great entrepreneurs, chairpersons, statesmen and scholars are known for their oratory that stems from their command of language.

(xii) Control your Emotions, but make an Emotional Appeal

Believe it that 'what comes from the heart goes to the heart'. Every human being is full of emotions. But an effective speaker cannot afford to be carried away by his own emotions. On the other hand, while exercising poise and maintaining composure, he can stir up his audience to action.

His job is not just to inform but also to convince and influence his audience. That is how many speeches become memorable.

MAKING IMPROMPTU SPEECHES

Every speaker can not deliver impromptu address. The ability to speak impromptu i.e., to speak on the spur of the moment is, in fact, more important than to prepare a speech on a subject/topic announced in advance for a particular occasion. It is all the more important in the context of an organization. We know that all organizational decisions are group decisions, taken mostly in a committee room or around a table. This situation involves a group. Each member of group is supposed to contribute to the decision-making process. Nobody can exactly visualize in advance what turn the discussion will take. Speaking impromptu is, therefore, a necessary part of day-to-day communication in an organization. Moreover, the demands leave hardly any time for long preparation. The following guidelines are of immense help in this regard.

(i) *Practicing to speak impromptu*: It is not everyone's cup of tea to speak impromptu because everyone is not really good or effective in speaking impromptu. It is quite a common sight to see a speaker nervous, sweating, losing fluency or fidgeting when asked to speak without notice. That is why it is very important for almost everybody to practice speaking impromptu.

(ii) *Various techniques have been developed for this purpose*. One such technique is a game that can be easily played in a group. Some topics are written on small pieces of paper that is folded and dropped into a box. The box is then shaken and passed from person to person by turns. A person picks up a folded paper from the box at random. On unfolding it, he finds a topic on which he is supposed to speak. As it is a game, people like to participate in it and get useful practice in speaking impromptu.

Another game is the linkage technique. In it, a member of a group, or a student in a class, starts telling a story and abruptly stops. Then the person sitting next to him picks up the thread of the story and starts telling the next part that he thinks would be the logical next stage in the story. And thus it goes on, leading to very stimulating, funny or thrilling episodes in a long story. Participating in games, like these, gives one sufficient practice in speaking without preparation.

(iii) *"Don't talk impromptu—give an impromptu talk"*—says Dale Carnegie. There is a big significant meaning in this exhortation. Let us ask ourselves—"Do we really talk impromptu?" The fact is that as soon as we are asked to speak on any topic, our mind starts organizing our thoughts on it. In this way what really takes place is an impromptu talk that has a logical structure in the same way as a long, prepared speech. The only difference is that in a prepared speech, we have had sufficient time to organize our thinking, gather sufficient and relevant material/ data, and come out with a well thought out conclusion. An impromptu talk has also a similar structure. How well structured our impromptu talk will be depends on how much we have been practicing to speak impromptu. The more we practice, the better structured our impromptu talk will be.

(iv) *Be mentally prepared to speak impromptu*: It is indeed a good practice to keep visualizing what we would say about something if we were suddenly asked to stand up/take the microphone in a larger gathering, and speak. Let us analyze how much we know about a certain subject and what we would like to say about it. It naturally implies that we must keep gathering as much information as possible. Not only that: we must create/find out newer areas of interest and be mentally prepared to speak on it on our own or to add to what someone else is speaking on it. In this way, it is a matter of conditioning ourselves to speak impromptu.

(v) *Give examples from your experience*: With passing years, a man, more so a business executive gets experience of working in different situations. A man's life is, in fact, a store-house of experiences. The best way to gain confidence in an impromptu speech is to give examples from our own experience. It not only gives substance to our speech but also involves the audience in a more meaningful relationship with us. Telling about our own experience requires no preparation. That is why we are advised by communication experts to enlist our significant experiences and come out with relevant examples whenever we are required to speak.

(vi) *Genuine interest in the audience*: Just as our interest in our experiences and examples therefrom are a source of confidence in an impromptu talk so is our interest in the audience. If we care to know about the interest and inclinations of the audience, we will be able to talk impromptu without much difficulty.

(vii) *Remember quotations, proverbs, maxims, etc*. We know that from the very beginning of our education, we are exposed to all kinds of writings and specially taught to remember pithy, meaningful quotations for all occasions. For an impromptu speech, they are very useful. Every good newspaper and magazine gives us memorable quotations every day. It is a good practice to note them and use them whenever the need arises. We must have a sharp, tenacious memory for this purpose.

(viii) *Remember jokes, humorous anecdotes, etc.*: Along with daily routine and business related work, everybody needs some moments of entertainment. Therefore, everybody is interested in jokes and humorous anecdotes. They are easy to remember and very useful for an impromptu speaker. One can always start-off with a joke or an anecdote without unnecessarily being self-conscious.

(ix) Make use of incidents in the lives of great men. It is said that every one has a model seated in his/her psyche to imitate and follow. All of us read a lot about great men and remember almost all the major incidents in their lives. By repeatedly turning them out in our minds, we make them, consciously or unconsciously, our models. Since we remember them so well, it is always easy to see their relevance to any situation and start-off an impromptu speech with a suitable reference or to find a place for them somewhere in the course of our speech.

(x) Size up the patience level of the audience: While the points given above serve as guidance, it is important to have an eye on the mood and patience level of the audience. Almost all the listeners know about all the great figures that we have in our mind and to whose lives we choose to make reference. So, we have also to keep in mind that the audience can't be patient with the repetition of what they already know.

(xi) The speaker has to be sharp enough to see what to say, when, and in what connection.

Get involved, don't get participation: Communication is contextual in nature. Therefore, one can't make a successful impromptu speech getting involved in a communication situation at the moment. At such a moment, the listeners are really in a mood to receive what we say. But they are certainly not in a mood to be 'told' or sermonized or pontificated.

The style of a long, prepared and circulated, or read-out speech may at times assume the overtones of pontification or serious words of advice. But an impromptu speech is best.

GROUP COMMUNICATION

"The pervasiveness of groups helps explain why the ability to work as a team player is often regarded as more important than an employee's individual brilliance."

—Ronald B. Adler and Janne Marquardt Elmhorst

Introduction

Understanding of business communication is incomplete without the study of the group communication. We observe people communicating verbally and non-verbally and forming interpersonal relations in a group. In the present business environment, working with others has become a vital part of every job. Today's professionals work in team to handle complicated and complex problems.

Working in a group not only provides the advantage of enhanced efficiency and accuracy but also generates more enthusiasm from the members. People are more committed to a decision when they have a part in making it. Therefore, companies deliberately create groups in the form of committees, quality circles, autonomous work groups, parallel group to get maximum out of different individuals' initiative, intelligence and imagination. As the number of groups in an organisation is increasing, communication in group is assuming added importance.

What is Group?

A group may be defined as two or more persons interacting and influencing each other through the process of communication. Usually, the members of the group subscribe themselves to common values, beliefs and objectives and interrelate with one another in a dynamic way.

Types of Groups

Groups can be of following types:

Formal and Informal

Formal Groups are explicitly as part of the organisation structure such as committees, task forces, etc. In these groups, important objectives and roles of different members are predetermined.

On the other hand, informal groups emerge spontaneously without deliberate design in the organisation hierarchy. These informal groups can be of members who join together because of their common interest and needs for social belongingness. The objective and roles in these groups arise from the current interactions of members.

Primary and Secondary Groups

A group can also be classified as primary or secondary depending upon its size, the degree of face-to-face interaction and the type of influence it exerts on its members.

Primary Groups are groups with a small size in which face-to-face contacts are frequent and relationships among members tend to be close and intimate as family, sports team, social setting among close friends, impersonal and large scale association.

However, professional association, a company, ethic-religious group, a university alumni body, are examples of secondary groups.

The term reference group is often used to indicate a secondary group. These groups may posses certain attractions due to which different individuals wish to form them and identify themselves in some way.

Such groups reflect and affect the beliefs, values and feelings of their members, even though they may involve no face-to-face contact.

Reasons for Joining Groups

The reason for joining a group may be:

Protection

Joining group may be self-protection strategy of individuals. For example, they prefer to join trade union because it protects their rights.

Need for Social Belonging

People by nature have need for social belongingness and companionship. Therefore, they join the groups. Job may be interesting but with belongingness to a work group, they feel themselves encouraged and elevated.

Identification

People feel need to be identified with specific type of like-minded people. They also want their affections and sympathy. Therefore, they join the group. Sometimes loyalty to the group can override loyalty to the organisation.

Need for Power

People sometimes join groups because they want to control and dominate others through exercise of power. They want some surrounding where they can play leadership role which a group provides.

Characteristics of Groups

The following key characteristics of groups need to be discussed:

(1) Norms
(2) Cohesiveness
(3) Communication and interactions
(4) Structural factors
(5) Group Dynamics

Norms

Social norms—the collective shared value of members of the group—regulate the relationship between and among individuals in the groups and guide their behaviour. These norms have the following characteristics:

Acceptable to the majority of people.

Focus on the group behaviour rather than the thoughts and feelings of members.

Facilitates the process of managing people.

Enables to predict the behaviour of group members.

Develop slowly and change slowly.

Accompanied by implicit reward and punishment for compliance and non-compliance of these norms.

The purpose of these norms is:

To inspire the members and project to others the nature of the group.

To ensure the predictability of the behaviour of different individuals.

To assist the group members in avoiding embarrassing situations like abstaining from discussing issues likely to hurt the feelings of particular member(s).

To help the group to survive.

Cohesiveness

Cohesiveness is the extent to which members find the group attractive and tightly or loosely held together. The members of a highly cohesive group are more likely to remain together, cooperate and participate in common endeavours. As a result, communication among them will be more frequent and smooth, and productivity and performance will improve.

This group cohesiveness is determined by the following factors:

Similarity of attitude and goals: People with similar attitudes and objectives will find each other's company as a source of satisfaction and are likely to remain together.

Time spent together: Spending greater time together promotes more cohesiveness as people spending more time together are given inter-personal attraction. A close relationship is likely to exist between group members who are located near to each other than those living far apart.

Threats: The cohesiveness of group increases when it faces external threats. At the time of external threat, the cohesiveness of the group is solidified.

Size: The smaller the size, the greater are the chances of inter-personal attraction. This results in enhanced cohesiveness. On the other hand, if the size of group increases, it results in development of bureaucratic rules and procedures that dilute the informal nature of relations and communication among group members.

Entry restriction: The more stringent the entry requirements are the more cohesive the group will be. The stringent entry requirement facilitates to protect the group norms which guide the behaviour of different group members.

Rewards: Incentives based upon group performance cultivate a group centred perspective where cooperation and collaboration rather than internal competition prevail. This cooperation promotes the group cohesiveness. On the other hand, reward system based upon individual performance breeds competition among group members that affects cohesiveness in adverse way.

Communication and Interaction

Communication and interaction among members is the main characteristic of a group. With the communication among members, different communication networks are formed. In their studies of the communicative networks, *Alex Bevelar and Harold Leavitt* compared the speed and accuracy with which the members of four different networks solved problems and the effects these patterns had on their members' morale.

In a communication experiment, different persons were divided into five nember-groups who had to communicate with one another by passing written notes. Each person in a group received a list of symbols—like star, circle, and wavy line. The task was to find out as quickly as possible which the common symbol is. The situations depicted in this experiment were found in large organisations where a number of people in different parts of the organisation are in touch with one another.

The results of the study revealed that the problems were solved more quickly with fewer mistakes in centralized network, i.e. the wheel. The person at the centre enjoys the position of a perceived leader. In decentralized network, i.e. the circle—the performance was found slower and erratic, but people enjoyed there.

A study by *Shaw* suggests that centralized networks such as 'the wheel', lead to efficient and expeditious execution of simple and structured tasks, but for highly complex problems, decentralized networks such as 'circles' network where everybody communicates freely and flawlessly with others, are more suitable. Moreover, in wheel network, the central person is more overwhelmed and overloaded when dealing with incoming messages and manipulating data in the complex task. Another study by *Alvin Sandowsky* showed that centralized communication networks are more efficient on all types of task performance (actual), but decentralized networks developed better plans for performing complex tasks.

Structural Factors

Work groups have a structure that influences the behaviour of their members. These structural factors include:

The nature of the structure; atmosphere; status; composition; size; leadership.

Structure and Atmosphere

the structure and atmosphere of a group play a major role in facilitating the performance of tasks and the satisfaction of individual needs. The groups with organic structure—which are flexible, are more aware about organizational objectives and lesser governed by formalities—tend to be more innovative in generating and implementing new ideas. These types of groups have a high level of autonomy in matters connected with the use of technology.

The other extreme of structure is the mechanistic group, bound by rules with established norms for making decisions. Such a structure is suitable for performing standardized jobs on mass scale. Communication in organic structure tends to be open and free whereas it is more formal in mechanical structures.

Roles

Group members play a particular role in the group. A role is defined as a set of expected pattern of behaviour attributed to a person occupying a particular position.

Usually a role is prescribed in the role occupants' job description. How the group member perceives and performs his role in the group, affects the functioning of the group. Sometimes, role conflicts arise when a person performs more than one role and the performance of one role makes performance in the other more difficult.

Status

Status is the social ranking a person enjoys because of his position in the group. This status depends upon various factors such as seniority, salary, power, professional knowledge, etc. The person enjoying good status can exert more influence in the functioning of the group.

Composition

When the composition of group is considered, we observe that there can be homogeneity or heterogeneity. A homogeneous group is said to exist when the profile of the members e.g. their age, experience, education, specialization, etc. are similar in many ways. In heterogeneous groups, the profile of the members is dissimilar.

Size

The size of the group may be smaller or larger. Small groups give their people more opportunity to interact freely and frankly whereas large groups, working on bureaucratic practice, become more formalized.

Leadership

Leadership is one of the important structural characteristics of a group. This can be both formal and informal. *Formal* leadership is reflected in the authority bestowed on the leader to use rewards and sanctions for influencing the behaviour of other members. *Informal leadership* derives a mandate from the group members to act as their spokesman or guide.

Group Dynamics

Each member of the group affects others and is also affected in an unconscious and subtle way. "A psychoanalytical view of the dynamics of a group recognizes the group's emotional impact as the individual's behaviour because of considerations of conformity, loyalty and identification with and reaction to the group", *Eugene McKenna* remarks.

For example, an atmosphere of hostility in a group does not come out of nowhere; members unconsciously contribute to it even though they may deny it.

Bich recognizes the existence of a mechanism below the unconscious surface of the group, made up of three functions; which have the express purpose of resolving group tension.

(a) Flight or fight
(b) Dependency
(c) Pairing

Flight or Fight

The group experiences its survival as being dependent on either fighting; being aggressive or flighting being passive or withdrawing from the scene.

Dependency

The group tends to depend on procedural matters so that it can feel secure. It likes to alleviate the feeling of insecurity by becoming dependent on the leader.

Pairing

Two members of the group, enter into discussion while the remaining members listen and are attentive.

GROUP DEVELOPMENT

Groups tend to move through a series of development phases. Bruce Tuckman identifies these stages as: Forming, storming, norming and performing. Rodney Napier & Matti Gershelfield identified a fifth phase called reforming.

Forming

At this stage, the group is concerned with testing the boundaries of appropriate behaviour in very careful and conscious way. Members at this stage are dependent upon the group leader.

Storming

At this stage, conflict emerges among members as they tend to seek personal recognition. Understanding issues at this stage is concerned with prestige and power.

Norming

At this stage, the counter movements develop to soften the hostility with open communication and reorganizing the group. Personal feelings are subordinated to the group interest.

Performing

At this stage, the members of the group channelise their energies into work after solving the structural problems and their inter-personal differences. At this stage, the members feel greater degree of freedom and assume a sense of shared responsibility for the group goals.

Reforming

Sometimes, tension remains and working groups are not continuously feeling harmony. Therefore, group members initiate to reform with new norms to strengthen the group.

GROUP DISCUSSION

The term discussion is derived from the Latin root 'discutere', which means to shake or strike. Discussion is an activity in which a subject or theme is thoroughly shaken and examined. Thus group discussion involves enquiry or examination on a particular theme among group members.

At group discussion, various members contribute to the theme with arguments in favour and against. Despite the members' contradictory arguments, the discussion attempts to find the solution to the problem.

Features of Group Discussion

Purpose

The group discussion has a clear purpose. If the purpose is not clear, members will indulge in frivolous and aimless talking. With this process, time and energy of the participants is wasted.

Planning

Group discussion is always planned in advance. Its agenda is prepared which states the theme to be discussed.

Notice is given in advance specifying the date, time and venue of the meeting.

Participation

Since group discussion is the process of co-operative pooling of available information, each individual member of the group is encouraged to participate and contribute to the discussion.

Often, a discussion is dominated by a handful of members. But others can actively listen.

Free Communication

Free and flawless communication is essential to ensure the effectiveness of discussion.

Leadership

Every group discussion has to be led by a leader whose role is to navigate the discussion like a ship through troubled waters. In fact, leadership is indispensable for the group discussion.

Procedure to Communicate in Group Discussion

Each member of the group must follow the following rules to contribute to the group discussion:

Plan the topic in advance by searching the material with facts and figures.

Listen patiently and emphatically to the arguments of others.

Try to strike the problems than personality.

Ensure that the voice is audible to the other participants.

Avoid criticizing the others in destructive way.

Try to build consensus in the group through co-operative and collaborative efforts.

SEMINAR

A Seminar is group communication in which one person makes a presentation or speech on a topic by highlighting its contents in the light of present pressing problems. This presentation or speech is following by questions and experts' comments from the audience.

Thus seminar is a mixture of speech and group discussion. During a seminar, one person acts as Chairman of the session and conducts the seminar by introducing the topic and the speaker.

At the end of the session, he asks the audience to raise questions and ensures that the discussion follows in the light of the theme.

Seminar as a tool of group communication can be used with advantage.

It is used as a teaching and learning aid to provide and promote new ideas in business organizations and universities.

It is used as an instrument to share information on a particular theme.

It is used as a means to influence the thinking of various politicians and policy-makers.

METHOD OF MAKING SEMINAR EFFECTIVE

The effectiveness of a seminar depends upon how different parties and persons play their role in effective way. These parties and persons include organizers, speakers, chairpersons and audience.

Organizers' Role

To make seminar effective, organizers should—

Plan the seminar in advance by deciding the date, venue and theme of seminar.

Publish the relevant material in advance.

Advertise it in newspapers and invite various participants within time.

Ensure the proper arrangement of OHP, slides, lighting and other audio visual aids.

Facilitate arrangements of sitting, tea or lunch, etc.

Speaker's Role

The speaker of the seminar should—

Prepare the topic before hand by searching the material from library and websites, organizing the topic in logical order and pondering over the various relevant issues.

Ensure that his speech is informative, illuminating and interesting.

Use the appropriate visual aids like OHP transparencies, slides, etc.

Take the time limits into consideration.

Try to answer maximum questions of the audience at the end.

Convey thanks to the audience for their patient listening.

Chairperson's Role

The chairperson of the session should—

Introduce the topic briefly. This should be followed by the speaker's introduction in brief by highlighting the area of his specialization and his achievements.

Ensure that the speaker finishes his speech within time limit.

Invite questions from audience at the end of the speech.

Ensure that the discussion follows in the light of the theme and no one should hurt the feelings of another during question/answer session.

Sum up the findings of the speech after question-answer session. This is a reinforcement effort to emphasise upon the important points and relate them subtly to the objective of the seminar. While criticism is consciously avoided, effort is made to do the summing up in a way to drive home the broad message at the core of the seminar. It is normally the job of an expert on the subject and skilled in communication.

Thank the speaker and audience at the end.

Audience's Role

The audience should—

Occupy seats before the start of the seminar.

Listen patiently to the speeches of various speakers.
Note down important points and citations.
Avoid disturbing the speaker during the speech.
Stay till the conclusion of the seminar.

CHAPTER

19

Meetings, Committees and Conferences

"Two heads are always better than one"

—An old proverb

Executives, employees or experts gather as a group to discuss and debate upon certain matters for the purpose of taking collective decisions. Such gatherings with specific agenda or purpose or work may assume the form of meetings, committees and conferences. With their organization, different possible proposals are discussed in the light of their pros and cons. Consensus is generated through interaction and influence among various persons, and various constructive suggestions are brought on the subject.

In practice, it is very difficult to distinguish and demarcate meetings, committees and conferences. Their dividing line is very thin. They can not be packed into watertight compartments.

Both committees and conferences function through meetings. Both in meetings and conferences, the emphasis is on discussion whereas in committees emphasis is on decision-making.

Whether there is meeting, committee or conference, there is face-to-face oral communication in the group.

MEETINGS

> "Meeting is any focused conversation that has a specific purpose mentioned in its agenda".

Business meetings are held on—

Sharing information or comparing notes of the findings of different members.

Solving certain problems or taking action through consensus.

Performing certain ritual or social activities.

Convening certain meetings is compulsory as per the law of the land. For example, under Companies Act, every company has to hold:

A statutory meeting between one month to six months of the incorporation of the company for the purpose of informing members about shares allotted, cash received and paid, contracts, etc.

An annual general meeting in each calendar year for the presentation of accounts, declaration of dividend, appointment of directors and auditors, and other special matters including Corporate Governance, Environment Accounting, Corporate Social Responsibility, etc.

Board meeting at least once in every three months and at least four in every year to discuss and decide on various company matters, etc.

In addition to this, it is also legally compulsory (mandatory) that every meeting should have:

Proper and timely notice and agenda.

Quorum (Attendance of minimum number of members).

Chairman.

Minutes of the meeting duly recorded.

(A) Planning the Meeting

Meetings, especially problem-solving meetings, need meticulous planning as necessitated in case of interview, presentations, letters, and memos.

Decision about holding Meetings

Meetings should be called—

When it is a legal compulsion.

When the individual tasks are interdependent.

When the job is beyond the capacity of one person.

When chances of differences among employees or executives are lesser.

When the important information is to be conveyed immediately.

When important decision is to be taken with the consensus of members.

As meetings translate into sacrifice of important time and resources, therefore, they should be called and convened selectively.

Holding of meetings is not justified in the following cases:

When the matter could be handled over the phone.

When key persons are not available to attend.

When memo, email or fax could achieve the same goal.

When members are not prepared.

Agenda and Notice

For every meeting, timely notice must be sent to the concerned members stating the time, location (venue), date and possible time-length of the meeting. Along with notice, agenda, a list of topics to be covered in the meeting, must be attached

Specimen of Notice and Agenda is given on the next page:

A.K. Chemicals Limited
G.T. Road, Phagwara, Distt. Kapurthala

Notice of the Meeting

Notice is hereby given that the Sixteenth Annual General Meeting of the members of A.K. Chemicals Ltd. will be held on June 29, 2010 at 11.00 AM at the Registered Office of the Company at G.T. Road, Phagwara, District Kapurthala, to transact the following business:

Ordinary Business

(1) To receive, consider and adopt the balance sheet as on March 31, 2010 and Profit & Loss Account for the year ending on that date and Directors' and the Auditor's reports thereon.
(2) To declare dividend on the paid up Equity share capital for the year ending 31st March, 2010.
(3) To appoint a Director in place of Shri Atul Narain who retires by rotation and, being eligible, offers himself for re-appointment.
(4) To appoint Auditors of the company to hold the office from the conclusion of this meeting until the conclusion of next Annual General Meeting and fix their remuneration. The Complex Associates, Chartered Accountants, the retiring auditors of the company, are eligible and offer themselves for re-appointment.

Special Business

To consider, and if thought fit, to pass with or without modification, the following resolution, as an ordinary resolution.

"Resolved that pursuant to the provisions of Foreign Exchange Management Act (FEMA), 1973, read with the guidelines prescribed by the Central Government from time to time for investment by the non-resident Indians and overseas corporate bodies under the portfolio investment scheme, the consent of the company be and is hereby accorded for making investment in the company by non-resident Indians and overseas corporate bodies under the portfolio investment scheme to the extent of 24% of total paid-up equity capital of the company".

"Resolved further that the board of directors be and is hereby authorized to convey to the Reserve Bank of India and other concerned authorities that the company does not have any objection for non-resident Indians and overseas corporate bodies making investment in the company by purchasing its shares through stock exchange under the portfolio investment scheme subject to such approvals as may be required to be obtained by each of them in this connection and to take other necessary steps to implement the resolution."

By the order of The Board

For A.K. Chemicals Ltd. Chairman

Ashutosh Sharma
Company Secretary

Place: Phagwara
Dated: June 1, 2003

Preparatory Work before the Meeting

Before the start of the meeting, all preliminary works should be completed like arrangement of any written or visual aids, seating arrangement, refreshment arrangement, etc.

Whether one is the Chairman or only Invitee, one must go to the meeting well prepared. For this, study of the problems to be discussed should be done in advance. One should also study the anticipated responses or reactions of the other members.

(B) Conducting the Meeting

Since conduct of the meeting involves the sacrifice of priceless time of various executives and employees, it is essential that the results of the meeting should surpass its cost (both tangible and intangible). For successful conduct of the meeting, preparation and punctuality of members is must. In addition to these, the following points must be kept in mind:

At the beginning of the Meeting

As the Chairman starts with the cheerful and positive tone he/she—

Clarifies the goals to be accomplished through meeting by reading the agenda of the meeting;

Provides necessary background information and explains the context of the meeting to all the members; and

Tells that now the members present can contribute to the solution of the problem within the time constraint.

Conducting Business

The chairman being leader of the group should—

Encourage participation of members by giving everyone an equal chance to speak out. For this he can—

Give every member a turn to speak.

Ask question to the group as a whole or to a particular individual.

Ask the members to write their ideas on a piece of paper and comment on them later on.

It should be ensured that participation is not unbalanced, dominated by vocal members or by persons having authority or popularity. Unbalanced participation discourages the people to talk and prevents the group from considering potentially useful ideas.

Keep the discussion on track by reminding the relevance of the arguments.

Avoid criticizing and commenting in destructive or discouraging way or making any personal attack.

Handle the members' differences tactfully and impartially with mature and objective judgment in the light of the situation. The chairman should remind them not to offend or defend their points but try to get education and evaluation out of the discussion.

Enhance the value of members' comments by thanking them for their valuable contributions.

As a *member of the meetings,* one should—

Speak at his turn with constructive solution and concrete arguments.

Control his negative emotions.

Avoid condemning or unnecessarily praising someone.

Be aware of contributing to the solution, not to the problem.

(c) Concluding the Meeting

The chairman of the meeting should ensure the conclusion of meeting at the arrival of the scheduled time or when the agenda has been covered.

He should:

Point out that the time is almost over, summarise the accomplishment of meeting and future course of action and convey thanks to the group members for their constructive and creative contributions.

After the meeting

After the meeting, the company secretary should record the minutes of the proceedings of the meeting. Such minutes should be concise and duly numbered

Minutes of the Board Meeting
Ashoka Chemicals Limited

Minutes of the Board Meeting held at the registered office of the company at 13, Model Town, Ludhiana on July 20, 2009 at 3 p.m.

Present:
Shri Kuldip Singh (in the chair)
Shri Vinod Mittal
Shri Rupesh Handa
Shri Narinder Khanna

In attendance
Shri Darvesh Arora, Secretary

No. of	Subject of Minutes	Details of Minutes
1.	Minutes of the previous meeting	The minutes of the previous Board meeting held on July 20, 2009 were read out by the secretary and confirmed by the meeting
2.	Export of Chemicals	Resolved: "That Shri Vinod Mittal and Shri Rupesh Handa will visit Russia to explore the possibilities of exporting chemicals."
3.	Issue of Debentures	Resolved: "That the company will issue 16% Debentures redeemable within 7 years to finance the expansion projects."
4.	Purchase of land	Resolved: "That Mr. Narinder Khanna is authorized to negotiate for the purchase of land near Jalandhar By-Pass, Ludhiana."
5.	Next Meeting	The next meeting of the Board was fixed for Sept. 13, 2000 at 3 p.m. at the Registered Office of the Company.

Dated : June 16, 2010

Signed Kuldeep Singh
Chairman
Signed Darvesh Arora
Secretary

COMMITTEES

A committee is a group of people, either appointed or elected, committed with certain task(s) or matter(s).

Its use in business is widespread for investigating specific matters and taking decisions. Its use is increasing with the passage of time. The Committee is also known by other names: boards, commissions or task forces. One of the most outstanding examples of committee is the board of directors, established according to provisions of the law.

Types of Committees

We come across many types of committees like finance committee, bonus committee, nominating committee, grievance committee, audit committee, etc.

The names suggest and indicate their tasks and powers. Usually committees can be classified into the following categories:

1. *Executive and Advisory Committees*

Executive Committee is an organization of generally elected members empowered to take decisions in routine matters in the light of the broad organizational objectives. Advisory committee is committee of experts from different groups, entrusted with the function of advising in taking decisions.

2. *Formal and Informal Committees*

A formal committee is a committee formally constituted with definite tasks and responsibilities. The finance committee, the budget committees are created for the purpose of group thinking or group decision-making. They have no formal authority and fixed agenda, but are constituted to advise the management.

3. *Standing and ad hoc Committees*

Standing Committees are permanent committees whereas *ad hoc* committees are constituted for a specific purpose; these are disbanded (wound up) as the task is accomplished.

ADVANTAGES OF COMMITTEES

Assured Integrated Group Efforts

Many problems are so complicated that they require efforts of various persons from different fields to find satisfactory solution. Committees provide the advantage of group efforts of different persons with versatile knowledge and experience directed at solution of the problems. When committee is organized, much useful knowledge and experience is pooled and various dimensions of the decision arrived at are considered.

To Generate New Ideas

When different expert members sit together, discuss and think, new ideas emerge spontaneously. These ideas are very useful for the future of business. A Committee can boost creativity of members, if they are organized in congenial environment with focus on the objective or purpose or problem.

For Promoting Coordination and Cooperation

The various specialists are usually concerned with their own problems and think that their problems should deserve top priority. But as they come closer and listen to other specialists, they try to understand the problem from organizational point of view and at whole organizational level. Then they willingly cooperate and offer themselves for the solution of the problem and thereby the needed harmony is maintained. They pull together and do not pull apart.

Provides Training for Executives

Committees are not only helpful for generating ideas and making decisions but also they provide opportunity for training the executives. It is through meetings that young executives acquire in-depth knowledge and experience through deliberations. It is through meetings that the executives develop perspective from company's point of view for taking decisions. Moreover, with constitution of committees, the spirit of thinking from organizational point of view is strengthened.

Participation Prevents Concentration of Authority

Committees prevent the concentration of authority in the hands of one or a few persons. The committees help to democratize the process of decision-making and encourage decentralization in the organization and encourage delegation of power. With this, the abuses and misuses of authority are prevented and second rung executives are developed for

Bibliography

Ahuja, Pramla, Ahuja, G.C., "How to Listen Better", Sterling Publishers Pvt. Ltd., New Delhi, 1990.

Balasubrahmanian, M., "Business Communication"; Kalyani Publishers, New Delhi, 1999.

Berlo, D.K., "The Process of Communication", New York: Holt, Rinehart & Winston, 1960

Dance, F.E.X., The Concept of Communication, *Journal of Communication*, 20, No. 2, 1970.

Pal, Rajendra and Korlahalli, J.S.; Essentials of Business Communication, (New Delhi: 1979), Sultan Chand & Sons.

Davis, K., "Management Communication and Grapevine in a Governmental Organization", Personnel Psychology, Summer, 1968, pp. 223-30.

Harriman, B. "Up and Down the Communication Ladder", *Harvard Business Review*, September-October 1974.

Hegde, Y.S., Krishna Rajeshwari, "The A to Z to Management Skills", UBS Publishers and Distributors Ltd., Calcutta, 1994.

Holt, David, "Management—Principles and Practices", Prentice Hall, New Jersey, 1990.

Rice, R.E. and Shook, D.E., "Relationships of Job Categories and Organizational Level to Use of Communication Channels, Including Electronic mail: A Meta Analysis and Extension", *Journal of Management Studies*, March 1990.

Rao, Nageshwara and Rajendra P. Das, (Delhi: 2006), Himalaya Publishing House.

Ray, Reuben, "Communication Management", Himalaya Publishing House, Mumbai, 2000.

Robbins, S.P., "Organizational Behaviour", Prentice Hall of India Pvt. Ltd., New Delhi, 1999.

Saboo, R., "Social Family Skills", Secretary-General, India Jaycees, New Delhi, 1984.

Sharma, R.C., and Mohan Krishna, "Business Correspondence and Report Writing", Tata-McGraw Hill Publishing Co. Ltd., New Delhi, 1993.

Thayer Lee, "Communication Concept and Perspectives", Macmillan & Co. Ltd., London, and Spartan Books, Washington, 1967.

Tiwari, S.K., How Much Clear is Your Communication? Prabandh, January-March 1981.

Index